C-441   CAREER EXAMINATION SERIES

This is your
PASSBOOK for...

Lieutenant, Fire Department

Test Preparation Study Guide
Questions & Answers

NATIONAL LEARNING CORPORATION®

COPYRIGHT NOTICE

This book is SOLELY intended for, is sold ONLY to, and its use is RESTRICTED to individual, bona fide applicants or candidates who qualify by virtue of having seriously filed applications for appropriate license, certificate, professional and/or promotional advancement, higher school matriculation, scholarship, or other legitimate requirements of education and/or governmental authorities.

This book is NOT intended for use, class instruction, tutoring, training, duplication, copying, reprinting, excerption, or adaptation, etc., by:

1) Other publishers
2) Proprietors and/or Instructors of "Coaching" and/or Preparatory Courses
3) Personnel and/or Training Divisions of commercial, industrial, and governmental organizations
4) Schools, colleges, or universities and/or their departments and staffs, including teachers and other personnel
5) Testing Agencies or Bureaus
6) Study groups which seek by the purchase of a single volume to copy and/or duplicate and/or adapt this material for use by the group as a whole without having purchased individual volumes for each of the members of the group
7) Et al.

Such persons would be in violation of appropriate Federal and State statutes.

PROVISION OF LICENSING AGREEMENTS – Recognized educational, commercial, industrial, and governmental institutions and organizations, and others legitimately engaged in educational pursuits, including training, testing, and measurement activities, may address request for a licensing agreement to the copyright owners, who will determine whether, and under what conditions, including fees and charges, the materials in this book may be used them. In other words, a licensing facility exists for the legitimate use of the material in this book on other than an individual basis. However, it is asseverated and affirmed here that the material in this book CANNOT be used without the receipt of the express permission of such a licensing agreement from the Publishers. Inquiries re licensing should be addressed to the company, attention rights and permissions department.

All rights reserved, including the right of reproduction in whole or in part, in any form or by any means, electronic or mechanical, including photocopying, recording, or by any information storage and retrieval system, without permission in writing from the Publisher.

Copyright © 2025 by
National Learning Corporation

212 Michael Drive, Syosset, NY 11791
(516) 921-8888 • www.passbooks.com
E-mail: info@passbooks.com

PASSBOOK® SERIES

THE *PASSBOOK® SERIES* has been created to prepare applicants and candidates for the ultimate academic battlefield – the examination room.

At some time in our lives, each and every one of us may be required to take an examination – for validation, matriculation, admission, qualification, registration, certification, or licensure.

Based on the assumption that every applicant or candidate has met the basic formal educational standards, has taken the required number of courses, and read the necessary texts, the *PASSBOOK® SERIES* furnishes the one special preparation which may assure passing with confidence, instead of failing with insecurity. Examination questions – together with answers – are furnished as the basic vehicle for study so that the mysteries of the examination and its compounding difficulties may be eliminated or diminished by a sure method.

This book is meant to help you pass your examination provided that you qualify and are serious in your objective.

The entire field is reviewed through the huge store of content information which is succinctly presented through a provocative and challenging approach – the question-and-answer method.

A climate of success is established by furnishing the correct answers at the end of each test.

You soon learn to recognize types of questions, forms of questions, and patterns of questioning. You may even begin to anticipate expected outcomes.

You perceive that many questions are repeated or adapted so that you can gain acute insights, which may enable you to score many sure points.

You learn how to confront new questions, or types of questions, and to attack them confidently and work out the correct answers.

You note objectives and emphases, and recognize pitfalls and dangers, so that you may make positive educational adjustments.

Moreover, you are kept fully informed in relation to new concepts, methods, practices, and directions in the field.

You discover that you are actually taking the examination all the time: you are preparing for the examination by "taking" an examination, not by reading extraneous and/or supererogatory textbooks.

In short, this PASSBOOK®, used directedly, should be an important factor in helping you to pass your test.

LIEUTENANT, FIRE DEPARTMENT

DUTIES:
Under the general supervision of a fire officer of a higher grade; carries out the following tasks:

Size-up: Evaluates the incident scene to determine initial, as well as subsequent actions to be taken, as a fire or other emergency incident progresses; inspects scene noting such factors as type of structure, wind conditions, temperature, and water availability; determines conditions at scene by observing, smelling, or listening for smoke, flames, leaks, spills, building condition, and other factors; physically evaluates scene; based on size-up, determines tactical priorities and strategy, chooses equipment needed to accomplish strategic objectives and directs that tactical operations be carried out to accomplish such objectives.

On-Scene Communication: Communicates, both while en route and at an emergency scene, to ensure proper coordination of apparatus and personnel; while en route to incidents, communicates and coordinates actions with other fire companies; upon arrival at the scene, receives information regarding the assignment of personnel and apparatus from the officer in command; contacts fire alarm office to report conditions, request additional resources, and update personal assignment/status; communicates with other fire personnel at the scene about progress, conditions, resource needs, and size-up and relays orders from superiors to subordinate members.

On-Scene Resource Allocation and Coordination: Evaluates resource needs and assigns personnel, resources, and equipment to various functions and positions at the emergency scene; assumes command of emergency scenes as appropriate; calls in specialized units (e.g., HAZMAT), as appropriate; directs the movement and location of equipment and apparatus at the scene; assigns fire personnel to perform specific tasks at the emergency scene (for example, laying supply lines, raising ladders, evacuating civilians, treating injured victims, etc.); and directs that necessary safety precautions be taken.

Performance Evaluation: Observes subordinate performance to identify strengths and weaknesses and assess training needs and conducts informal or formal counseling sessions with subordinates to discuss performance; conducts post-incident critiques and questions subordinates on operation.

Training Delivery: Ensures that all subordinate personnel are properly trained to carry out their assigned duties by planning, developing, conducting, and evaluating training sessions and drills; informally trains fire service personnel in apparatus operations, equipment use, EMS procedures, and other routine duties.

Internal Inspections: Inspects/observes the inspection of personal gear, equipment, apparatus, and station facilities to ensure proper and safe operation and takes steps to ensure that observed deficiencies are corrected and necessary maintenance is performed; observes or is advised of deficiencies; and performs related duties as required.

SCOPE OF THE EXAMINATION
The written examination will be designed to test, where practicable, the following knowledge's, abilities and skills that have been established as qualifications for the position:

1. Knowledge of principles and practices of fire ground operations (both strategy and tactics) and the chemistry and physics of fire as related to fire ground operations including, for example: rescue, ventilation, hydraulics, ladder and pump operations, overhaul and salvage, common and special fire hazards, major emergency planning, and safety as related to capabilities, limitations, care and maintenance of tools, equipment and apparatus, and health and safety programs;

2. Knowledge of building design, construction and materials, as related to the fire service, including, for example: life safety, fire safety, structural failure, fire prevention, fire protection, and fire suppression (spread of fire, spread of heat and smoke, and extension of fire);

3. Knowledge of supervision and training, including, for example: motivation, performance evaluation, discipline, training;

4. Knowledge of law as it applies to the fire service;

5. Knowledge of fire prevention, including building inspection as it relates to the fire service, including, for example: occupancies of assembly, education, health care, business, storage, etc;

6. Knowledge of fire protection, including portable extinguishers, fixed extinguishing systems (including sprinklers) and public and private alarm systems;

7. Knowledge of principles and practices of fire cause determination; and

8. Knowledge of hazardous materials, including principles and practices of response to non-fire emergencies.

LIEUTENANT, FIRE DEPARTMENT

DUTIES

A Lieutenant has complete charge of operations at scenes of fires in the absence, or pending the arrival, of a superior officer.

Assigns firefighters to lay out and connect hose lines and nozzles, turns water off and on, raises ladders and ventilates buildings. Responds to all alarms assigned to his company. Supervises the work of firefighters at scenes of fire and in stations. Inspects property at scene of fire to prevent re-ignition. Supervises the cleaning, checking and replacement of tools and equipment after a fire. Inspects equipment, grounds and station to insure proper order and condition. Inspects buildings and premises for fire hazards. Makes reports of personnel and activities. Trains and drills firefighters. Performs related functions.

SUBJECT OF EXAMINATION:

A written test designed to evaluate knowledge, skills and/or abilities in the following areas:
1. Fire prevention;
2. Firefighting practices and equipment;
3. On-the-job training of fire personnel;
4. Rescue techniques and basic emergency medical response;
5. Preparing written material; and
6. Supervision.

HOW TO TAKE A TEST

I. YOU MUST PASS AN EXAMINATION

A. WHAT EVERY CANDIDATE SHOULD KNOW

Examination applicants often ask us for help in preparing for the written test. What can I study in advance? What kinds of questions will be asked? How will the test be given? How will the papers be graded?

As an applicant for a civil service examination, you may be wondering about some of these things. Our purpose here is to suggest effective methods of advance study and to describe civil service examinations.

Your chances for success on this examination can be increased if you know how to prepare. Those "pre-examination jitters" can be reduced if you know what to expect. You can even experience an adventure in good citizenship if you know why civil service exams are given.

B. WHY ARE CIVIL SERVICE EXAMINATIONS GIVEN?

Civil service examinations are important to you in two ways. As a citizen, you want public jobs filled by employees who know how to do their work. As a job seeker, you want a fair chance to compete for that job on an equal footing with other candidates. The best-known means of accomplishing this two-fold goal is the competitive examination.

Exams are widely publicized throughout the nation. They may be administered for jobs in federal, state, city, municipal, town or village governments or agencies.

Any citizen may apply, with some limitations, such as the age or residence of applicants. Your experience and education may be reviewed to see whether you meet the requirements for the particular examination. When these requirements exist, they are reasonable and applied consistently to all applicants. Thus, a competitive examination may cause you some uneasiness now, but it is your privilege and safeguard.

C. HOW ARE CIVIL SERVICE EXAMS DEVELOPED?

Examinations are carefully written by trained technicians who are specialists in the field known as "psychological measurement," in consultation with recognized authorities in the field of work that the test will cover. These experts recommend the subject matter areas or skills to be tested; only those knowledges or skills important to your success on the job are included. The most reliable books and source materials available are used as references. Together, the experts and technicians judge the difficulty level of the questions.

Test technicians know how to phrase questions so that the problem is clearly stated. Their ethics do not permit "trick" or "catch" questions. Questions may have been tried out on sample groups, or subjected to statistical analysis, to determine their usefulness.

Written tests are often used in combination with performance tests, ratings of training and experience, and oral interviews. All of these measures combine to form the best-known means of finding the right person for the right job.

II. HOW TO PASS THE WRITTEN TEST

A. NATURE OF THE EXAMINATION

To prepare intelligently for civil service examinations, you should know how they differ from school examinations you have taken. In school you were assigned certain definite pages to read or subjects to cover. The examination questions were quite detailed and usually emphasized memory. Civil service exams, on the other hand, try to discover your present ability to perform the duties of a position, plus your potentiality to learn these duties. In other words, a civil service exam attempts to predict how successful you will be. Questions cover such a broad area that they cannot be as minute and detailed as school exam questions.

In the public service similar kinds of work, or positions, are grouped together in one "class." This process is known as *position-classification*. All the positions in a class are paid according to the salary range for that class. One class title covers all of these positions, and they are all tested by the same examination.

B. FOUR BASIC STEPS

1) Study the announcement

How, then, can you know what subjects to study? Our best answer is: "Learn as much as possible about the class of positions for which you've applied." The exam will test the knowledge, skills and abilities needed to do the work.

Your most valuable source of information about the position you want is the official exam announcement. This announcement lists the training and experience qualifications. Check these standards and apply only if you come reasonably close to meeting them.

The brief description of the position in the examination announcement offers some clues to the subjects which will be tested. Think about the job itself. Review the duties in your mind. Can you perform them, or are there some in which you are rusty? Fill in the blank spots in your preparation.

Many jurisdictions preview the written test in the exam announcement by including a section called "Knowledge and Abilities Required," "Scope of the Examination," or some similar heading. Here you will find out specifically what fields will be tested.

2) Review your own background

Once you learn in general what the position is all about, and what you need to know to do the work, ask yourself which subjects you already know fairly well and which need improvement. You may wonder whether to concentrate on improving your strong areas or on building some background in your fields of weakness. When the announcement has specified "some knowledge" or "considerable knowledge," or has used adjectives like "beginning principles of..." or "advanced ... methods," you can get a clue as to the number and difficulty of questions to be asked in any given field. More questions, and hence broader coverage, would be included for those subjects which are more important in the work. Now weigh your strengths and weaknesses against the job requirements and prepare accordingly.

3) Determine the level of the position

Another way to tell how intensively you should prepare is to understand the level of the job for which you are applying. Is it the entering level? In other words, is this the position in which beginners in a field of work are hired? Or is it an intermediate or advanced level? Sometimes this is indicated by such words as "Junior" or "Senior" in the class title. Other jurisdictions use Roman numerals to designate the level – Clerk I, Clerk II, for example. The word "Supervisor" sometimes appears in the title. If the level is not indicated by the title, check the description of duties. Will you be working under very close supervision, or will you have responsibility for independent decisions in this work?

4) Choose appropriate study materials

Now that you know the subjects to be examined and the relative amount of each subject to be covered, you can choose suitable study materials. For beginning level jobs, or even advanced ones, if you have a pronounced weakness in some aspect of your training, read a modern, standard textbook in that field. Be sure it is up to date and has general coverage. Such books are normally available at your library, and the librarian will be glad to help you locate one. For entry-level positions, questions of appropriate difficulty are chosen – neither highly advanced questions, nor those too simple. Such questions require careful thought but not advanced training.

If the position for which you are applying is technical or advanced, you will read more advanced, specialized material. If you are already familiar with the basic principles of your field, elementary textbooks would waste your time. Concentrate on advanced textbooks and technical periodicals. Think through the concepts and review difficult problems in your field.

These are all general sources. You can get more ideas on your own initiative, following these leads. For example, training manuals and publications of the government agency which employs workers in your field can be useful, particularly for technical and professional positions. A letter or visit to the government department involved may result in more specific study suggestions, and certainly will provide you with a more definite idea of the exact nature of the position you are seeking.

III. KINDS OF TESTS

Tests are used for purposes other than measuring knowledge and ability to perform specified duties. For some positions, it is equally important to test ability to make adjustments to new situations or to profit from training. In others, basic mental abilities not dependent on information are essential. Questions which test these things may not appear as pertinent to the duties of the position as those which test for knowledge and information. Yet they are often highly important parts of a fair examination. For very general questions, it is almost impossible to help you direct your study efforts. What we can do is to point out some of the more common of these general abilities needed in public service positions and describe some typical questions.

1) General information

Broad, general information has been found useful for predicting job success in some kinds of work. This is tested in a variety of ways, from vocabulary lists to questions about current events. Basic background in some field of work, such as sociology or economics, may be sampled in a group of questions. Often these are principles which have become familiar to most persons through exposure rather than through formal training. It is difficult to advise you how to study for these questions; being alert to the world around you is our best suggestion.

2) Verbal ability

An example of an ability needed in many positions is verbal or language ability. Verbal ability is, in brief, the ability to use and understand words. Vocabulary and grammar tests are typical measures of this ability. Reading comprehension or paragraph interpretation questions are common in many kinds of civil service tests. You are given a paragraph of written material and asked to find its central meaning.

3) Numerical ability

Number skills can be tested by the familiar arithmetic problem, by checking paired lists of numbers to see which are alike and which are different, or by interpreting charts and graphs. In the latter test, a graph may be printed in the test booklet which you are asked to use as the basis for answering questions.

4) Observation

A popular test for law-enforcement positions is the observation test. A picture is shown to you for several minutes, then taken away. Questions about the picture test your ability to observe both details and larger elements.

5) Following directions

In many positions in the public service, the employee must be able to carry out written instructions dependably and accurately. You may be given a chart with several columns, each column listing a variety of information. The questions require you to carry out directions involving the information given in the chart.

6) Skills and aptitudes

Performance tests effectively measure some manual skills and aptitudes. When the skill is one in which you are trained, such as typing or shorthand, you can practice. These tests are often very much like those given in business school or high school courses. For many of the other skills and aptitudes, however, no short-time preparation can be made. Skills and abilities natural to you or that you have developed throughout your lifetime are being tested.

Many of the general questions just described provide all the data needed to answer the questions and ask you to use your reasoning ability to find the answers. Your best preparation for these tests, as well as for tests of facts and ideas, is to be at your physical and mental best. You, no doubt, have your own methods of getting into an exam-taking mood and keeping "in shape." The next section lists some ideas on this subject.

IV. KINDS OF QUESTIONS

Only rarely is the "essay" question, which you answer in narrative form, used in civil service tests. Civil service tests are usually of the short-answer type. Full instructions for answering these questions will be given to you at the examination. But in case this is your first experience with short-answer questions and separate answer sheets, here is what you need to know:

1) Multiple-choice Questions

Most popular of the short-answer questions is the "multiple choice" or "best answer" question. It can be used, for example, to test for factual knowledge, ability to solve problems or judgment in meeting situations found at work.

A multiple-choice question is normally one of three types—
- It can begin with an incomplete statement followed by several possible endings. You are to find the one ending which *best* completes the statement, although some of the others may not be entirely wrong.
- It can also be a complete statement in the form of a question which is answered by choosing one of the statements listed.

- It can be in the form of a problem – again you select the best answer.

Here is an example of a multiple-choice question with a discussion which should give you some clues as to the method for choosing the right answer:

When an employee has a complaint about his assignment, the action which will *best* help him overcome his difficulty is to
- A. discuss his difficulty with his coworkers
- B. take the problem to the head of the organization
- C. take the problem to the person who gave him the assignment
- D. say nothing to anyone about his complaint

In answering this question, you should study each of the choices to find which is best. Consider choice "A" – Certainly an employee may discuss his complaint with fellow employees, but no change or improvement can result, and the complaint remains unresolved. Choice "B" is a poor choice since the head of the organization probably does not know what assignment you have been given, and taking your problem to him is known as "going over the head" of the supervisor. The supervisor, or person who made the assignment, is the person who can clarify it or correct any injustice. Choice "C" is, therefore, correct. To say nothing, as in choice "D," is unwise. Supervisors have and interest in knowing the problems employees are facing, and the employee is seeking a solution to his problem.

2) True/False Questions

The "true/false" or "right/wrong" form of question is sometimes used. Here a complete statement is given. Your job is to decide whether the statement is right or wrong.

SAMPLE: A roaming cell-phone call to a nearby city costs less than a non-roaming call to a distant city.

This statement is wrong, or false, since roaming calls are more expensive.

This is not a complete list of all possible question forms, although most of the others are variations of these common types. You will always get complete directions for answering questions. Be sure you understand *how* to mark your answers – ask questions until you do.

V. RECORDING YOUR ANSWERS

Computer terminals are used more and more today for many different kinds of exams.

For an examination with very few applicants, you may be told to record your answers in the test booklet itself. Separate answer sheets are much more common. If this separate answer sheet is to be scored by machine – and this is often the case – it is highly important that you mark your answers correctly in order to get credit.

An electronic scoring machine is often used in civil service offices because of the speed with which papers can be scored. Machine-scored answer sheets must be marked with a pencil, which will be given to you. This pencil has a high graphite content which responds to the electronic scoring machine. As a matter of fact, stray dots may register as answers, so do not let your pencil rest on the answer sheet while you are pondering the correct answer. Also, if your pencil lead breaks or is otherwise defective, ask for another.

Since the answer sheet will be dropped in a slot in the scoring machine, be careful not to bend the corners or get the paper crumpled.

The answer sheet normally has five vertical columns of numbers, with 30 numbers to a column. These numbers correspond to the question numbers in your test booklet. After each number, going across the page are four or five pairs of dotted lines. These short dotted lines have small letters or numbers above them. The first two pairs may also have a "T" or "F" above the letters. This indicates that the first two pairs only are to be used if the questions are of the true-false type. If the questions are multiple choice, disregard the "T" and "F" and pay attention only to the small letters or numbers.

Answer your questions in the manner of the sample that follows:

32. The largest city in the United States is
    A. Washington, D.C.
    B. New York City
    C. Chicago
    D. Detroit
    E. San Francisco

1) Choose the answer you think is best. (New York City is the largest, so "B" is correct.)
2) Find the row of dotted lines numbered the same as the question you are answering. (Find row number 32)
3) Find the pair of dotted lines corresponding to the answer. (Find the pair of lines under the mark "B.")
4) Make a solid black mark between the dotted lines.

VI. BEFORE THE TEST

Common sense will help you find procedures to follow to get ready for an examination. Too many of us, however, overlook these sensible measures. Indeed, nervousness and fatigue have been found to be the most serious reasons why applicants fail to do their best on civil service tests. Here is a list of reminders:

- Begin your preparation early – Don't wait until the last minute to go scurrying around for books and materials or to find out what the position is all about.
- Prepare continuously – An hour a night for a week is better than an all-night cram session. This has been definitely established. What is more, a night a week for a month will return better dividends than crowding your study into a shorter period of time.
- Locate the place of the exam – You have been sent a notice telling you when and where to report for the examination. If the location is in a different town or otherwise unfamiliar to you, it would be well to inquire the best route and learn something about the building.
- Relax the night before the test – Allow your mind to rest. Do not study at all that night. Plan some mild recreation or diversion; then go to bed early and get a good night's sleep.
- Get up early enough to make a leisurely trip to the place for the test – This way unforeseen events, traffic snarls, unfamiliar buildings, etc. will not upset you.
- Dress comfortably – A written test is not a fashion show. You will be known by number and not by name, so wear something comfortable.

- Leave excess paraphernalia at home – Shopping bags and odd bundles will get in your way. You need bring only the items mentioned in the official notice you received; usually everything you need is provided. Do not bring reference books to the exam. They will only confuse those last minutes and be taken away from you when in the test room.
- Arrive somewhat ahead of time – If because of transportation schedules you must get there very early, bring a newspaper or magazine to take your mind off yourself while waiting.
- Locate the examination room – When you have found the proper room, you will be directed to the seat or part of the room where you will sit. Sometimes you are given a sheet of instructions to read while you are waiting. Do not fill out any forms until you are told to do so; just read them and be prepared.
- Relax and prepare to listen to the instructions
- If you have any physical problem that may keep you from doing your best, be sure to tell the test administrator. If you are sick or in poor health, you really cannot do your best on the exam. You can come back and take the test some other time.

VII. AT THE TEST

The day of the test is here and you have the test booklet in your hand. The temptation to get going is very strong. Caution! There is more to success than knowing the right answers. You must know how to identify your papers and understand variations in the type of short-answer question used in this particular examination. Follow these suggestions for maximum results from your efforts:

1) Cooperate with the monitor
The test administrator has a duty to create a situation in which you can be as much at ease as possible. He will give instructions, tell you when to begin, check to see that you are marking your answer sheet correctly, and so on. He is not there to guard you, although he will see that your competitors do not take unfair advantage. He wants to help you do your best.

2) Listen to all instructions
Don't jump the gun! Wait until you understand all directions. In most civil service tests you get more time than you need to answer the questions. So don't be in a hurry. Read each word of instructions until you clearly understand the meaning. Study the examples, listen to all announcements and follow directions. Ask questions if you do not understand what to do.

3) Identify your papers
Civil service exams are usually identified by number only. You will be assigned a number; you must not put your name on your test papers. Be sure to copy your number correctly. Since more than one exam may be given, copy your exact examination title.

4) Plan your time
Unless you are told that a test is a "speed" or "rate of work" test, speed itself is usually not important. Time enough to answer all the questions will be provided, but this does not mean that you have all day. An overall time limit has been set. Divide the total time (in minutes) by the number of questions to determine the approximate time you have for each question.

5) Do not linger over difficult questions

If you come across a difficult question, mark it with a paper clip (useful to have along) and come back to it when you have been through the booklet. One caution if you do this – be sure to skip a number on your answer sheet as well. Check often to be sure that you have not lost your place and that you are marking in the row numbered the same as the question you are answering.

6) Read the questions

Be sure you know what the question asks! Many capable people are unsuccessful because they failed to *read* the questions correctly.

7) Answer all questions

Unless you have been instructed that a penalty will be deducted for incorrect answers, it is better to guess than to omit a question.

8) Speed tests

It is often better NOT to guess on speed tests. It has been found that on timed tests people are tempted to spend the last few seconds before time is called in marking answers at random – without even reading them – in the hope of picking up a few extra points. To discourage this practice, the instructions may warn you that your score will be "corrected" for guessing. That is, a penalty will be applied. The incorrect answers will be deducted from the correct ones, or some other penalty formula will be used.

9) Review your answers

If you finish before time is called, go back to the questions you guessed or omitted to give them further thought. Review other answers if you have time.

10) Return your test materials

If you are ready to leave before others have finished or time is called, take ALL your materials to the monitor and leave quietly. Never take any test material with you. The monitor can discover whose papers are not complete, and taking a test booklet may be grounds for disqualification.

VIII. EXAMINATION TECHNIQUES

1) Read the general instructions carefully. These are usually printed on the first page of the exam booklet. As a rule, these instructions refer to the timing of the examination; the fact that you should not start work until the signal and must stop work at a signal, etc. If there are any *special* instructions, such as a choice of questions to be answered, make sure that you note this instruction carefully.

2) When you are ready to start work on the examination, that is as soon as the signal has been given, read the instructions to each question booklet, underline any key words or phrases, such as *least, best, outline, describe* and the like. In this way you will tend to answer as requested rather than discover on reviewing your paper that you *listed without describing*, that you selected the *worst* choice rather than the *best* choice, etc.

3) If the examination is of the objective or multiple-choice type – that is, each question will also give a series of possible answers: A, B, C or D, and you are called upon to select the best answer and write the letter next to that answer on your answer paper – it is advisable to start answering each question in turn. There may be anywhere from 50 to 100 such questions in the three or four hours allotted and you can see how much time would be taken if you read through all the questions before beginning to answer any. Furthermore, if you come across a question or group of questions which you know would be difficult to answer, it would undoubtedly affect your handling of all the other questions.

4) If the examination is of the essay type and contains but a few questions, it is a moot point as to whether you should read all the questions before starting to answer any one. Of course, if you are given a choice – say five out of seven and the like – then it is essential to read all the questions so you can eliminate the two that are most difficult. If, however, you are asked to answer all the questions, there may be danger in trying to answer the easiest one first because you may find that you will spend too much time on it. The best technique is to answer the first question, then proceed to the second, etc.

5) Time your answers. Before the exam begins, write down the time it started, then add the time allowed for the examination and write down the time it must be completed, then divide the time available somewhat as follows:
    - If 3-1/2 hours are allowed, that would be 210 minutes. If you have 80 objective-type questions, that would be an average of 2-1/2 minutes per question. Allow yourself no more than 2 minutes per question, or a total of 160 minutes, which will permit about 50 minutes to review.
    - If for the time allotment of 210 minutes there are 7 essay questions to answer, that would average about 30 minutes a question. Give yourself only 25 minutes per question so that you have about 35 minutes to review.

6) The most important instruction is to *read each question* and make sure you know what is wanted. The second most important instruction is to *time yourself properly* so that you answer every question. The third most important instruction is to *answer every question*. Guess if you have to but include something for each question. Remember that you will receive no credit for a blank and will probably receive some credit if you write something in answer to an essay question. If you guess a letter – say "B" for a multiple-choice question – you may have guessed right. If you leave a blank as an answer to a multiple-choice question, the examiners may respect your feelings but it will not add a point to your score. Some exams may penalize you for wrong answers, so in such cases *only*, you may not want to guess unless you have some basis for your answer.

7) Suggestions
    a. Objective-type questions
        1. Examine the question booklet for proper sequence of pages and questions
        2. Read all instructions carefully
        3. Skip any question which seems too difficult; return to it after all other questions have been answered
        4. Apportion your time properly; do not spend too much time on any single question or group of questions

5. Note and underline key words – *all, most, fewest, least, best, worst, same, opposite,* etc.
6. Pay particular attention to negatives
7. Note unusual option, e.g., unduly long, short, complex, different or similar in content to the body of the question
8. Observe the use of "hedging" words – *probably, may, most likely,* etc.
9. Make sure that your answer is put next to the same number as the question
10. Do not second-guess unless you have good reason to believe the second answer is definitely more correct
11. Cross out original answer if you decide another answer is more accurate; do not erase until you are ready to hand your paper in
12. Answer all questions; guess unless instructed otherwise
13. Leave time for review

   b. Essay questions
1. Read each question carefully
2. Determine exactly what is wanted. Underline key words or phrases.
3. Decide on outline or paragraph answer
4. Include many different points and elements unless asked to develop any one or two points or elements
5. Show impartiality by giving pros and cons unless directed to select one side only
6. Make and write down any assumptions you find necessary to answer the questions
7. Watch your English, grammar, punctuation and choice of words
8. Time your answers; don't crowd material

8) Answering the essay question

Most essay questions can be answered by framing the specific response around several key words or ideas. Here are a few such key words or ideas:

M's: manpower, materials, methods, money, management
P's: purpose, program, policy, plan, procedure, practice, problems, pitfalls, personnel, public relations
   a. Six basic steps in handling problems:
1. Preliminary plan and background development
2. Collect information, data and facts
3. Analyze and interpret information, data and facts
4. Analyze and develop solutions as well as make recommendations
5. Prepare report and sell recommendations
6. Install recommendations and follow up effectiveness

   b. Pitfalls to avoid
1. *Taking things for granted* – A statement of the situation does not necessarily imply that each of the elements is necessarily true; for example, a complaint may be invalid and biased so that all that can be taken for granted is that a complaint has been registered

2. *Considering only one side of a situation* – Wherever possible, indicate several alternatives and then point out the reasons you selected the best one
3. *Failing to indicate follow up* – Whenever your answer indicates action on your part, make certain that you will take proper follow-up action to see how successful your recommendations, procedures or actions turn out to be
4. *Taking too long in answering any single question* – Remember to time your answers properly

IX. AFTER THE TEST

Scoring procedures differ in detail among civil service jurisdictions although the general principles are the same. Whether the papers are hand-scored or graded by machine we have described, they are nearly always graded by number. That is, the person who marks the paper knows only the number – never the name – of the applicant. Not until all the papers have been graded will they be matched with names. If other tests, such as training and experience or oral interview ratings have been given, scores will be combined. Different parts of the examination usually have different weights. For example, the written test might count 60 percent of the final grade, and a rating of training and experience 40 percent. In many jurisdictions, veterans will have a certain number of points added to their grades.

After the final grade has been determined, the names are placed in grade order and an eligible list is established. There are various methods for resolving ties between those who get the same final grade – probably the most common is to place first the name of the person whose application was received first. Job offers are made from the eligible list in the order the names appear on it. You will be notified of your grade and your rank as soon as all these computations have been made. This will be done as rapidly as possible.

People who are found to meet the requirements in the announcement are called "eligibles." Their names are put on a list of eligible candidates. An eligible's chances of getting a job depend on how high he stands on this list and how fast agencies are filling jobs from the list.

When a job is to be filled from a list of eligibles, the agency asks for the names of people on the list of eligibles for that job. When the civil service commission receives this request, it sends to the agency the names of the three people highest on this list. Or, if the job to be filled has specialized requirements, the office sends the agency the names of the top three persons who meet these requirements from the general list.

The appointing officer makes a choice from among the three people whose names were sent to him. If the selected person accepts the appointment, the names of the others are put back on the list to be considered for future openings.

That is the rule in hiring from all kinds of eligible lists, whether they are for typist, carpenter, chemist, or something else. For every vacancy, the appointing officer has his choice of any one of the top three eligibles on the list. This explains why the person whose name is on top of the list sometimes does not get an appointment when some of the persons lower on the list do. If the appointing officer chooses the second or third eligible, the No. 1 eligible does not get a job at once, but stays on the list until he is appointed or the list is terminated.

X. HOW TO PASS THE INTERVIEW TEST

The examination for which you applied requires an oral interview test. You have already taken the written test and you are now being called for the interview test – the final part of the formal examination.

You may think that it is not possible to prepare for an interview test and that there are no procedures to follow during an interview. Our purpose is to point out some things you can do in advance that will help you and some good rules to follow and pitfalls to avoid while you are being interviewed.

What is an interview supposed to test?

The written examination is designed to test the technical knowledge and competence of the candidate; the oral is designed to evaluate intangible qualities, not readily measured otherwise, and to establish a list showing the relative fitness of each candidate – as measured against his competitors – for the position sought. Scoring is not on the basis of "right" and "wrong," but on a sliding scale of values ranging from "not passable" to "outstanding." As a matter of fact, it is possible to achieve a relatively low score without a single "incorrect" answer because of evident weakness in the qualities being measured.

Occasionally, an examination may consist entirely of an oral test – either an individual or a group oral. In such cases, information is sought concerning the technical knowledges and abilities of the candidate, since there has been no written examination for this purpose. More commonly, however, an oral test is used to supplement a written examination.

Who conducts interviews?

The composition of oral boards varies among different jurisdictions. In nearly all, a representative of the personnel department serves as chairman. One of the members of the board may be a representative of the department in which the candidate would work. In some cases, "outside experts" are used, and, frequently, a businessman or some other representative of the general public is asked to serve. Labor and management or other special groups may be represented. The aim is to secure the services of experts in the appropriate field.

However the board is composed, it is a good idea (and not at all improper or unethical) to ascertain in advance of the interview who the members are and what groups they represent. When you are introduced to them, you will have some idea of their backgrounds and interests, and at least you will not stutter and stammer over their names.

What should be done before the interview?

While knowledge about the board members is useful and takes some of the surprise element out of the interview, there is other preparation which is more substantive. It *is* possible to prepare for an oral interview – in several ways:

1) Keep a copy of your application and review it carefully before the interview

This may be the only document before the oral board, and the starting point of the interview. Know what education and experience you have listed there, and the sequence and dates of all of it. Sometimes the board will ask you to review the highlights of your experience for them; you should not have to hem and haw doing it.

2) Study the class specification and the examination announcement

Usually, the oral board has one or both of these to guide them. The qualities, characteristics or knowledges required by the position sought are stated in these documents. They offer valuable clues as to the nature of the oral interview. For example, if the job involves supervisory responsibilities, the announcement will usually indicate that knowledge of modern supervisory methods and the qualifications of the candidate as a supervisor will be tested. If so, you can expect such questions, frequently in the form of a hypothetical situation which you are expected to solve. NEVER go into an oral without knowledge of the duties and responsibilities of the job you seek.

3) Think through each qualification required

Try to visualize the kind of questions you would ask if you were a board member. How well could you answer them? Try especially to appraise your own knowledge and background in each area, *measured against the job sought*, and identify any areas in which you are weak. Be critical and realistic – do not flatter yourself.

4) Do some general reading in areas in which you feel you may be weak

For example, if the job involves supervision and your past experience has NOT, some general reading in supervisory methods and practices, particularly in the field of human relations, might be useful. Do NOT study agency procedures or detailed manuals. The oral board will be testing your understanding and capacity, not your memory.

5) Get a good night's sleep and watch your general health and mental attitude

You will want a clear head at the interview. Take care of a cold or any other minor ailment, and of course, no hangovers.

What should be done on the day of the interview?

Now comes the day of the interview itself. Give yourself plenty of time to get there. Plan to arrive somewhat ahead of the scheduled time, particularly if your appointment is in the fore part of the day. If a previous candidate fails to appear, the board might be ready for you a bit early. By early afternoon an oral board is almost invariably behind schedule if there are many candidates, and you may have to wait. Take along a book or magazine to read, or your application to review, but leave any extraneous material in the waiting room when you go in for your interview. In any event, relax and compose yourself.

The matter of dress is important. The board is forming impressions about you – from your experience, your manners, your attitude, and your appearance. Give your personal appearance careful attention. Dress your best, but not your flashiest. Choose conservative, appropriate clothing, and be sure it is immaculate. This is a business interview, and your appearance should indicate that you regard it as such. Besides, being well groomed and properly dressed will help boost your confidence.

Sooner or later, someone will call your name and escort you into the interview room. *This is it.* From here on you are on your own. It is too late for any more preparation. But remember, you asked for this opportunity to prove your fitness, and you are here because your request was granted.

What happens when you go in?

The usual sequence of events will be as follows: The clerk (who is often the board stenographer) will introduce you to the chairman of the oral board, who will introduce you to the other members of the board. Acknowledge the introductions before you sit down. Do not be surprised if you find a microphone facing you or a stenotypist sitting by. Oral interviews are usually recorded in the event of an appeal or other review.

Usually the chairman of the board will open the interview by reviewing the highlights of your education and work experience from your application – primarily for the benefit of the other members of the board, as well as to get the material into the record. Do not interrupt or comment unless there is an error or significant misinterpretation; if that is the case, do not hesitate. But do not quibble about insignificant matters. Also, he will usually ask you some question about your education, experience or your present job – partly to get you to start talking and to establish the interviewing "rapport." He may start the actual questioning, or turn it over to one of the other members. Frequently, each member undertakes the questioning on a particular area, one in which he is perhaps most competent, so you can expect each member to participate in the examination. Because time is limited, you may also expect some rather abrupt switches in the direction the questioning takes, so do not be upset by it. Normally, a board member will not pursue a single line of questioning unless he discovers a particular strength or weakness.

After each member has participated, the chairman will usually ask whether any member has any further questions, then will ask you if you have anything you wish to add. Unless you are expecting this question, it may floor you. Worse, it may start you off on an extended, extemporaneous speech. The board is not usually seeking more information. The question is principally to offer you a last opportunity to present further qualifications or to indicate that you have nothing to add. So, if you feel that a significant qualification or characteristic has been overlooked, it is proper to point it out in a sentence or so. Do not compliment the board on the thoroughness of their examination – they have been sketchy, and you know it. If you wish, merely say, "No thank you, I have nothing further to add." This is a point where you can "talk yourself out" of a good impression or fail to present an important bit of information. Remember, *you close the interview yourself.*

The chairman will then say, "That is all, Mr. _____, thank you." Do not be startled; the interview is over, and quicker than you think. Thank him, gather your belongings and take your leave. Save your sigh of relief for the other side of the door.

How to put your best foot forward

Throughout this entire process, you may feel that the board individually and collectively is trying to pierce your defenses, seek out your hidden weaknesses and embarrass and confuse you. Actually, this is not true. They are obliged to make an appraisal of your qualifications for the job you are seeking, and they want to see you in your best light. Remember, they must interview all candidates and a non-cooperative candidate may become a failure in spite of their best efforts to bring out his qualifications. Here are 15 suggestions that will help you:

1) Be natural – Keep your attitude confident, not cocky

If you are not confident that you can do the job, do not expect the board to be. Do not apologize for your weaknesses, try to bring out your strong points. The board is interested in a positive, not negative, presentation. Cockiness will antagonize any board member and make him wonder if you are covering up a weakness by a false show of strength.

2) Get comfortable, but don't lounge or sprawl

Sit erectly but not stiffly. A careless posture may lead the board to conclude that you are careless in other things, or at least that you are not impressed by the importance of the occasion. Either conclusion is natural, even if incorrect. Do not fuss with your clothing, a pencil or an ashtray. Your hands may occasionally be useful to emphasize a point; do not let them become a point of distraction.

3) Do not wisecrack or make small talk

This is a serious situation, and your attitude should show that you consider it as such. Further, the time of the board is limited – they do not want to waste it, and neither should you.

4) Do not exaggerate your experience or abilities

In the first place, from information in the application or other interviews and sources, the board may know more about you than you think. Secondly, you probably will not get away with it. An experienced board is rather adept at spotting such a situation, so do not take the chance.

5) If you know a board member, do not make a point of it, yet do not hide it

Certainly you are not fooling him, and probably not the other members of the board. Do not try to take advantage of your acquaintanceship – it will probably do you little good.

6) Do not dominate the interview

Let the board do that. They will give you the clues – do not assume that you have to do all the talking. Realize that the board has a number of questions to ask you, and do not try to take up all the interview time by showing off your extensive knowledge of the answer to the first one.

7) Be attentive

You only have 20 minutes or so, and you should keep your attention at its sharpest throughout. When a member is addressing a problem or question to you, give him your undivided attention. Address your reply principally to him, but do not exclude the other board members.

8) Do not interrupt

A board member may be stating a problem for you to analyze. He will ask you a question when the time comes. Let him state the problem, and wait for the question.

9) Make sure you understand the question

Do not try to answer until you are sure what the question is. If it is not clear, restate it in your own words or ask the board member to clarify it for you. However, do not haggle about minor elements.

10) Reply promptly but not hastily

A common entry on oral board rating sheets is "candidate responded readily," or "candidate hesitated in replies." Respond as promptly and quickly as you can, but do not jump to a hasty, ill-considered answer.

11) Do not be peremptory in your answers

A brief answer is proper – but do not fire your answer back. That is a losing game from your point of view. The board member can probably ask questions much faster than you can answer them.

12) Do not try to create the answer you think the board member wants

He is interested in what kind of mind you have and how it works – not in playing games. Furthermore, he can usually spot this practice and will actually grade you down on it.

13) Do not switch sides in your reply merely to agree with a board member

Frequently, a member will take a contrary position merely to draw you out and to see if you are willing and able to defend your point of view. Do not start a debate, yet do not surrender a good position. If a position is worth taking, it is worth defending.

14) Do not be afraid to admit an error in judgment if you are shown to be wrong

The board knows that you are forced to reply without any opportunity for careful consideration. Your answer may be demonstrably wrong. If so, admit it and get on with the interview.

15) Do not dwell at length on your present job

The opening question may relate to your present assignment. Answer the question but do not go into an extended discussion. You are being examined for a *new* job, not your present one. As a matter of fact, try to phrase ALL your answers in terms of the job for which you are being examined.

Basis of Rating

Probably you will forget most of these "do's" and "don'ts" when you walk into the oral interview room. Even remembering them all will not ensure you a passing grade. Perhaps you did not have the qualifications in the first place. But remembering them will help you to put your best foot forward, without treading on the toes of the board members.

Rumor and popular opinion to the contrary notwithstanding, an oral board wants you to make the best appearance possible. They know you are under pressure – but they also want to see how you respond to it as a guide to what your reaction would be under the pressures of the job you seek. They will be influenced by the degree of poise you display, the personal traits you show and the manner in which you respond.

ABOUT THIS BOOK

This book contains tests divided into Examination Sections. Go through each test, answering every question in the margin. We have also attached a sample answer sheet at the back of the book that can be removed and used. At the end of each test look at the answer key and check your answers. On the ones you got wrong, look at the right answer choice and learn. Do not fill in the answers first. Do not memorize the questions and answers, but understand the answer and principles involved. On your test, the questions will likely be different from the samples. Questions are changed and new ones added. If you understand these past questions you should have success with any changes that arise. Tests may consist of several types of questions. We have additional books on each subject should more study be advisable or necessary for you. Finally, the more you study, the better prepared you will be. This book is intended to be the last thing you study before you walk into the examination room. Prior study of relevant texts is also recommended. NLC publishes some of these in our Fundamental Series. Knowledge and good sense are important factors in passing your exam. Good luck also helps. So now study this Passbook, absorb the material contained within and take that knowledge into the examination. Then do your best to pass that exam.

EXAMINATION SECTION

EXAMINATION SECTION
TEST 1

DIRECTIONS: Each question or incomplete statement is followed by several suggested answers of completions. Select the one that BEST answers the question or complete the statement. *PRINT THE LETTER OF THE CORRECT ANSWER IN THE SPACE AT THE RIGHT.*

1. During a civil disorder in the city, the fire officer in charge of the first arriving apparatus finds that he is being prohibited from hooking up to hydrants because crowds of young toughs refuse to move away from the hydrants to allow the completion of operations. Of the following, the action generally considered to be MOST advisable for the officer to take under these circumstances is to
    - A. have the company leave the immediate area and request police protection
    - B. empty the contents of the booster tank, if apparatus is so equipped, on any visible fire
    - C. explain to the crowds the consequences of their actions
    - D. ask a member of the company of the same ethnic background as the gang leaders to ask for their cooperation

1._____

2. A fire officer whose company is effecting forcible entry notices that the smoke seems to be drawing back toward the fire within when the street entrance door is opened. Of the following, the MOST appropriate conclusion the fire officer should generally draw from this occurrence is that
    - A. heavy exterior streams are being directed into the upper floors
    - B. the seat of the fire is at a considerable distance from the door and at a higher level in the structure
    - C. another company has gained entry and is in the process of extinguishing the fire within
    - D. a potential backdraft explosion condition is present

2._____

3. The officer of the first engine company to arrive at a fire in a detached, five-story vacant building finds the two upper floors fully involved with fire. He orders the first of two lines to the exposure four side, a vacant lot between the fire building and a similar building. The officer's line placement is
    - A. *correct*, chiefly because the fire was too far advanced for an interior attack
    - B. *incorrect*, chiefly because line #1 should cover the front of the fire building with a large caliber stream and line #2 should cover the rear
    - C. *correct*, chiefly because exposure four was the main exposure with a possible extension hazard present
    - D. *incorrect*, chiefly because line #1 should have been used in the exposure with line #2 stretched to the fire floor via aerial ladder

3._____

4. Foamed plastic ceiling and wall insulation have excellent insulating properties but can be dangerously combustible. Following are three statements that MAY or MAY NOT apply to the fire characteristics of plastic foam insulation:
    - I. When left exposed, all plastic foam surfaces can ignite quite easily
    - II. Covering plastic foam insulation surfaces with port-land cement plaster, wall board, or meta sheeting will prevent decomposition of the foam by heat
    - III. A conventional sprinkler system has proved incapable of controlling fire spread when both walls and ceiling were foam-coated.

4._____

Which of the following choices is generally CORRECT with respect to the above statements?
- A. I and II are true, but III is not.
- B. I and III are true, but II is not.
- C. II and III are true, but I is not.
- D. I, II, and III are true.

5. When a fire officer arrives at an operation involving electrified track of a subway or other railroad system, his FIRST consideration should be whether the
   - A. power is to remain on or be turned off
   - B. response is for afire or other emergency
   - C. situation requires a hose line to be stretched
   - D. supervisor of the subway or railroad involved should be contacted directly or through the Fire Department dispatcher

6. Increasing the nozzle pressure from 75 psi to 100 psi on a master stream fog nozzle operating in the 60° position will result in which of the following changes?
   The width
   - A. and range *increase*
   - B. and range *decrease*
   - C. increases and the range *decreases*
   - D. decreases and the range *increases*

7. A suspicious fire occurred in a four-story occupied apartment building during the early evening hours. Afterwards the lieutenant in charge of the first arriving engine company supplied the fire marshal with the following information:
   I. At the time of arrival, flames had broken out through the windows of the apartment on the second-floor front of the building
   II. A number of persons had already gathered on the sidewalk across the street to watch the firefighting operations
   III. The entry hall and the stairwell were heavily charged with thick, black smoke when the first firemen entered the building
   IV. One civilian kept trying to help the firemen despite their repeated objections
   Which of these items would be LEAST helpful to the fire marshal?
   - A. I
   - B. II
   - C. III
   - D. IV

8. Emergency access to a ship's hold may be provided by the
   - A. vertical ventilation shaft
   - B. escape hatch
   - C. propeller shaft tunnel
   - D. forward peak tank

9. As an experiment, fires were set in the basement of an old school building to test the effect on upper floor exits and exit passageways of the heat and smoke generated. Its findings GENERALLY were that
   - A. heat caused the corridors to become untenable first
   - B. smoke caused the corridors to become untenable first
   - C. both heat and smoke caused the corridors to become untenable at about the same time
   - D. the interaction of heat and smoke was too complex to permit determination of their individual effects on tenability of corridors

10. Unsafe acts during drills give the company officer an opportunity to take corrective action and emphasize the importance of safety.
Corrective action would NOT be required when a member
   A. anchors a hose by standing on it while the apparatus is used to make a stretch
   B. mounts to the aerial ladder turntable with hose over his shoulder
   C. hauls hose onto a roof by pulling it up rather than walking it on
   D. climbs a scaling ladder with hands on rungs instead of on the beam or spar

11. As a unit performed field inspection duty in a large industrial plant, the officer pointed out to new men that the piping was color coded and that the code was the one established by the United States of America Standards Institute (USASI, now the American National Standards Institute, Inc.).
In this system, fire protection materials and equipment are identified by the color
   A. red   B. yellow (orange)   C. green   D. bright blue

12. Upon arriving at an LP gas tank truck fire, the officer in command of an engine company gave the following orders:
   I. *Stretch line and approach fire from upwind*
   II. *Keep nozzle low and aim it upward*
   III. *Keep all spectators at least 500 feet from front and rear of tank*
The one of the following choices that contains ONLY those of the officer's orders which are correct is:
   A. I, II, III   B. I, II   C. I, III   D. II, III

13.

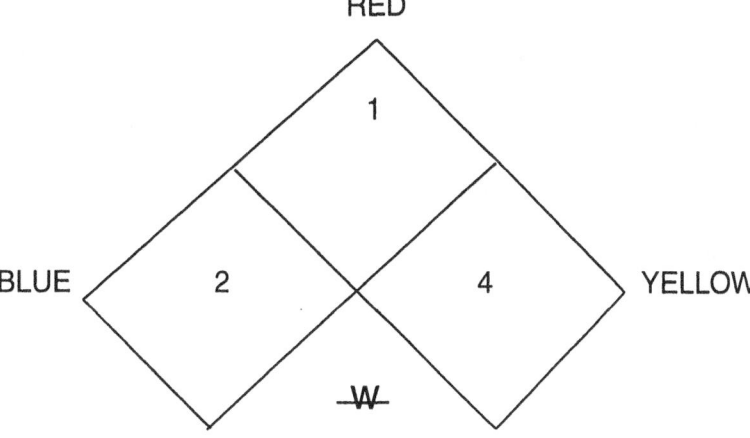

On arriving at a railroad incident involving a freight train, an officer finds the above label attached to one of the freight cars.
The numbers in the label were colored as identified in the above diagram. A light white smoke could be seen coming from the freight car.
From the label and the smoke, the officer concludes:
   I. No water should be used on the products within the car
   II. The most serious hazard presented by the car's contents is flammability
   III. Even a very short exposure to the material in the car could be extremely hazardous to health
   Which of the officer's conclusions is generally CORRECT?
   A. I   B. II
   C. III   D. None is correct

14.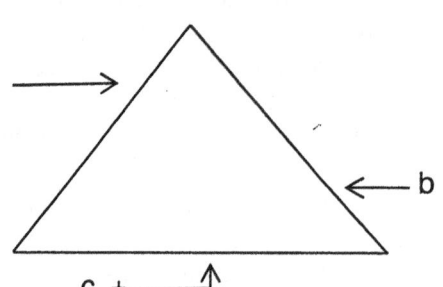

DIAGRAM I   DIAGRAM II

The lines marked a, b, and c in each diagram above represent saw cuts made by a power saw. The triangular shape of each diagram is that of the hole that would be opened up by the power saw's cuts.
Which one of the following choices CORRECTLY describes the hole shape that should be cut in a brick wall or in a peaked roof, and the proper sequence in which the saw cuts should be made in each case?
Cut the hole shaped as shown in Diagram I in _____ making saw cut _____;
Cut the hole shaped as shown in Diagram II in _____, making saw cut _____.
   A. brick walls; a first, then c, and last b; peaked roofs; a first, then b, and last c
   B. brick walls; b first, then c, and last a; peaked roofs; c first, then b, and last a
   C. peaked roofs; c first, then a, and last b; brick walls; b first, then a, and last c
   D. peaked roofs; b first, then c, and last a; brick walls; c first, then a, and last b

15. Polyvinyl chloride (PVC) is being used increasingly in the manufacture of a wide variety of articles.
Which one of the following is NOT a correct statement about polyvinyl chloride?
PVC
   A. is not easily ignited, but when heated it softens at 175°F and melts extensively at 220°F
   B. when burning, produces acrid fumes which can be corrosive
   C. burns readily once ignited, releasing quantities of heat
   D. in plasticized form, has fire characteristics largely determined by the amount and nature of the plasticizer

(KEY CORRECT ANSWERS)

1. A	6. D	11. A
2. D	7. B	12. B
3. B	8. A	13. A
4. B	9. B	14. D
5. A	10. C	15. C

TEST 2

DIRECTIONS: Each question or incomplete statement is followed by several suggested answers of completions. Select the one that BEST answers the question or complete the statement. *PRINT THE LETTER OF THE CORRECT ANSWER IN THE SPACE AT THE RIGHT.*

1. During overhauling operations at a fire, a lieutenant observes that a member has wet down all the clothing in a clothes closet. In the post-mortem discussion of the fire, the member states that he found some of the clothing smoldering and wet all of it as a safety precaution.
   The member's action was
   A. *correct*, mainly because some of the clothing that was undamaged could have been ignited by the smoldering clothing
   B. *incorrect*, mainly because the smoldering clothing should have been wet down outside the apartment
   C. *correct*, mainly because the member could direct his efforts to more important work sooner
   D. *incorrect*, mainly because the clothing should have been sorted first and only the smoldering items wet down

   1.____

2. When nailed-up dumbwaiter doors delay forcible entry to a dumbwaiter shaft fire, the tillerman of the first ladder company to arrive GENERALLY should
   A. go to the roof and open the skylight over the shaft
   B. force entry for the nozzleman on whatever floor he obtains water
   C. provide horizontal ventilation at the top floor by breaking windows from the roof
   D. go directly to the top floor to assist in operations at the point of attack on the fire

   2.____

3. High-stacked storage of idle wooden pallets creates potential sources of intense fires. The MOST generally accepted of the following ways of limiting the fire hazard of stacked wooden pallets is to
   A. suspend *fire stopping* asbestos cloth between the stringers of the upper and lower deck of the pallet
   B. add a board across one open end of the pallet
   C. use pallets constructed of fire-retardant lumber
   D. keep the pallets outdoors and at a distance from buildings

   3.____

4. If necessary to search for any extension of fire, there should be no hesitation about opening up wall paneling.
   This guideline is GENERALLY
   A. *inappropriate*, chiefly because paneling is expensive and its removal adds heavily to the fire loss
   B. *appropriate*, chiefly because the entire wall is usually replaced since matching old paneling is very difficult
   C. *inappropriate*, chiefly because small inspection holes could be cut and later easily patched
   D. *appropriate*, chiefly because adhesive holding paneling to a wall is extremely flammable

   4.____

5. Hose headers found in some large area industrial occupancies are part of the _____ System.
    A. Standpipe
    B. Automatic wet sprinkler
    C. Yard hydrant
    D. Water deluge

6. The one of the following generally considered to be the BEST method of extinguishing an oil spill fire where burning liquid is running down a ditch, gutter, or depression is to
    A. whip a fog nozzle stream across the surface of the burning liquid
    B. direct a solid stream on the ground in advance of the fire
    C. bounce a foam stream onto the burning surface
    D. form a heavy foam blanket below the point of the fire ahead of the flow of burning oil

7. Water, in any form, shall not be played against electrical equipment when operating at fires in electrical generating stations and substations without the advice of the power company representative.
Such a warning would GENERALLY be
    A. proper, chiefly because any form of water stream conducts electric current that endangers personnel on the line
    B. improper, chiefly because a fog stream is both an effective extinguishing medium and safe for members on the line
    C. proper, chiefly because water runoff may cause short circuits in other equipment starting new fires
    D. improper, chiefly because delay in directing water on the fire results in dangerous and costly power blackouts

8. The constant pressure feature of the FT-2 fog tip stops operating when the nozzle pressure (in pounds per square inch) is outside the range of

    A. 55-95   B. 65-95   C. 65-105   D. 75-105

9. The MOST appropriate of the following statements regarding the maintenance or use of the portable power saw is that
    A. the capacity of the fuel tank is generally sufficient for thirty-five to forty minutes of continuous operation
    B. one slap on the back of the operator by the guide man indicates Shut down saw
    C. the saw should not be refueled when the engine is hot
    D. a schedule of periodic servicing requirements for the saw should include daily checkups

10. The officer of an engine company in a relay supplying water for a tower ladder stream generally would be CORRECT to order
    A. water supplied to the base of the tower ladder at 150 psi
    B. two water sources to supply the base of the tower
    C. intake pressure to be in excess of 80 psi at the relay pumper closest to the tower ladder
    D. water shut down first at the tower ladder gate siamese

11. Which one of the following orders would be LEAST appropriate if given by the lieutenant of the first company to arrive at the scene of a fire in a vault containing cellulose nitrate storage?
    A. *Stay outside the vault area until the cellulose nitrate has been consumed.*
    B. *Protect the exposures and evacuate the immediate area.*
    C. *Open up doors to the vault as quickly as possible.*
    D. *Ventilate the building thoroughly before entering.*

11.____

12. Except for life-saving purposes, members are never to be ordered into a sanitation scow hopper which has been involved in fire.
    Of the following, the PRINCIPAL reason for this guideline is the
    A. presence of toxic gases caused by decomposition of organic material
    B. likelihood of falling through a burnt-out area
    C. lack of oxygen in the hopper enclosure
    D. possibility of hopper machinery starting up

12.____

13. If a nozzle on a line is replaced with a nozzle of smaller diameter and the engine pressure remains the same, the nozzle pressure will increase.
    This statement is CORRECT because the smaller nozzle discharges _____ gallons per minute and, therefore, the friction loss will _____ with the _____ flow.
    A. *fewer; decrease;* smaller
    B. *more; decrease;* larger
    C. *fewer; increase;* smaller
    D. *more; increase;* larger

13.____

14. To ensure that the pumper feeds the sprinkler system after one line is connected to the siamese, the lieutenant orders the chauffeur to gradually close the discharge gate supplying the siamese while leaving the throttle setting unchanged. He also orders the chauffeur to report the effect on the engine discharge manifold pressure reading and on the engine speed.

    The MAIN reason the lieutenant's actions are correct is that, if the gate were actually feeding the sprinkler system,
    A. both the engine discharge manifold pressure and the engine speed would start to increase
    B. the engine discharge manifold pressure would increase and the engine speed would start to decrease
    C. the engine discharge manifold pressure would decrease and the engine speed would start to increase
    D. both the engine discharge manifold pressure and the engine speed would start to decrease

14.____

15. A 10% increase in engine pressure will usually result in a 10% increase in nozzle pressure when the line is equipped with an MST, but this will NOT necessarily occur when the same line is equipped with an FT-1 or an FT-2.
This statement is
   A. *correct*, chiefly because a specific increase in engine pressure results in an identical increase in nozzle pressure when the FT-1 or FT-2 is used
   B. *incorrect*, chiefly because it applies only when rapid water is used with the FT-1 or FT-2 while plain water is used with the MST
   C. *correct*, chiefly because the variable orifice in the FT-1 or FT-2 permits K in the Underwriters' Formula [$EP = NP(1.1+KL)$] to vary
   D. *incorrect*, chiefly because the shut-off to which the FT-1 or FT-2 is attached allows control of the flow of water through the tips

15.____

(KEY CORRECT ANSWERS)

1. D	6. D	11. A
2. D	7. C	12. B
3. D	8. C	13. A
4. B	9. D	14. A
5. B	10. C	15. C

EXAMINATION SECTION
TEST 1

DIRECTIONS: Each question or incomplete statement is followed by several suggested answers or completions. Select the one that BEST answers the question or completes the statement. *PRINT THE LETTER OF THE CORRECT ANSWER IN THE SPACE AT THE RIGHT.*

1. A fireman permanently assigned to an engine company is detailed for training to another unit within his division for one tour of duty on the following day. The fireman asks his company officer if he is entitled to compensation at the rate of time-and-one-half of his regular salary for travel time to the other unit. The officer tells him that he is.
   The company officer's answer to the question is basically

   A. *incorrect,* MAINLY because company officers are the only members entitled to travel-time compensation
   B. *correct,* MAINLY because the company officer has the authority to decide whether the fireman is entitled to travel-time compensation
   C. *incorrect,* MAINLY because a member who is detailed to another unit for training is not entitled to travel-time compensation
   D. *correct,* MAINLY because a member is always entitled to travel-time compensation when he is detailed to another unit

1.____

2. A company relocates into the quarters of another company. Of the following calls, the one the relocating company is NOT required to respond to is a

   A. simultaneous call if the company in which they are relocated is assigned
   B. subsequent 2nd alarm for a fire or emergency at which the original company is operating
   C. special call for the company in which they are relocated
   D. 5th alarm for a fire at which the original company is operating

2.____

3. Radio code signal 10-36 should be transmitted for a condition involving a(n)

   A. civilian in need of assistance
   B. odor of smoke
   C. defective alarm system
   D. automobile accident

3.____

4. A lieutenant acting as commanding officer at the scene of a fire in an apartment building finds it necessary to remove a Federal government lock from a mail box.
   Of the following, the BEST course of action for him to take regarding the lock is to

   A. give it to the tenant whose name appears on the mail box
   B. have one of his members deliver it to the Division Commander's office
   C. send it, as soon as possible, to the official in charge of the nearest United States post office
   D. hand it over to the senior police officer at the scene and obtain a receipt

4.____

5. According to regulations, company officers should be prepared for annual company inspections by deputy chiefs during the months of

   A. April and May   B. June and July
   C. January and February   D. March and April

5.____

6. Code number 4 in the uniform filing system identifies subject matter of the primary section pertaining to

   A. operations
   B. fire prevention
   C. personnel
   D. training

7. A lieutenant notifies the battalion chief immediately upon discovering alcoholic beverages in quarters. The lieutenant then questions the members. Before preferring charges, he warns the members of their rights.
   This series of actions is

   A. *proper,* chiefly because members must be warned of their rights before charges are preferred
   B. *improper,* chiefly because members must be warned of their rights before being questioned
   C. *proper,* since the presence of the alcoholic beverages represents an overt act the lieutenant may question members without warning them of their rights
   D. *improper,* since the presence of the alcoholic beverages represents an overt act, the lieutenant may prefer charges without questioning members or warning them of their rights

8. An engine company officer conducting a drill on apparatus maintenance attempts to control the discussion and direct it into areas of knowledge he considers to be the most important aspects of the drill.
   The officer's approach is

   A. *appropriate,* CHIEFLY because it enables him to demonstrate his leadership to the members
   B. *inappropriate,* CHIEFLY because his restraining of the discussion by the members may cause resentment and resistance to the material being taught
   C. *appropriate,* CHIEFLY because such control and direction are necessary to assure the effectiveness of the drill as a learning experience
   D. *inappropriate,* CHIEFLY because participation and *learning by doing* should be the most important aspects of the drill

9. A public school teacher telephones a lieutenant in quarters and requests permission for her class to pay a visit to the firehouse.
   Of the following, the MOST appropriate action for the lieutenant to take would be to

   A. make the necessary arrangements for the firehouse visit of the class
   B. refer the request to the bureau of community relations
   C. ask the teacher to call back during the company commander's tour of duty
   D. advise the teacher that such visits are permitted during *Open House* periods

10. While a lieutenant and his company are returning to quarters after a fire call, a battalion chief stops the apparatus and tells the lieutenant he is going to prefer charges because a member is riding the rear step without wearing a fire helmet.
    The PROPER action would be to file charges AGAINST

    A. all members of the company, because they did nothing to stop their colleague from violating a departmental safety rule

B. the offending member only, because he was the one violating a departmental safety rule
C. the lieutenant only, because as the officer in command he is responsible for the actions of the entire company
D. the lieutenant and the offending member, because in such circumstances both are held to account under the rules

11. Employees of a tenant in a 30-story office building tell a lieutenant performing AFID that they have not been given a written copy of the sections of the building's fire safety plan applying to them.
Of the following, the MOST appropriate action for the lieutenant to take is to

   A. forward an A-8 indicating that the tenant shall distribute a written copy of the applicable material to all his employees
   B. arrange for the fire wardens to give verbal instructions to the employees regarding the applicable sections of the safety plan
   C. forward an A-8 indicating that the building management shall distribute written copies of the applicable parts of the safety plan to the employees
   D. point out to the employees that as long as a copy of the safety plan is posted on each floor, distribution of copies of the plan to employees is not required

11._____

12. A fire occurs at 3 o'clock in the afternoon of a workday on the fifth story of a centrally air-conditioned 25-story office building. A lieutenant, the first officer to arrive, assigns a member to find the fire safety director.
Of the following, the BEST way to accomplish this would be for the lieutenant to order the member to proceed immediately to the

   A. mechanical equipment room, where the fire safety director should be stopping the air supply to the fire floor
   B. fire command station, where the fire safety director should be in order to meet responsibilities assigned to him *in* the fire safety plan
   C. office of the fire safety director, where the fire safety director should be controlling the operations of the fire brigade
   D. floor below the fire, where the fire safety director should be to best aid the lieutenant in beginning firefighting operations

12._____

13. A lieutenant inspecting a multiple dwelling erected in 1960 is accompanied by the building manager. They find a sign reading *Gas Meter Room - No Storage Permitted* lying on the floor inside the gas meter room.
Of the following, the MOST appropriate action for the lieutenant to take would be to point out to the building manager that, according to the building code, the sign must be posted on the

   A. exterior of the gas meter room door
   B. interior of the gas meter room door
   C. wall adjacent to the gas meters in the gas meter room
   D. wall outside the gas meter room adjacent to the gas meter room door

13._____

14. A fireman inspecting a factory building constructed in 1967 finds that, during working hours, the doors leading from the factory workrooms to the stairs are locked from the stair side, but are unlocked from the workroom side offering easy egress to the stairs. The fireman is uncertain about the legality of this condition and asks his lieutenant for guidance.
    In this situation, it would be MOST appropriate for the lieutenant to tell the fireman that this condition is

    A. *lawful,* CHIEFLY because the doors could be opened readily from the workroom side
    B. *unlawful,* CHIEFLY because panic bolts of an approved type have not been provided
    C. *lawful,* CHIEFLY because there is ready egress from the workroom to the stairs during factory working hours
    D. *unlawful,* CHIEFLY because the doors should be readily openable from both sides during working hours

15. According to the fire prevention code, a solution made up of half a gallon of wood alcohol and two pounds of sulphide of sodium would MOST appropriately be used for

    A. coating old flammable motion picture film to render it less hazardous
    B. emulsifying gasoline spills before flushing into sewers
    C. removing spray paint from fluorescent lights in spray booths
    D. scrubbing the floor of explosive magazines to decompose nitroglycerine stains

16. A lieutenant inspecting a tenement finds a gate on a window giving access to a fire escape. The building owner, accompanying the lieutenant, points out that the gate is of a type approved by the Underwriters Laboratory (UL).
    Of the following, the MOST appropriate response for the lieutenant to make to the owner is that the gate is

    A. *unlawful* unless it is of a type approved by the fire department
    B. *lawful* if it is of a type approved by the city board of standards and appeals
    C. *lawful* because it has UL approval
    D. *unlawful* because all such gates are unlawful

17. Certain office buildings must have floor areas located more than 40 feet above curb level subdivided into spaces not to exceed 7500 square feet.
    Following are criteria that might determine whether an office building's floor areas shall be subdivided:
    The office building('s)
    I. does not have smoke detectors
    II. is 100 feet or more in height
    III. is unsprinklered
    IV. floor areas exceed 7500 square feet, excluding any areas enclosing stairs, corridors, elevators, and shafts

    Which one of the following choices lists ALL of the above criteria which conform to the building code?

    A. I, II
    B. I, III, IV
    C. II, III, IV
    D. I, II, III, IV

18. The controls in an elevator in a high-rise office building are being operated on *firemen service.* In this situation, certain operating conditions established must be met. Which one of the following is NOT such a condition? The

    A. manual controls in the elevator car override any other keyed switch controls and elevator landing call buttons
    B. elevator is operable only by a person in the elevator car
    C. elevator car and hoistway doors remain open only while the Door Open button is depressed
    D. controls permit the operator inside the car to change the direction of travel prior to reaching the originally selected floor

19. The test of a required sprinkler system in a converted dwelling must be made by a licensed plumber or sprinkler system contractor AT LEAST once

    A. each month
    B. every three months
    C. every six months
    D. each year

20. Apartment doors opening into any stair or public hall connected therewith in old law tenements more than four stories in height MUST

    A. have a fire resistance rating of at least 1 hour for those doors on the fourth or higher story unless the stair or public hall is protected by a sprinkler system
    B. have a fire resistance rating of at least 3/4 hour for those doors on the third or higher story
    C. have a fire resistance rating of at least 1 hour unless the stair or public hall is protected by a sprinkler system
    D. be non-combustible

KEY (CORRECT ANSWERS)

1.	C	11.	A
2.	B	12.	B
3.	D	13.	A
4.	C	14.	D
5.	A	15.	D
6.	D	16.	B
7.	B	17.	D
8.	C	18.	C
9.	A	19.	D
10.	D	20.	A

TEST 2

DIRECTIONS: Each question or incomplete statement is followed by several suggested answers or completions. Select the one that BEST answers the question or completes the statement. *PRINT THE LETTER OF THE CORRECT ANSWER IN THE SPACE AT THE RIGHT.*

Questions 1-5.

DIRECTIONS: Questions 1 through 5 are based on the following description of an eight-story factory building, 95 feet high, erected in 1940. It has a continuous frontage consisting of 250 feet on A Street, 200 feet on 1st Avenue, and 250 feet on B Street, the last featuring a truck-loading dock. Fire extinguishing features include a central station-connected automatic sprinkler system, a standpipe, and portable extinguishers.

1. The eighth floor is occupied by a firm using inflammable paint to spray and dip metallic parts for lamps and is required to comply with the paint spraying rules of the Board of Standards and Appeals. There are several spray booths and also a dip tank through which articles pass on a conveyor so that hinged covers are impractical.
The rules mandate that in this occupancy

   A. cabinets for the main storage of 75 gallons of inflammable spray materials need not be vented to the outer air
   B. sprinkler heads shall be provided in cabinets and storage rooms
   C. the extinguishing system over the dip tank shall be designed for automatic operation only
   D. the conveyor shall be interlocked with the extinguishing system so that it will stop when the system operates

2. With respect to using the exterior enclosed fireproof stairway as a means of access to the upper stories of this building for firefighting, according to the labor law, it would be INCORRECT to say that

   A. the doors leading into the building from these stairs can be equipped with locks
   B. the lighting of the stairs may be on the same circuit as that supplying the regular factory lighting
   C. stretching of hose might be facilitated if there is a balcony opening upon an open space of at least 100 square feet
   D. the stairways and landings may be constructed of incombustible material

3. The fifth floor of the building is tenanted entirely by a manufacturer of women's dresses. Three 5-gallon cans containing a cleaning fluid are on the premises. The labels indicate that the fluid is an inflammable mixture manufactured and sold with a fire department certificate of approval.
Of the following, it would be MOST appropriate to state that this condition is

   A. *not permitted* in an occupancy where dry goods or similar material is manufactured
   B. *permitted* only in buildings which meet the requirements of the building code regulating high-hazard occupancies
   C. *permitted* if the containers are stored as required by the fire department
   D. *not permitted* in this occupancy because the containers exceed one-gallon capacity

4. Within the past year a garment factory has occupied the third floor of the building and installed several steam pressing machines. Steam is generated by an oil burner located in the occupancy. Oil is stored in an 1100-gallon storage tank buried in the basement and is pumped to a 275-gallon day tank on the third floor. A transfer pump in the basement supplies oil to a booster pump which supplies oil at the required pressure to the day tank. The one of the following that is CORRECT under these conditions is that the

   A. installation of an oil burner above the lowest floor for other than space heating is illegal in a building this high
   B. pump between the transfer pump and the day tank is not an approved installation
   C. day tank should not exceed 50 gallons in capacity
   D. day tank must have either a concrete curb surrounding it or an overflow switch which can cause an alarm to sound in case of oil overflow

5. The truck loading dock is protected by a system of dry sprinklers controlled by a dry pipe valve which is actuated by the release of compressed air.
Which of the following is NOT a requirement to which this portion of the building's sprinkler system should conform?

   A. The air pressure which must be maintained in the system is specified in the code as 75 psi.
   B. The compressed air shall be supplied from a source capable of restoring normal air pressure in the system within thirty minutes.
   C. Air pressure must be maintained throughout the year.
   D. The air compressor shall be provided with an approved relief valve set to open as specified by the dry-valve manufacturer.

6. When a roof is opened up to improve ventilation for companies attempting to reach the fire, it is generally recommended that a protective hose line be available at the opening. Water from this hose line on the roof generally should NOT be applied

   A. to cover the firemen working on the roof
   B. through the hole to extinguish fire in the space below the roof
   C. on exposures to reduce the effects of heat and flames escaping through the roof hole
   D. to the roof to limit the flame action around the roof hole

7. When operating the Stang Intelligent Nozzle in the portable position, a member should limit horizontal rotation to a 90 angle to either side from the straight ahead position over the Siamese inlet.
Of the following, the MAIN reason for this is that the

   A. looped barrel will not countercheck thrust forces if the nozzle is turned beyond these limits
   B. need for rope security will be eliminated
   C. safety stop lock will override at horizontal angles greater than 90
   D. stability of the platform will be assured

8. The one of the following that is NOT a correct statement concerning a 2 1/2 gallon pressurized water extinguisher filled with an aqueous film-forming foam charge is that the

A. solution remaining in a partially expended extinguisher can be held in reserve in case of re-ignition
B. agent is compatible with dry chemical and foam extinguishers on Class B fires
C. film formed will be effective if applied gently on the surface of burning oil
D. film formed is more effective when the charge is combined with a wetting agent

9. A covering officer assigned to a rescue unit is giving a drill on the concrete core cutter. In the course of his instruction, the officer makes each of the following points:
The
   I. carbide core bit can cut an 8" diameter hole through solid concrete
   II. drill can be used in any one of three positions: overhead, laterally, or downward
   III. cutting rate is approximately one inch per minute provided no metal reinforcing rods are encountered

Of the following choices, the one containing only the CORRECT statements made by the officer is

A. I, II   B. II, III   C. I, III   D. I, II, III

10. Rubber-lined hose should be used with a foam nozzle. The one of the following which is the CHIEF reason for doing this is that unlined hose

A. has a rough interior surface which increases friction loss
B. kinks more readily because it lacks rigidity
C. clogs the nozzle strainer with its lint
D. is porous and results in pressure loss at the nozzle

11. The following are firefighting practices that might be followed when pesticides are involved in fire:
   I. Fight the fire from the windward side or at right angles to the wind
   II. Use foam wherever possible to reduce toxic runoff
   III. Contain contaminated runoff water wherever possible

The one of the following choices containing ALL of the above practices that are generally correct is

A. I, II   B. II, III   C. I, III   D. I, II, III

12. During his inspection of a sprinklered factory, a lieutenant notices that underneath the countertop work tables are cabinets and drawers. The bottoms of the cabinets and the lowest drawers are practically at floor level. The lieutenant advises the plant supervisor that it would probably be best to avoid using the bottom six inches of space for the storage of material.
The one of the following which is the BEST explanation for following this practice is that it will generally

A. reduce the amount of time needed for workers to obtain needed material
B. prevent the accumulation of scraps in locations subject to spontaneous heating
C. limit potential water damage losses to stock
D. impede the spread of fire by decreasing the fire loading

13. Recently a fire involved the upper floors of a 30-story telephone company switching center under construction in the general vicinity of City Hall.
    A lesson learned from operations at this special occupancy building that will improve operations at future similar fires is that

    A. officers should examine the interiors of buildings where air conditioner intakes constitute a part of the exposure hazard as a part of *brand patrol*
    B. sound-powered telephone systems are more reliable than handie-talkie communications between company officers and chauffeurs
    C. hose stretched in the street is best protected against damage from falling brands by the use of heavy streams such as deckpipes
    D. engine pressures in the 300 psi range cannot be safely supplied to provide adequate nozzle pressures

14. A BLEVE (Boiling Liquid Expanding Vapor Explosion) potential may exist when tanks containing liquified flammable gases are exposed to heat and flame.
    Following are three statements that may or may not serve as guidelines for dealing with the fire control problems in a situation where a BLEVE potential exists:
      I. Application of water must be at the point of flame contact
      II. The most critical and highest priority for cooling is the tank's liquid-containing spaces
      III. Accurate direction of fire streams is of major importance
    Which of the following choices contains ONLY those guidelines which are correct?

    A. I, II   B. II, III   C. I, III   D. I, II, III

15. The MOST appropriate of the following statements regarding departmental mask procedures at fire operations in contaminated locations is that a

    A. lieutenant who has been exposed to the effects of toxic fumes and heavy smoke, without the protection of a mask, shall not be permitted to return to the contaminated location, even if he has put on a mask
    B. lieutenant operating under contaminated conditions in a below-grade level may remove his mask in order to more effectively supervise his men who are working with masks
    C. member of a mask-equipped team who is required to leave the contaminated area shall be escorted to a safe area by two members
    D. member who has used a mask under heavy exertion and heat conditions shall not be permitted to operate in contaminated areas without a mask during finishing up stages unless he is properly rested

16. Of the following, the MAIN purpose of a large-caliber stream is to

    A. contain the fire
    B. break up heat waves
    C. effect ventilation
    D. protect exposures by forming a water curtain

17. The officer of the first engine company to arrive at a fire in a building equipped with both sprinkler and stand-pipe systems shall, if the standpipe's use is vital at the fire, order the first line connected to the

    A. standpipe Siamese and the second line connected to the first floor outlet of the standpipe system
    B. standpipe Siamese and the second line connected to the sprinkler Siamese
    C. sprinkler Siamese and the second line connected to the standpipe Siamese
    D. standpipe Siamese and the third line connected to the sprinkler Siamese

18. Of the following kinds of gas, the one which would be present in the HIGHEST percentage at a fire involving cable insulation in a Con Edison manhole is

    A. acetylene
    B. sulphur dioxide
    C. phosgene
    D. hydrogen

19. Recovery is usually rapid following administration of artificial respiration in cases resulting from

    A. carbon monoxide poisoning
    B. drug overdose
    C. anatomic obstruction
    D. electrical shock

20. Debris tunneling may be necessary to effect the rescue of victims in a serious structural collapse. The recommended method for constructing a debris tunnel is by the use of frames and forepoling.
    The one of the following components which is generally NOT a part of a debris tunnel is a

    A. crown bar
    B. collar
    C. sole plate
    D. footing

KEY (CORRECT ANSWERS)

1.	D	11.	D
2.	B	12.	C
3.	C	13.	A
4.	B	14.	C
5.	A	15.	A
6.	B	16.	A
7.	D	17.	B
8.	D	18.	D
9.	A	19.	C
10.	C	20.	D

EXAMINATION SECTION
TEST 1

DIRECTIONS: Each question or incomplete statement is followed by several suggested answers or completions. Select the one that BEST answers the question or completes the statement. *PRINT THE LETTER OF THE CORRECT ANSWER IN THE SPACE AT THE RIGHT.*

1. A lieutenant conducting a company drill describes a scene in which a sudden unexpected structural collapse trapped an unknown number of members. The units that were clearly more effective in the rescue and firefighting effort proved to be those in which the officer retained control because the members were well-trained and consequently responded to orders quickly and efficiently. The units that were less effective were those in which the officer lost control and members operated independently.
For the lieutenant to mention that some members have this tendency to operate independently and inefficiently in such unusual situations is generally

   A. *appropriate,* chiefly because routine chain-of-command procedures are ineffective in handling unusual incidents
   B. *inappropriate,* chiefly because unusual incidents are handled routinely by those officers present and aware of the situation
   C. *appropriate,* chiefly because members should be aware that people often follow the lead of those around them during unusual incidents
   D. *inappropriate,* chiefly because unusual incidents inspire firefighters to save life, leading to their following the correct course of action naturally

1.____

2. A lieutenant makes a regular practice of holding a critique in company quarters after each working fire. He notices that some of the members become defensive when asked to describe or explain their actions at the fire.
Of the following, the MOST appropriate conclusion the lieutenant should draw is that members who become unduly defensive during the discussion are generally displaying feelings of

   A. competitiveness
   B. jealousy
   C. belligerency
   D. guilt

2.____

3. The three statements listed below may or may not be correct reasons for a company officer to exercise authority to accomplish fire department goals. Authority
   I. is a mechanism for creating coordination and control within the company
   II. eliminates the necessity for the officer to be sensitive to his subordinates' needs
   III. is a means by which the behavior of individual subordinates may be influenced

   Which of the following choices lists ONLY those of the above statements that are generally considered to be correct reasons for the exercise of authority?

   A. I, II   B. II, III   C. I, III   D. I, II, III

3.____

4. A company officer sees a fireman assigned to do committee work in the bunkroom come to the office to take a personal phone call and spend several minutes on the phone. An hour later, the officer inspects the bunkroom only to discover half the room swept, and the broom, dust pan, and mop left standing in the corner. The officer then goes downstairs where he finds the fireman at work with other members performing a maintenance check on the apparatus. When the company officer begins to reprimand him about the condition of the bunkroom, the fireman interrupts him with an apology and explains that he had been distracted by the phone call, but would return immediately to complete his committee work. Before allowing the fireman to return, the officer completes his criticism of the member's inattention to committee work, stressing the preventive maintenance aspects of all such housekeeping chores.
The action taken by the company officer generally is

   A. *advisable,* chiefly because the fireman's inattention to duties may carry over to fire-fighting situations where there is hazard to life
   B. *inadvisable,* chiefly because he is unnecessarily criticizing a subordinate who has realized his mistake and is about to take steps to correct it
   C. *advisable,* chiefly because such public criticism may serve as a useful lesson to the entire company
   D. *inadvisable,* chiefly because a company officer should allow members to learn by discovering and correcting their own mistakes

5. A lieutenant is to conduct a company drill in quarters on the use of an exhaust fan for better ventilation in fire situations. He has the fan and several copies of its operations manual available.
Of the following, the MOST effective method for training the members of the company in the use of this fan is for the lieutenant to

   A. hand out the manuals to the members and, after they have read them, lecture them on the use of the fan
   B. demonstrate the use of the fan and instruct the members to study the manuals carefully
   C. discuss the material in the manuals with the members and direct the members believed to be most proficient to demonstrate its use
   D. instruct the members in the use of the fan with reference to the manuals and observe each one in his performance with it

6. The MOST appropriate of the following guidelines for a company officer to employ in a coaching interview with a subordinate is to

   A. use a job-centered rather than a man-centered approach
   B. act in an authoritarian manner if this is his usual pattern
   C. begin the interview with a review of the deficiencies in the man's work and end with a summary of his strengths
   D. let the subordinate do most of the talking, avoiding comments of approval or disapproval

7. Lieutenant Smith has recently been transferred to a new company on a permanent basis. He finds that some of the procedures established by the lieutenant he has replaced are inefficient and unproductive.
Of the following, it would be LEAST acceptable for Lieutenant Smith to handle this situation by

   A. changing all inefficient and unproductive procedures immediately
   B. changing the most time-consuming of the unproductive procedures first and gradually changing the others
   C. making only those changes which are acceptable to the members of his company
   D. making only urgent changes until his informal authority is established among the members of the company

7.____

8. A lieutenant recently transferred to an engine company in another borough finds the firemen under his new command lax, generally apathetic, and very slow in complying with orders. To remedy this situation, the lieutenant sets forth certain restrictions and rules to guide the conduct of the members. He then uses his authority to enforce his orders when any member does not comply.
The lieutenant's use of his authority as a means of restricting the behavior of the firemen is likely to be MOST effective in a situation where

   A. he is attempting to change the general attitude of the firemen rather than their performance of a specific activity
   B. a change in behavior depends on an interchange of information between the lieutenant and the firemen
   C. uniformity of action by the firemen is critical
   D. speed in performing a task is not a factor

8.____

9. In order to enlist the help of members in effecting change, a fire officer may sometimes take the leaders of their informal groups into his confidence.
This method of effecting change is MOST suitable when a fire officer wishes to

   A. convince members that they stand to gain from the change
   B. ensure that a new procedure is not made public
   C. inform members of the effect of the change on their public relations image as professional firefighters
   D. notify members of the full details of new procedures involved in the change

9.____

10. Supervisors usually employ direct orders or, when possible, put orders in the form of questions, for example, *Would you....* The best method of giving orders, however, if circumstances permit, is to help subordinates analyze a situation in such a way that the situation itself suggests the order, with the supervisor and subordinate reaching agreement on the wisest course of action.
Which of the following is the MAJOR advantage of this type of indirect order?

   A. Subordinates generally realize the importance to the supervisor of the order and are thus more fearful of the consequences of disobedience.
   B. Subordinates will generally carry out the order without suggesting any modifications to deal with new developments that arise during performance of the order.
   C. Such orders are usually carried out more intelligently than unexplained commands.
   D. Such orders usually provide detailed standards against which work performance can be fairly evaluated.

10.____

11. A battalion chief criticizes a lieutenant, telling him that his reports are too long. *I'm too busy to read all that. Give it to me on one page, condensed to a single paragraph.* Although brevity of reports is generally desirable, the order given to this lieutenant demanding condensation of each report to only one paragraph is defective MAINLY because requiring brevity

    A. fails to provide an opportunity for exercise of writing skill
    B. encourages omission of information and endangers understanding
    C. creates the misleading impression that a serious matter is unimportant
    D. results in obscuring a main point in favor of technical details

12. Work load analysis is a supervisory tool which may help a lieutenant deal with problems arising in connection with work assignments.
    Which of the following is MOST likely to be an indication of the need for a work–load study?

    A. A member who habitually attempts to shirk his duties
    B. A general competitiveness with members of other companies
    C. The complete absence of backlogged work
    D. The continual *business* of a few members, while others are often idle

13. After every significant fire at which his unit operated, a lieutenant conducted a post-fire critique. At the beginning of the critique, he and the most experienced members present generally outlined their opinions of conditions on arrival at the fire scene and their size-up and actions taken. The lieutenant was proud that a favorable consensus usually became obvious early in the discussion. He attributed this to the high level of proficiency which the unit had achieved through training and drilling. The MOST appropriate of the following views of the lieutenant's assessment of his critiques and their outcomes is that he probably was

    A. making a realistic judgment based upon his knowledge of the way in which the members had been trained
    B. forgetting that conducting critiques is an unproductive activity because the opinion of the chief officer-in-charge at the fire is more important
    C. assuming correctly that the less experienced members would have little of value to contribute to the critique
    D. neglecting the possibility that other members might withhold expressions contrary to his and to those of the more experienced members

14. While in quarters, a lieutenant occasionally exchanges thoughts with his subordinates about the best way for the company to carry out non-routine assignments. He encourages them to think aloud and give their immediate reactions. He also expresses his own ideas. This interchange is completely informal and no one is expected to state firm conclusions.
    This approach is generally

A. *inadvisable,* mainly because subordinates' suggestions which are poor may be difficult to refuse
B. *advisable,* mainly because sincere give-and-take discussions may bring doubts and misunderstandings into the open
C. *inadvisable,* mainly because a supervisor should be direct and sure of himself
D. *advisable,* mainly because a supervisor should himself behave as he expects subordinates to behave

15. Rules and regulations are essential to the effective operation of an organization. But rules may become too specific and detailed, or they may be applied too rigidly. Disadvantages likely to result from the establishment of unnecessary rules or the excessively rigid application of rules are indicated in all of the following choices EXCEPT 15.____

   A. inconsistent treatment of matters involved
   B. weakening of the supervisor's ability to use discretion
   C. development of resentment and dissatisfaction among staff
   D. difficulty in adapting to changing conditions

KEY (CORRECT ANSWERS)

1.	C	6.	A
2.	D	7.	C
3.	C	8.	C
4.	B	9.	A
5.	D	10.	C
	11.	B	
	12.	D	
	13.	D	
	14.	B	
	15.	A	

TEST 2

DIRECTIONS: Each question or incomplete statement is followed by several suggested answers or completions. Select the one that BEST answers the question or completes the statement. *PRINT THE LETTER OF THE CORRECT ANSWER IN THE SPACE AT THE RIGHT.*

1. Below are three statements which may or may not be applicable with respect to organization leadership. Since there are informal leaders in most work groups, the company officer seeking to establish and maintain an effective working relationship with an informal leader should be guided by those of the following statements which are correct.
    I. The very fact that an informal leader cooperates with management may result in his losing status with the work group.
    II. The work group may have different informal leaders for different purposes.
    III. An informal leader who obtains easier work or special favors is likely to lose his position as informal leader.

    Which of the following choices lists ALL of the above statements that should serve as guides to the company officer?

    A. I, II   B. II, III   C. I, III   D. I, II, III

1.___

2. A lieutenant in charge of a ladder company doing overhauling and examination work in a fire building noticed a badly damaged and weakened section of flooring. Calling it to the attention of Fireman Smith who was working nearby opening up the ceiling and walls, the lieutenant told Fireman Smith: *Block off that weak section of flooring as soon as you can; it's a real safety hazard and someone might be hurt.* Shortly thereafter, Fireman Brown injured his leg when he fell through the weakened section of flooring, which had not been blocked off. The lieutenant asked Fireman Smith why he had not carried out his order. Fireman Smith explained that he thought the order was to be carried out as soon as he could after completing the search for possible hidden fire.
   In this situation, Fireman Smith has

   A. misunderstood the order due to the fact that the order was not sufficiently explicit
   B. demonstrated poor judgment by failing to ask the lieutenant for additional help to finish opening the ceiling sooner
   C. evaded orders, for which he should be reprimanded by the lieutenant
   D. disobeyed orders, thereby warranting the preferring of charges

2.___

3. A lieutenant explaining a new procedure to subordinates is MOST likely to ensure correct understanding if he uses

   A. proper technical terminology
   B. substantial re-emphasis
   C. non-verbal cues
   D. examples from his actual experience

3.___

4. Many cities have centralized fire training facilities which reproduce fire conditions realistically.
   Which of the following is LEAST likely to be an advantage of this method of training?

   A. Errors in firefighting will be made out of public view and are thus unlikely to provoke uninformed criticism.
   B. The need for adaptations of evolutions at a working fire is eliminated.
   C. Such training facilities permit uniform introduction throughout the department of newly developed fire-fighting methods.
   D. Life and property losses would be reduced by this kind of experience in firefighting.

4.___

5. If a lieutenant reading a new departmental procedure for the first time is dissatisfied with certain aspects of it, he should FIRST

   A. submit a suggestion to eliminate the procedure
   B. attempt to learn the basis for the procedure
   C. develop a proposal for an alternative procedure
   D. express his dissatisfaction with his peers

6. A fire officer must be wary of assuming that a member's training in a specific operation is completed once peak skill level has been achieved.
   Overlearning through continued repetition needs to be encouraged CHIEFLY to

   A. facilitate rote performance without conscious thought
   B. develop understanding of the basic purpose of the operation
   C. diminish the likelihood that forgetting will occur
   D. overcome differences in motivation and morale

7. Under certain circumstances, face-to-face communications are more effective than written orders.
   Of the following, probably the GREATEST advantage of face-to-face communications is that they

   A. enhance informal organizational relationships
   B. establish specific responsibility for orders and their execution
   C. result in a more lasting effect through visual and emotional impact
   D. provide an opportunity for improved comprehension through immediate feedback

8. Assume that a superior officer asks a lieutenant for an evaluation of a fireman under his supervision.
   In order to be fair, the lieutenant's opinion should be based MAINLY on the fireman's

   A. overall work results
   B. general attitude
   C. comprehension of objectives
   D. leadership ability

9. A fire company has been operating for a long time at a hot smoky fire and is tired. Upon being relieved on their line, the company members sit down on the running board of the nearby apparatus. Just then a battalion chief orders the lieutenant to stretch a line to the roof of exposure number 2 via an aerial ladder. The lieutenant briefly explains to the chief how long and hard the unit has worked and that they have just begun to take the break. The chief listens and then orders the lieutenant to carry out the order.
   Of the following, the PROPER course of action for the lieutenant to take is to order the men to stretch the line and

   A. explain that the chief ordered the action taken
   B. seek out the deputy chief to explain the problem
   C. refrain from making any comment to them
   D. suggest that the members institute a grievance

10. A lieutenant wishes to plan and schedule work so that he can avoid overlooking tasks and can set necessary priorities. He begins by making a list of all the tasks that he can think of, writing them down as they come to mind, without regard to their relative importance.
    This approach to planning and scheduling is generally

    A. *good,* mainly because priorities are best determined if a listing is made in order that each task can be described in full detail
    B. *poor,* mainly because setting priorities encourages postponement of work tasks which are less important but still necessary
    C. *good,* mainly because listing the tasks helps avoid missing any of them while priorities can be assigned afterward
    D. *poor,* mainly because planning and scheduling reduces supervisory flexibility and adaptability to changing circumstances

11. A lieutenant who fails to delegate effectively may know the appropriate principles of supervision but cannot or will not apply them.
    Which of the following is MOST likely to characterize the actions of such an officer?
    He

    A. tends to compliment subordinates on their ingenuity
    B. delegates some tasks, even those he could accomplish better himself
    C. lets subordinates make errors that are minor, easily corrected, and cause no injury or expense, to develop their skills
    D. sets up controls to monitor the detailed actions of his subordinates, rather than their deviations from general plans

12. Members of a company are MOST likely to be highly motivated by a lieutenant who

    A. relies on the willingness of the members to get the work done
    B. stresses those human needs that can be satisfied within the structure of the organization
    C. encourages competition in as many ways as possible
    D. attempts to satisfy all the needs of his men

13. A lieutenant, while conducting a company drill, becomes annoyed by the conduct of a fireman who repeatedly displays an antagonistic attitude toward the drill. The lieutenant controls his growing exasperation with the fireman for some time, but finally tells the fireman in no uncertain terms that he is out of line and is expected to participate in the drill. The lieutenant's behavior in this matter is

    A. *improper,* chiefly because showing impatience demonstrates lack of maturity
    B. *proper,* chiefly because describing how he feels may take some of the edge off the lieutenant's exasperation
    C. *improper,* chiefly because the fireman will recognize the effect of his disruptive tactics and will be encouraged to continue them
    D. *proper,* chiefly because the fireman will act defensively and thus improve his performance

14. Of the following statements, which one gives the BEST reason for adopting standardized methods of performing firefighting operations?
Members may

    A. be objectively evaluated as to performance by superior officers using standard criteria
    B. be transferred to other companies without impairing efficiency
    C. gain better comprehension of the value of skilled teamwork
    D. perform evolutions without the need for situational adaptation

15. Authority delegation is not responsibility delegation. For a supervisor dealing with subordinates, the MOST likely inference from this statement is that a

    A. supervisor is responsible for seeing that the authority which he delegates to his subordinates is exercised properly
    B. significant cause of mismanagement is the assigning of responsibility to subordinates without corresponding authority
    C. supervisor should not hold subordinates responsible for achieving results unless they have been properly trained and instructed
    D. subordinate without specified authority is likely to overburden his supervisor with decision making

KEY (CORRECT ANSWERS)

1. D
2. A
3. B
4. B
5. B
6. C
7. D
8. A
9. C
10. C
11. D
12. B
13. B
14. B
15. A

EXAMINATION SECTION
TEST 1

DIRECTIONS: Each question or incomplete statement is followed by several suggested answers or completions. Select the one that BEST answers the question or completes the statement. *PRINT THE LETTER OF THE CORRECT ANSWER IN THE SPACE AT THE RIGHT.*

1. Regulations state that officers may order use of 1 1/2" hose when compatible with fire conditions in certain situations. The one of the following which is NOT included in the approved usage of 1 1/2" hose is

   A. as initial hose lines at fires above first floor in residence buildings
   B. as initial hose lines at rubbish or trash fires in commercial buildings
   C. at marine or pier fires when used from punts or rafts
   D. at brush fires

2. At a fire in the subway system, it became necessary to order the shut-off of power to a section of tracks. The member transmitting the order called the dispatcher by radio and waited at the radio for four minutes until the dispatcher confirmed that the power had been shut off; then he reported back to his company officer.
The member's actions in this situation were

   A. in accordance with department regulations
   B. not in accordance with department regulations because he did not report back immediately
   C. not in accordance with department regulations because he did not notify the trainmaster also
   D. not in accordance with department regulations because he did not personally confirm that power had been shut off

3. Restoration of fire escape drop ladders and counterbalanced stairways to their normal position is the responsibility of the officer in command of

   A. fire operations
   B. the company which lowered the drop ladder or stairway
   C. the last ladder company to leave the scene of operations
   D. the last company to leave the scene of operations

4. The one of the following statements that is MOST in accord with department regulations is that *either* 4 1/2" soft hydrant connections or 4 1/2" suction connections may be used by companies when

   A. first to arrive on first alarms
   B. other than first to arrive on first alarms
   C. arriving at second or greater alarms
   D. drafting operations are indicated

5. According to departmental regulations, persons using department ladders at fires are to be assisted by members

   A. in all cases
   B. in all cases except for able-bodied men

29

C. in all cases where the height of the ladder is greater than ten feet above ground
D. in all cases except when such assistance is declined

6. Department regulations require company officers to cause an inspection to be made when notified of structural or occupancy hazards dangerous to life.
The one of the following statements that is MOST accurate and complete is that when such inspections are made, information is to be transmitted to the

   A. battalion chief on duty
   B. deputy and battalion chiefs on duty
   C. deputy and battalion chiefs on duty and a report forwarded to the Division of Fire Prevention
   D. deputy and battalion chiefs on duty and reports forwarded to the Division of Fire Prevention and the Chief of Department

7. The report *Recurrent Injury to Members* is to be completed by the

   A. officer on duty immediately after the occurrence
   B. unit commander at the first opportunity
   C. Medical Division after the diagnosis is made
   D. unit commander after receipt of the diagnosis from the Medical Division

8. When a tag summons is served, the member issuing the summons MUST swear to a complaint before the officer on duty at

   A. his own company quarters
   B. the nearest police precinct stationhouse
   C. the nearest company quarters
   D. the Enforcement Unit of the Division of Fire Prevention

9. According to regulations, when a fire is encountered while responding to another location,

   A. only one company may stop to extinguish the fire
   B. only one engine company and one ladder company may stop to extinguish the fire
   C. the number of companies stopping to extinguish the fire may not exceed three, one of which should be an engine company and one a ladder company
   D. as many companies may stop to extinguish the fire as are required by the circumstances

10. The signal 13-65-2 is used as a preliminary signal indicating

    A. Marine company not required
    B. air raid warning alert
    C. restricted use of radio system established
    D. radio system temporarily inoperative

11. According to regulations, when an off-duty member who volunteers his service at a fire administers rescue breathing, he is to notify the

    A. officer in command of the fire
    B. medical officer on emergency duty
    C. officer of the assigned unit
    D. officer on duty at his next regular tour

12. According to regulations, information relative to fire or emergency operations may be given to accredited news reporters at the scene

    A. only by the officer in command
    B. by any chief officer
    C. by any member of the department having knowledge of the situation
    D. by the officer in command or a member designated by the Fire Commissioner

13. According to departmental regulations, the Photography Unit is to respond when notified by the dispatcher that an accident has occurred involving damage to apparatus or death or injury to members or civilians.
    The apparatus involved in the accident is NOT to be moved before photography work is completed unless

    A. the apparatus is undamaged and was responding to an alarm
    B. injuries and damage are obviously minor
    C. the apparatus is leaking gasoline which is in danger of ignition
    D. traffic conditions make its movement imperative

14. The MAXIMUM quantity of paints which may be manufactured or stored without a permit, according to the Fire Prevention Code, is _____ gallons.

    A. 20   B. 25   C. 30   D. 50

15. Oil separators are required by the Administrative Code before issuance of a permit to a garage for the storage of volatile inflammable oil if the garage accommodates _____ or more motor vehicles.

    A. four   B. five   C. six   D. ten

16. The term cellar, as used in the Building Code, shall mean *a story having _____ of its height, measured from finished floor to finished ceiling, below the curb level at the center of the street front.*
    The one of the following which, when filled in the blank space, BEST completes the sentence is

    A. more than one-half   B. no more than one-half
    C. more than three-quarters   D. no more than three-quarters

17. The Oil Burner Rules of the Board of Standards and Appeals state *No movable combustible materials shall be stored or maintained within _____ feet of heating apparatus, except where same is protected by fire-retarding material.*
    The one of the following numbers which, when inserted in the blank space above, MOST accurately completes the sentence is

    A. 2   B. 3   C. 4   D. 5

18. The Rules of the Board of Standards and Appeals require that combustible materials used for decorative purposes within special occupancy structures be made flameproof. Approval of flameproof materials is

    A. valid for an indefinite period   B. limited to a period of 6 months
    C. limited to a period of 1 year   D. limited to a period of 2 years

19. A multiple dwelling, according to the Multiple Dwelling Law, is a dwelling occupied as the residence of _____ or more families living independently of each other.
The one of the following numbers which, when inserted in the blank space above, MOST accurately completes the sentence is

   A. 2   B. 3   C. 4   D. 5

20. The one of the following statements that is MOST accurate is that in multiple dwellings, windows at grade levels at sidewalks, yards, or courts may

   A. not have bars
   B. have bars provided that they are easily removed from the inside of the window
   C. have bars but at least one window in each room must be without bars
   D. have bars but at least one window in each apartment must be without bars

21. The number of extra sprinkler heads which must be kept in the premises of a building with an automatic sprinkler system, according to the Building Code, is

   A. 10
   B. 10 percent of the number of sprinkler heads in the entire system
   C. 6
   D. 6 percent of the number of sprinkler heads in the entire system

22. The Building Code requires that standpipe systems be equipped with pressure reducing valves where the normal hydrostatic pressure at a 2 1/2" hose outlet valve exceeds _____ lbs. per square inch.

   A. 50   B. 55   C. 60   D. 65

23. Walls of structures used for public entertainment may be covered with combustible wall coverings, according to the Building Code, provided that the

   A. wall covering is pasted or cemented directly to the plaster surfaces of the wall
   B. wall covering does not extend more than six feet in height
   C. building is a Class 1 fireproof structure
   D. building has a seating capacity of 600 people or less

24. The Fire Prevention Code requires that a permit be obtained for the storage of more than the equivalent of five barrels of oils and fats.
The one of the following which is excluded from this requirement is

   A. lubricating oils   B. grease
   C. edible oils   D. soap stock

25. The Fire Prevention Code requires that rooms in dry cleaning establishments in which washing tanks are located be equipped with

   A. asbestos cloths or blankets
   B. carbon dioxide or dry chemical extinguishers
   C. buckets of sand
   D. automatic fire alarm device

26. A lieutenant, in an effort to improve training results, made a training progress table on which he listed the men in his group and the various skills he expected to teach in each lesson. As a member performed each task, the lieutenant placed a check or cross on the chart which indicated satisfactory or unsatisfactory performance.
The use of a training table in this manner is

   A. *desirable,* mainly because it enables the lieutenant to keep track of the members' progress and the tasks that require additional training
   B. *undesirable,* mainly because it reduces the amount of time available for teaching and observing
   C. *desirable,* mainly because it helps the lieutenant to rate his subordinates
   D. *undesirable,* mainly because the emphasis is placed on the performance of the parts of the operation rather than on the operation as a whole

26.____

27. *An experienced officer teaching probationary firemen often overlooks so-called minor points because of his great familiarity with the job. When an instructor takes such points for granted, he leaves gaps in his instruction.*
Of the following, the BEST way of preventing this type of oversight is to

   A. ask the probationary firemen if they have any questions during the explanation and demonstration
   B. observe the probationary firemen closely as they perform the operation for errors or misconceptions
   C. utilize visual aids in demonstrating the operation
   D. break down the operation into simple parts when planning the lesson

27.____

28. When conducting drills, a lieutenant made an effort to devote approximately the same amount of time to each member of the group.
This procedure GENERALLY is

   A. *good* because the members will realize that they all are receiving equal treatment
   B. *bad* because some members require more training than others
   C. *good* because the lieutenant is less likely to neglect any member
   D. *bad* because the lieutenant has to devote too much effort to keeping track of the time spent with each member

28.____

29. For a lieutenant occasionally to devote a drill period to the use of basic tools, such as the axe or the hook, is GENERALLY

   A. *necessary,* mainly because such drills will help keep the members in good physical condition
   B. *unnecessary,* mainly because there are more important subjects requiring attention
   C. *necessary,* mainly because faulty habits may develop if fundamentals are not reviewed
   D. *unnecessary,* mainly because members have many opportunities to use these tools at fires

29.____

30. A lieutenant conducting A.F.I.D. enters a luncheonette and discovers that the owner, the only person on duty, apparently does not understand English.
The one of the following which would be the BEST action for the lieutenant to take in this situation is to attempt to

30.____

A. make the owner understand by speaking English in a loud, clear voice
B. make the owner understand by using sign language
C. find a customer or passerby who can act as an interpreter
D. question the owner closely to determine whether he really does not understand English

31. During the height of extinguishment operations at a fire in a taxpayer, a lieutenant observes a newly assigned probationary fireman attempting, in an awkward and dangerous manner, to ventilate by chopping a hole in the roof with an axe.
In this situation, the BEST of the following courses for the lieutenant to follow is to

   A. briefly demonstrate the proper axe technique
   B. assign an experienced fireman to cut the hole and give the probationary fireman another assignment
   C. assign an experienced fireman to assist the probationary fireman
   D. permit the probationary fireman to finish, but avoid similar assignments until after he receives additional training in the handling of axes

32. An officer who frequently changes the standard operating procedures in routine matters is *probably*

   A. open minded and receptive to new ideas
   B. insecure and emotionally unstable
   C. hasty and inclined to act without careful consideration
   D. a perfectionist with very high standards

33. *Although it is inevitable that, on occasion, an officer will have doubts about the wisdom of an order which he receives from his superior, nothing in the officer's words or manner in transmitting this order to his subordinates should betray his opinion.*
The idea expressed in this statement is

   A. *valid,* mainly because a subordinate must be sure of his grounds before criticizing the orders of his superior officer
   B. *invalid,* mainly because the officer is denied the normal outlet for his feelings which may cause psychological problems
   C. *valid,* mainly because criticism of orders to subordinates, either expressed or implied, weakens discipline
   D. *invalid,* mainly because there are established means for suggesting improvements in departmental procedures

34. *The good leader encourages his men to work 'with him,' rather than 'for him.'*
The one of the following statements which MOST accurately gives the implication of this statement is that the leader should

   A. do a share of the unpleasant and hazardous tasks of the job
   B. instill the idea that he and his men have the same goals and interests
   C. maintain direct personal contact with his men whenever practicable
   D. encourage his men to exercise initiative and assume responsibility within the limits of their rank and assignment

35. On a number of occasions, a lieutenant found it necessary to criticize the careless and untidy work of a member when performing housekeeping chores. After a number of incidents, the lieutenant called the member into the office to discuss the problem. The lieutenant reviewed all the previous incidents and, at the end of the discussion said, *You have been a slob around here. If you don't improve immediately, I will prefer charges against you.*
The MOST serious error made by the lieutenant in dealing with this situation was his

    A. failure to prefer charges immediately
    B. threat to prefer charges for future incidents
    C. criticism of the member's character
    D. reference to past incidents

36. A lieutenant in command at a fire with a great hazard of explosion made a great effort to give orders in his normal tone of voice and generally to conduct himself in his normal manner, as though the situation was routine and without danger.
In this situation, the lieutenant's behavior was

    A. *improper,* mainly because the men under his command are not alerted to their danger
    B. *proper,* mainly because danger is part of a fireman's job and should be faced without flinching
    C. *improper,* mainly because the lieutenant is not behaving normally or honestly
    D. *proper,* mainly because the men under his command also will tend to act calmly

37. The MAIN reason for a superior officer to delegate authority to a subordinate officer is to

    A. develop the leadership potential of the subordinate
    B. make the authority equal to the responsibility of an assignment
    C. free the superior officer for more important tasks
    D. obtain new and better methods of performing the duties assigned

38. During inspection of quarters, a battalion chief criticizes the method employed in compiling a certain report and orders the lieutenant on duty to modify the procedure. The modification is in conflict with the explicit orders of the company commander.
In this situation, the lieutenant should

    A. suggest to the battalion chief that he first discuss the matter with the company commander
    B. report the matter to the company commander before putting into effect the new method
    C. modify the record keeping method and inform the company commander of the change at the first opportunity
    D. modify the record keeping method as directed without notification to the company commander since the battalion chief usually informs the company commander of his orders

39. A try test of a pumper, conducted in quarters, to determine whether it can draft water should NOT last longer than _____ rninute(s).

    A. 1 B. 1 1/2 C. 2 D. 2 1/2

40. To prevent the accumulation of sludge in the crankcase of a motor vehicle, it is BEST to avoid

    A. overheating the motor
    B. running the motor for short periods at a time
    C. unnecessary idling of the motor
    D. quick starting and acceleration of the vehicle

41. Excessive leakage at the stuffing box of a centrifugal pump is MOST likely caused by a(n)

    A. air leak into the pump through stuffing boxes
    B. obstruction in the impeller
    C. seal ring improperly located in stuffing box, preventing water from entering the space to form seal
    D. bent or worn pump shaft

42. When adding water to storage batteries in departmental vehicles, care should be exercised to prevent overfilling. Of the following, the MAIN reason for avoiding overfilling is that the excess water may cause

    A. rust to form on the connecting terminals
    B. loss of acid from the solution
    C. acid burns to the person filling the battery
    D. blockage of the vent in the cylinder cap

43. The loaded stream extinguisher is recommended for use on Class _____ fires.

    A. A only
    B. A and B only
    C. A and C only
    D. A, B, and C

44. The ladder angle recommended for use with a portable ladder pipe on the Mack-Magirus aerial ladder apparatus

    A. is 78°
    B. is 70°
    C. depends upon the height of the ladder
    D. depends upon the nozzle pressure used

45. The MAIN reason for keeping oils off cotton jacketed hose is that the oils will

    A. attack and weaken the jacket
    B. loosen the adhesive between the rubber lining and the jacket
    C. soften the rubber lining
    D. make the hose slippery and difficult to handle

46. The MOST likely cause of an off-scale reading when using the Jordan 710 ion chamber is that

    A. a short circuit exists in the instrument
    B. interference from light or radio frequency radiation is occurring
    C. the batteries are weak
    D. the radiation received is beyond the capacity of the instrument

47. When a knot is tied in a rope, the tensile strength of the rope is

   A. increased
   B. reduced
   C. not affected
   D. increased or reduced depending upon the kind and location of the knot

48. The range of the Baker cellar pipe, compared to the ranges of the bent cellar pipe and the Bresnan distributor is

   A. *larger* than either the bent cellar pipe or the Bresnan distributor
   B. *smaller* than either the bent cellar pipe or the Bresnan distributor
   C. *larger* than the bent cellar pipe and a smaller range than the Bresnan distributor
   D. *smaller* than the bent cellar pipe and a larger range than the Bresnan distributor

49. During a periodic inspection of a flashlight, some corrosion was observed on the inside of the case. The PROPER way of handling this problem is to

   A. replace the flashlight case
   B. scrape away the corroded area and change the batteries
   C. rub the corroded area with steel wool and turpentine
   D. wash the case with a solution of baking soda and water

50. When placing the American LaFrance or Mack Metal aerial ladder in position, the MAXIMUM permissible distance between the inboard side of the apparatus and the building upon which operations are being conducted is _____ feet.

   A. 30   B. 32   C. 35   D. 40

KEY (CORRECT ANSWERS)

1. B	11. C	21. C	31. B	41. D
2. A	12. D	22. B	32. C	42. B
3. C	13. D	23. A	33. C	43. B
4. B	14. A	24. C	34. B	44. B
5. A	15. B	25. A	35. C	45. B
6. C	16. A	26. A	36. D	46. D
7. D	17. D	27. D	37. C	47. B
8. C	18. C	28. B	38. C	48. D
9. B	19. B	29. C	39. A	49. D
10. D	20. D	30. C	40. B	50. C

TEST 2

DIRECTIONS: Each question or incomplete statement is followed by several suggested answers or completions. Select the one that BEST answers the question or completes the statement. *PRINT THE LETTER OF THE CORRECT ANSWER IN THE SPACE AT THE RIGHT.*

1. Department regulations require that after gasoline storage systems have been filled, the officer on duty must personally make certain that the fill box at the curb is tightly closed and that the plug is made wrench tight.
   The MAIN reason for this procedure is to prevent

   A. evaporation of gasoline
   B. theft of gasoline
   C. water seeping into the tank
   D. leakage from the tank

1.____

2. Summonses may be served by members of the Fire Department for double parking

   A. at any time when on duty
   B. only when a Fire Department vehicle is proceeding to or returning from an alarm or operating at the scene of an alarm
   C. only when a Fire Department vehicle is proceeding to an alarm or operating at the scene of an alarm
   D. only when a Fire Department vehicle is operating at the scene of an alarm

2.____

3. A radio-equipped single pumper is especially called to a grass fire which can be extinguished without additional help. According to regulations, no preliminary report is required unless operations will require at LEAST _____ minutes.

   A. 15   B. 30   C. 45   D. 60

3.____

4. The regulations provide that when a member fails to appear for a medical examination or treatment at the place and on the date and time specified, an investigation is to be made by the

   A. company commander of the member concerned
   B. chief in charge of the Medical Division
   C. battalion commander of the member concerned
   D. medical officer to whom the member was to report

4.____

5. Whenever a building or structure is moved from one location to another, or otherwise has a change of address, certain changes in company records are required.
   The one of the following statements which MOST accurately gives the record change or changes that are required is that

   A. a new Building Record card is prepared and the original Building Record card is placed in the Dead Record file
   B. a Transfer Card is filed under the new address
   C. the old address is crossed out, the new address is substituted, and a Transfer Card is filed in place of the Building Record card under the old address
   D. a new Building Record card is prepared, the original Building Record card is placed in the Dead Record file, and a Transfer Card is filed in place of the original record

5.____

6. The one of the following statements which is NOT in accordance with the regulations concerning operating a foam generator is that

   A. foam powder should be poured into hopper when flowing pressure reaches 75 lbs.
   B. one pound of foam powder mixed with one gallon of water produces approximately 8 gallons of foam
   C. the discharge lines from the generator to the nozzle should be limited to 100 feet for best results
   D. a salt water supply line produces efficient foam

7. Suppose that you are the officer on duty when a woman rushes into your firehouse and reports that a man has been struck by an automobile on the street nearby. According to department orders, you should

   A. permit the woman to use your telephone to summon a doctor
   B. summon assistance from the closest city hospital
   C. summon medical assistance through the dispatcher
   D. report the matter to the Police Department

8. If a fire is encountered by an engine company and a ladder company while returning to quarters, the dispatcher

   A. should be sent a 2-2-2 preliminary signal for only the first company on the scene
   B. should be sent 2-2-2 preliminary signals for both companies
   C. need not be sent any signal
   D. should be sent 2-2-2 signals for both companies only if a full first alarm assignment is required, otherwise no signal should be sent

9. The one of the following reports that is to be prepared by the officer on duty when necessary is

   A. Chimney Fire Violation   B. Hose, Burst or Porous
   C. Fuel, Inferior   D. Members Attending Court

10. The one of the following evolutions in which a hitch and binder knot is NOT used is

    A. stretching a hose line to the upper floors via the outside of the building
    B. replacing burst lengths of hose in a hose stretched to the roof via the outside of the building
    C. hoisting a 35-foot ladder to the roof of a building
    D. drafting water and supplying the deck pipe of a hose wagon

11. Company commanders are responsible for the inspection of all magazines used for the storage of explosives located within their administrative district. Regulations require that, where explosives are not delivered during night hours, such inspections be made each day

    A. once between the hours of 8 A.M. and 3 P.M. and, if storage of explosives is found at this inspection, a second inspection between the hours of 12 Midnight and 8 M.
    B. twice, at any hour, provided that there is no regularity or pattern of inspections
    C. once between the hours of 6 P.M. and 12 Midnight and, if storage of explosives is found at this inspection, a second inspection between the hours of 12 Midnight and 8 A.M.
    D. once between the hours of 6 P.M. and 12 Midnight and once between the hours of 12 Midnight and 8 A.M.

12. Regulations state that when two persons, or a very heavy person, are to be lowered by means of a roof rope, the number of turns of the rope through and around the life belt should be NOT less than

    A. 3 B. 4 C. 5 D. 6

13. Regulations require that when conducting the weekly tests of centrifugal and reciprocating fire pumps on fire boats,

    A. reciprocating pumps are to be tested to capacity and centrifugal pumps are to be tested to two-thirds of capacity
    B. centrifugal pumps are to be tested to capacity and reciprocating pumps are to be tested to two-thirds of capacity
    C. reciprocating pumps are to be tested to capacity and centrifugal pumps are to be tested to three-quarters of capacity
    D. centrifugal pumps are to be tested to capacity and reciprocating pumps are to be tested to three-quarters of capacity

14. The one of the following types of outside employment which is prohibited by regulations for all members is employment as

    A. salesmen of tickets of any kind
    B. accident insurance adjusters, solicitors, or investigators
    C. solicitors for the raising of funds
    D. salesmen of stocks, bonds, or mutual funds

15. When the need for repairs to apparatus has been reported, but the repairs have not been made within a reasonable time, it is the duty of the company commander, according to the regulations, to send a written report to the

    A. battalion commander
    B. division commander
    C. office of the chief of the department
    D. Division of Repairs and Transportation

16. The one of the following signals which is INCORRECTLY described is

    A. 6-5-2 Use telephone
    B. 4-5 Respond to box
    C. 7-7-7 Public ambulance
    D. 13-13-13 Telegraph emergency squad

17. The one of the following statements about the first alarm response assignment of the second section of a double company that is CORRECT is that when the first section responds,

    A. either a street alarm box or special building alarm, and shortly thereafter an alarm is received from either an associated street or special building alarm, the second section is not to respond
    B. either a street alarm box or special building alarm, and shortly thereafter an alarm is received from an associated street or special building alarm, the second section is to respond

C. street alarm box and shortly thereafter an alarm is received from an associated special building box, the second section is not to respond
D. special building alarm and shortly thereafter an alarm is received from an associated street alarm box, the second section is not to respond

18. According to the Building Code, a vertical iron ladder to an escape manhole opening in the sidewalk is required from a cellar room when the room is being used as a

    A. coal storage room   B. restaurant kitchen
    C. boiler room   D. factory

19. In a building of public assembly, the provisions of the Fire Prevention Code prohibit the use of decorations, drapes or scenery made of combustible material which have not been rendered fireproof.
    Of the following types of occupancies, the one that is exempt from the provisions of this section is a

    A. school   B. hospital   C. church   D. museum

20. As used in the Building Code, a *4-hour fire rating* of a wall means that in a standard fire test of four hours duration, the

    A. wall will not collapse
    B. unexposed side of the wall will not char or smolder
    C. temperature on the unexposed side of the wall will not rise
    D. temperature on the unexposed side of the wall will not rise more than a predetermined amount

21. The prohibition against smoking in retail stores applies

    A. to all stores
    B. only to stores employing more than 25 persons
    C. only to stores accommodating more than 300 persons
    D. only to stores employing more than 25 persons or accommodating more than 300 persons

22. As used in the Building Code, the term *horizontal exit* refers to a(n)

    A. exit door on the ground floor which is at the same level as the street grade
    B. corridor or hallway leading to the exit stairs
    C. fire escape with the balcony at the same level as the floor
    D. connection between two floor areas through a fire wall

23. According to the Building Code, a required exit stairway enclosure in a public building MUST have a fire resistance rating of _____ hour(s).

    A. 1   B. 2   C. 3   D. 4

24. A recently enacted section of the Fire Prevention Code places limitations on the use of kerosene-burning equipment. When all the provisions of this section of the Code are in full effect, the one of the following uses of kerosene-burning equipment which will NOT be permitted is equipment used exclusively for

A. cooking purposes
B. lighting purposes
C. demonstration and sales purposes
D. heating purposes in any building in an area not supplied with permanent piped gas

25. The provisions of the Building Code require that in a building more than two stories high, the required stairways must all continue to the roof EXCEPT in a(n)

    A. office building
    B. school building
    C. theater
    D. storage warehouse

26. Of the following reasons for requiring that negative reports be submitted, the MOST valid is that

    A. report procedures should be uniform throughout the department
    B. negative reports sometimes are more important than positive reports
    C. the habit of submitting reports regularly is reinforced
    D. reports which are late or missing are not counted as negative

27. Some officers regard the preparation of reports as a routine task to be performed by subordinates without careful review.
    This practice is unwise CHIEFLY because the

    A. officer may appear to be shirking an unpleasant duty
    B. subordinate preparing the reports may come to regard the reports as unimportant and prepare them carelessly
    C. person preparing the reports is not responsible for their accuracy
    D. officer will not have first-hand knowledge on conditions within his command

28. An officer who observes a fireman performing an operation in an incorrect or inefficient manner should promptly correct the fireman. However, for an officer to insist that all operations, even the most trivial, be performed *his way* is undesirable CHIEFLY because

    A. an officer cannot personally supervise every operation
    B. initiative of the subordinate may be weakened
    C. the officer's way of doing things may not always be the best way
    D. officers should not concern themselves with petty details

29. An elderly man approaches you, as officer on duty, to complain that the noise of apparatus responding to alarms wakes him in the middle of the night.
    Of the following, the BEST way for you to handle this situation is to

    A. quickly change the subject since the man obviously is a *crank*
    B. ask the man for specific instances of apparatus making noise at night
    C. explain the need for speed in response of apparatus
    D. promise to avoid making unnecessary noise at night

30. Flexibility of operations and ability to meet emergency situations are BEST developed in firemen by stressing, during training programs,

    A. speed and proficiency in drills
    B. concepts and principles of firemanics
    C. the unusual situations which may be encountered at fires
    D. the latest developments in firefighting techniques and apparatus

31. It has been observed that the men who receive the highest grades during a training course do not always perform as well when operating in the field.
Of the following, the BEST explanation of this discrepancy is that

    A. men learn only by doing
    B. training courses are theoretical rather than practical
    C. training courses do not duplicate completely field conditions
    D. most people function below their potentialities

32. *The skilled officer recognizes that he is dealing with a group and not just individuals and that the group has standards and purposes which influence the behavior of the individuals with whose work he is concerned.*
The implication of this statement for a company officer is that

    A. both individual differences and group reactions should be considered when dealing with any situation
    B. individual differences should be given less consideration than group reactions when making decisions
    C. members of a company tend to present a united front against officers
    D. cliques are inevitable in any large organization such as the fire department

33. Public praise of a member by a company officer is an effective way of improving morale provided that it

    A. is given with some degree of uniformity among all the members
    B. appears to be spontaneous
    C. is offset by occasional public criticism
    D. is not done excessively

34. The good leader has the capacity, not only to accept responsibility and exercise initiative himself, but also to develop these traits in his subordinates.
Of the following, the BEST method for a lieutenant to use to encourage firemen to use initiative and assume responsibility is to

    A. rotate routine assignments equally among all members of the company
    B. employ suggestions or implied commands rather than direct commands in other emergency situations
    C. encourage firemen to read books and take courses in leadership
    D. ask for volunteers to perform necessary company duties

35. An officer instructing his men on a new procedure asked, at frequent intervals, whether there were any questions. Asking for questions is a

    A. *good* practice chiefly because it affords the men an opportunity to participate actively in the lesson
    B. *poor* practice chiefly because it may result in wasting time on irrelevant matters
    C. *good* practice chiefly because it may reveal points that are not understood by the men
    D. *poor* practice chiefly because men generally are reluctant to ask questions

36. A lieutenant who was assigned to deliver a talk before a civic organization first made a detailed outline of his talk. Then, with the help of two members of his company, he prepared several demonstrations and charts.
The lieutenant's procedure was

   A. *good* chiefly because careful preparation increases the effectiveness of a talk
   B. *poor* chiefly because a talk should be guided by the question and comments of the audience and not follow a predetermined outline
   C. *good* chiefly because the audience will be impressed by the care that the lieutenant has taken in preparing the talk
   D. *poor* chiefly because the talk will appear rehearsed rather than spontaneous and natural

36.____

37. A lieutenant who was giving a series of lectures started each talk by asking a member to summarize the points covered in the previous talk.
This practice is

   A. *poor;* time is wasted in needless repetition
   B. *good;* the lieutenant is free to observe the attitude of the group while the member is speaking
   C. *poor; the* member may make erroneous statements and mislead the group
   D. *good;* the learning process is reinforced by the review

37.____

38. After giving one of his men an assignment, a lieutenant returns to find that the member had not done the work according to instructions.
The FIRST thing that the lieutenant should ascertain is whether the member had

   A. ever performed the work before
   B. personal problems which may be interfering with the performance of his duties
   C. previously failed to follow instructions
   D. understood the instructions

38.____

39. The one of the following which is NOT a recommended method of overcoming transmission or reception difficulty when using the Radio Pack Set is to

   A. speak loudly
   B. hold the set up in the air
   C. rotate yourself
   D. face the antenna toward the transmission point

39.____

40. When traveling at 20 miles per hour on a dry asphaltic pavement under normal driving conditions, the distance required to bring a pumper to a complete stop after re-applying the brakes is MOST NEARLY _____ feet.

   A. 40   B. 60   C. 80   D. 100

40.____

41. Wooden aerial ladders should be washed with

   A. fresh water only
   B. brown soap and rinsed with fresh water
   C. soap powder and rinsed with fresh water
   D. an oil soap and rinsed with fresh water

41.____

42. When using an O'Brien cutter to make holes in a floor for a large size distributor, it is necessary to drill

    A. one hole
    B. two overlapping holes
    C. three overlapping holes in cloverleaf pattern
    D. four overlapping holes in cloverleaf pattern

43. The water level in storage batteries should be maintained, according to the regulations, _____ the top of the battery plates.

    A. even with
    B. 1/8" above
    C. 1/2" above
    D. 1" above

44. When using a relay relief valve in a relay operation involving several pumpers, the valve should be placed on the pumper

    A. nearest the hose nozzle
    B. in the middle of the relay
    C. furthest from the hose nozzle
    D. which appears most likely to break down

45. The length of rope on a Roof Rope Reel is normally _____ feet.

    A. 75   B. 100   C. 125   D. 150

46. The one of the following statements regarding storage conditions for foam extinguishers that is MOST correct is that these extinguishers

    A. should be protected against both high and low temperatures
    B. need not be protected against either high or low temperatures
    C. should be protected against low temperatures but need not be protected against high temperatures
    D. should be protected against high temperatures but need not be protected against low temperatures

47. The one of the following statements which MOST accurately distinguishes the loaded stream type of fire extinguisher from all other types is that the loaded stream type

    A. has the greatest range
    B. retards flashback
    C. is not affected by freezing temperatures
    D. can be used effectively on Class A, B, and C fires

48. The air tank of apparatus equipped with air brakes should be blown out weekly in order to

    A. rid the tank of water due to condensation
    B. check the air supply lines to the brakes
    C. prevent excessive air pressure build-up
    D. rid the tank of gasoline vapors

49. When raising the aerial ladder of the new four-wheel drive ladder, it is important that all controls and components be in the proper position.
The one of the following controls or components which is in the WRONG position for this operation is the

   A. trailer jack down and engaged slightly
   B. gear lock pin disengaged
   C. ladder hand brake in off position
   D. ladder adjustment crank in IN position

50. The type of pump that does NOT have positive displacement per revolution is the _____ pump.

   A. centrifugal
   B. rotary gear
   C. double-acting piston
   D. vane-type

KEY (CORRECT ANSWERS)

1. C	11. C	21. D	31. C	41. D
2. B	12. B	22. D	32. A	42. C
3. C	13. B	23. C	33. D	43. B
4. B	14. C	24. D	34. B	44. A
5. C	15. B	25. B	35. C	45. D
6. A	16. A	26. D	36. A	46. A
7. C	17. D	27. D	37. D	47. B
8. D	18. C	28. B	38. D	48. A
9. A	19. C	29. C	39. A	49. D
10. C	20. D	30. B	40. A	50. A

EXAMINATION SECTION
TEST 1

DIRECTIONS: Each question or incomplete statement is followed by several suggested answers or completions. Select the one that BEST answers the question or completes the statement. *PRINT THE LETTER OF THE CORRECT ANSWER IN THE SPACE AT THE RIGHT.*

1. The Official Action Guide provides that if there is a fire on the Express Highway, ladders shall be raised against the side of the Highway nearer the location of the fire.
   The reason given for this operation is that it will

   A. be less dangerous to life
   B. permit the use of fire extinguishers
   C. avoid blocking more than one roadway
   D. allow the stretching of hose lines

   1.____

2. The one of the following which is the MOST economical type of fire for the operation of house heating apparatus, according to the Official Action Guide, is a(n)

   A. high full-bodied fire
   B. low fire which is fired automatically
   C. forced fire in a low pressure heating boiler
   D. egg coal fire where the system is equipped with a blower

   2.____

3. The reason given in the Official Action Guide for NOT permitting pumpers with first size pumping engines to be operated for draughting water from a barrel in connection with the testing of the pump is that

   A. this operation may be dangerous to life
   B. this method does not provide a good test
   C. the engine may be overheated during the process
   D. sufficient water cannot be supplied to the pump in this way

   3.____

4. According to the Official Action Guide, when a member is called upon to release someone caught in a high exit turnstile, he shall, before proceeding to help the person,

   A. notify the Board of Transportation
   B. obtain a special wrench from the railroad clerk at the station
   C. report the incident to the battalion commander
   D. obtain a prybar and special instructions for its use from the railroad clerk at the station

   4.____

5. One of the pieces of equipment carried by a rescue company is a pair of rubber wading trousers.
   According to the Official Action Guide, these are useful in cases where there is a(n)

   A. fire in a cellar
   B. emergency which involves entering a sewer
   C. waterfront fire
   D. heavy ammonia leak

   5.____

6. According to the Official Action Guide, oil should be drained from the crankcase of a gasoline engine only

   A. while the engine is running
   B. when the motor has reached the operating temperature
   C. when the engine is cold
   D. after all the oil in the system has been collected in the crankcase

7. The signal 7-7-3-3-3-124-5-18 is a call for

   A. an engine company
   B. three officers and four men
   C. three officers and fifteen men
   D. a hook and ladder company

8. The signal 4-4-4-9-21 is a

   A. call for a Gasoline-Oil Unit to be alerted
   B. notification that a Gasoline-Oil Unit is in service
   C. notification that a Searchlight Unit is in service
   D. call for a Searchlight Unit to be alerted

9. Engine Company 38, which was relocated at the quarters of Engine Company 16, received orders to proceed to the quarters of Engine Company 20.
   Upon arrival at Engine Company 20, the signal which should be sent to the Central Office is

   A. 4-4-4-16-20   B. 4-4-4-20-16
   C. 4-4-4-38-20   D. 4-4-4-20-38

10. The preliminary signal for relocating an engine company (both pumper and hose wagon) is

    A. 15-15   B. 15   C. 16   D. 16-16

11. The one of the following which is a Special Call for a Smoke Ejector to report to a box is

    A. 9-37-52   B. 9-52-37   C. 9-41-52   D. 9-52-41

12. While inspecting a garage, a fire inspector notices that a garage license has not been issued for the premises by the Department of Licenses.
    The inspector should

    A. discontinue his inspection pending a determination by the Department of Licenses of the allowable motor vehicle occupancy
    B. complete his inspection and forward it (including a statement of the allowable motor vehicle occupancy) with a request that a copy be sent to the Department of Licenses
    C. discontinue his inspection and request that a communication (inquiry form) be sent to the Department of Licenses asking for an explanation
    D. complete his inspection and forward it with a request that the Department of Licenses be asked to determine the allowable motor vehicle occupancy

13. According to a Civil Defense Directive, when a Civil Defense volunteer reports to company quarters as a result of being notified by the fire department through the *Department Copy* of the *referral* card, the officer in command shall

    A. take his name and address and tell him that he will be notified as soon as a training program has been set up
    B. interview the Civil Defense volunteer and determine what his interests are
    C. enroll him on a CD-1 card
    D. instruct him in his duties

14. If the signal 13-1-13 (one round on the primary, one round on the secondary) is received at a company, the officer in command shall

    A. direct the apparatus to be taken from the quarters to the curb line
    B. be on the alert but take no other action
    C. have the siren blown for a series of three, one minute steady blasts, separated by two minutes of silence
    D. direct the apparatus to be returned to quarters

15. According to the Official Action Guide, the proper distance from a building at which to place the butt ends of a raised 25-foot portable truss ladder is _____ feet.

    A. 6   B. 7   C. 8   D. 9

16. According to the Official Action Guide, when setting up to relay water from one pumper to another, after connecting a double female swivel reducer to the suction inlet nearest the first pumping engine and a Siamese connection to the reducer, the NEXT step is to

    A. stretch a hose line to the first engine
    B. open the hydrant and charge the pump of the first engine
    C. connect a double female connection to each branch of the Siamese
    D. take weight off the Siamese connection

17. If no play pipe is available when siamesing two lines into a 3" line to develop a heavy stream, the officer in charge, according to the Official Action Guide, should order a

    A. 3" x 2 1/2" reducer used in order to be able to employ available nozzles
    B. 3" x 1 3/8" controlling nozzle
    C. 3" x 1 1/2" open nozzle
    D. reduction in the engine pressure which will permit him to use available nozzles

18. According to the Official Action Guide, as a ladder which is being hoisted leaves the ground,

    A. it should be turned so that the hoisting rope is between it and the wall of the building
    B. it should be pushed out on its beam until the bowline knot can clear the ladder roller
    C. the rope should be held taut until the ladder swings into a vertical position
    D. the butt of the ladder should be released in order to permit it to spring free

19. According to the Official Action Guide, when operating a hose line from a standpipe system inside a building, the nozzle which should be used is a

A. 2 1/2" x 1 1/4" controlling nozzle
B. 2 1/2" x 1 1/4" open nozzle
C. play pipe 3" x 1 1/2"
D. 2 1/2" x 1 1/8" open nozzle

20. The Fire Code provides that, in a dry cleaning establishment, each room where a washing tank is located must be provided with an approved fire extinguishing system.
The type of system which is specified is a(n) _____ system.

    A. steam
    B. carbon dioxide
    C. foam
    D. ordinary sprinkler

21. According to the Fire Code, the MAXIMUM quantity of calcium carbide which may be lawfully stored without a permit is _____ lbs.

    A. 60
    B. 80
    C. 100
    D. 120

22. A Class C refrigerating system, as defined in the Fire Code, is one in which the quantity of refrigerant does NOT exceed _____ lbs.

    A. 20
    B. 25
    C. 30
    D. 35

23. According to the Building Code, a tank used to provide the required primary water supply to a standpipe system may also be used as a supply for an automatic sprinkler system

    A. in all cases where both have been installed
    B. where there are other acceptable sources of water supply for the sprinkler system
    C. only when the standpipe system has a direct connection to the public water system
    D. provided that its capacity is at least five thousand gallons greater than that required for the sprinkler system

24. For computing the capacity of water supplies other than the fire pump, the Building Code assumes that the average discharge in gallons per minute from a standard one-half inch sprinkler head is

    A. 20
    B. 25
    C. 30
    D. 35

25. The one of the following instructions for the care of life nets which is specifically counter to the rules and regulations is

    A. life nets shall be cleaned at least once each year with a water and non-alkali soap
    B. rope life nets shall be tar oiled at least once each year
    C. locks and spring rods of folding type life nets shall be kept greased
    D. all leather portions of the life and ladder belts shall be treated with neatsfoot oil

26. One of the men complains to you that you always give him the least desirable assignments.
You should

    A. refuse to discuss the matter with him
    B. discuss the matter with him
    C. tell him that if he is dissatisfied to request a transfer to another company
    D. point out to him that he has not been performing his house duties properly

27. About a week after you have been assigned to a new company, you overhear two of the men making unflattering remarks about your ability.
    You should

    A. ignore the incident but review your actions of the past week
    B. go up to the men and discuss the matter with them in a friendly manner
    C. report the incident to the company commander and ask that either you or the men be transferred
    D. state at the next formation that you take complete responsibility for your acts

28. With respect to your relations with the men in the company, it is important for you, as an officer, to

    A. recognize that you have your likes and dislikes and to compensate for them
    B. delegate your responsibility to the men who will ultimately perform the work
    C. avoid having likes and dislikes
    D. restrict your relations with the men to official business

29. Assume that while you are serving as a lieutenant, you observe a newly appointed fireman performing his house duties in a careless, indifferent fashion.
    Of the following actions, it is MOST desirable that you

    A. report the men to the company commander and ask him what to do
    B. say nothing to anyone and give the man a month or two to find himself
    C. show the man where his work is inadequate
    D. reprimand the man in front of the other men so that they can bring pressure on him

30. As a lieutenant, you wish to praise one of the men for having carried out his house duties in an exemplary manner. You should

    A. send him a letter through channels complimenting him
    B. compliment him at a formation, comparing him with individuals who have not been carrying their share of the load
    C. say nothing but give the man desirable assignments
    D. tell him what you think of his work

31. You have been given the assignment to train the men of the company in the use of a new piece of equipment.
    In order to get the BEST results, the emphasis should be on

    A. showing them how to operate the equipment properly by demonstrating its operation
    B. having the men operate the equipment under your direct supervision
    C. teaching the complicated parts of the procedure to the smarter men and the simpler parts to the others
    D. having a few men learn the operation and then have them teach the remainder of the company

32. When training a recruit, the BEST way to make him into a capable fireman is to

    A. tell him what to do at each point so that he will never make a mistake
    B. encourage him to make his own decisions as far as his assigned duties permit
    C. refuse to answer questions to which you believe he should know the answers
    D. have him memorize the Official Action Guide

33. A young lieutenant can, in general, expect some opposition from the older men in a company.
    The one of the following in which he should be prepared for the GREATEST amount of opposition is in attempting to

    A. train the men on new equipment
    B. enforce the departmental rules
    C. change the company's thinking on firefighting methods
    D. get information concerning the state of the company equipment

34. As a lieutenant, your MAJOR function is to

    A. discipline men who violate the Official Action Guide and the rules and regulations of the department
    B. improve the morale of the men in the company
    C. make certain that the equipment is ready for use at all times
    D. improve the quality of the service rendered by the company

35. Your company commander gives you a work assignment for the men which you believe to be unnecessary and which you know will be resented by the men.
    Of the following actions which you, as lieutenant, can take, it is MOST desirable that you

    A. make your point of view known to the captain before carrying out his orders
    B. carry out your superior's orders without comment
    C. carry out the orders but let the men know that the orders did not originate with you
    D. change the work assignment slightly in order to make it appear more purposeful

36. A fireman using a pickhead axe to remove a hinge pin forces the blade of the axe between the head of the pin and the top of the hinge and pries downward on the blade. The pin sticks. Inspection of the lower end of the pin shows no nut.
    The NEXT step is to

    A. strike the lower end of the pin with a sledge
    B. force another axe beneath the door
    C. push down on the pickhead of the axe
    D. get greater leverage by twisting the axe handle

37. The one of the following which is NOT a recommended way to free bars in masonry is to

    A. strike the bar with a sledge about ten inches above the sill
    B. strike the sill with a sledge at the end at which the bar is secured
    C. start a hammer-head pick in the masonry sill at the edge of the bar, then strike the head of the pick with the sledge
    D. wedge a hammerhead pick between two bars and strike the head of the pick with the sledge

38. When cutting wood of any kind with the pickhead axe, it should be done at an angle with the grain of the wood, instead of straight across it.
    The MOST effective angle is

    A. 75°-90°   B. 60°-75°   C. 45°-60°   D. 30°-45°

39. Whenever possible, in cutting with a pickhead axe through a lath and plaster wall, it is desirable to

   A. chop away from a stud in order to prevent excessive damage
   B. follow the lath down the center of studding to prevent excessive damage
   C. chop away from a stud in order to penetrate more easily
   D. follow the lath down the center of studding to make chopping easier

40. The grip of an axe handle should be

   A. *thin* to permit any man to get a good grip on it
   B. *thick* to prevent breaking should the axe be driven through the floor unexpectedly
   C. *thin* to provide elasticity
   D. *thick* to provide a solid grip

41. The one of the following which is NOT a rule to be followed when grinding an axe after it has been used at a fire is:

   A. Care must be taken while grinding to prevent overheating the cutting edge
   B. After sharpening the blade, it should be rubbed slightly over the stone to take off the keen edge
   C. The axe should be ground in such a way as to preserve the body thickness
   D. The axe should be cleaned with a light oil before grinding

42. When inspecting manila rope, it is customary to separate the strands at three-foot intervals and to examine the inner parts.
    If, during this inspection, a fine powder is observe, it would indicate the presence of

   A. mould   B. grit   C. broken fibres   D. burn

43. The one of the following which is a reason for NOT tightening the truss rods on the bed ladders is that it may

   A. prevent the bed ladders from being raised
   B. cause the ladder to go up too fast
   C. cause the fly to bend when raising the fly ladder
   D. damage the ladder locks

44. The capacity of an eighty-five foot aerial ladder with the top of the ladder supported is, under ordinary circumstances, _____ men.

   A. four   B. five   C. six   D. eight

45. A rotary type of priming pump reaches its MAXIMUM efficiency at a speed of _____ r.p.m.

   A. 600 to 800   B. 800 to 1000
   C. 1000 to 1200   D. 1200 to 1400

46. The length of time that the standard 50-pound can of foam powder will last if water is flowing through the inlet side of the generator at 100 P.S.I, and a 1 3/4" open nozzle is used, is MOST NEARLY _____ seconds.

   A. 50   B. 60   C. 70   D. 80

47. As lieutenant, you are in charge of a company working a line on the roof of a building. It is important that you do NOT

    A. use a gate
    B. lash the line to the hose roller
    C. use a controlling nozzle
    D. use an open nozzle

48. If there is a fire in a street or sidewalk transformer vault, the one of the following precautions which should be taken is to

    A. delay removing the cover until the current is turned off
    B. remove the manhole cover as soon as you arrive in order to permit poisonous fumes to escape
    C. let the fire burn itself out as the damage has all been done at the moment of electrical breakdown
    D. use a Baker cellar pipe if one is available

49. The Becket bend, which is illustrated below, is frequently used

    A. in first aid work
    B. to shorten a rope
    C. when operating a sledge as a battering tool
    D. to secure two lines of rope together

50. At a hot, smoky fire, the officer in charge of a hose line keeps his line away from the fire and directs the stream at the point from which the densest smoke is issuing. This procedure is

    A. *desirable;* it will reduce the number of casualties among the firemen
    B. *undesirable;* he should permit the nozzle man to use his own judgment about directing the stream
    C. *desirable;* the densest smoke usually issues from the danger points
    D. *undesirable;* it will frequently cause unnecessary water damage

KEY (CORRECT ANSWERS)

1. C	11. D	21. D	31. B	41. D
2. A	12. D	22. A	32. B	42. B
3. D	13. C	23. D	33. C	43. B
4. B	14. B	24. A	34. D	44. B
5. D	15. B	25. A	35. A	45. C
6. B	16. D	26. B	36. B	46. A
7. C	17. C	27. A	37. D	47. B
8. C	18. A	28. A	38. C	48. A
9. B	19. A	29. C	39. B	49. D
10. B	20. A	30. D	40. C	50. D

TEST 2

DIRECTIONS: Each question or incomplete statement is followed by several suggested answers or completions. Select the one that BEST answers the question or completes the statement. *PRINT THE LETTER OF THE CORRECT ANSWER IN THE SPACE AT THE RIGHT.*

1. According to the Rules and Regulations of the Fire Department, copies of all reports forwarded shall be preserved at points of origin 1.___

    A. for not more than six months
    B. for at least one year
    C. indefinitely
    D. only in special cases
    E. until otherwise directed

2. Of the following, the LEAST accurate statement concerning operation of house heating apparatus, according to the Official Action Guide, is that 2.___

    A. the temperature of the water in the hot water house supply must not exceed 160°F
    B. in calculating coal bin capacity, each cubic foot of space will hold 52 lbs. of coal
    C. the weight of coal carried in a Department ashcan is approximately 200 lbs. for buckwheat coal
    D. all flues and fire heating surfaces of all house heating appliances shall be cleaned weekly during the heating season
    E. when blowing a steam boiler, pressure of steam is raised to 8 lbs.

3. Of the following, the LEAST accurate statement concerning Field Violation Cards is that 3.___

    A. when all the violations listed on a Field Violation Card have been complied with, such card shall be placed in the Occupancy Folder
    B. not more than two Minor Violation Orders shall be recorded on any one card
    C. not more than two Major Violation Orders shall be recorded on any one card
    D. when the space on both sides is completely used for entries, such card is placed on file in the Occupancy Folder
    E. when subsequent violations are found for a building which previously complied with violations found, the additional entries shall be made on the same Field Violation Card

4. According to the Official Action Guide, when serving summonses, members shall procure certain information concerning the person upon whom the summons has been served and note such information on the back of both of both stubs of the summons. Which of the following is NOT an example of such information? 4.___

    A. Age
    B. Sex
    C. Approximate weight
    D. Place of birth
    E. Occupation

5. The one of the following items of information that need NOT be included in an *Operations at Fires - Company* report is the 5.___

    A. approximate number of pounds of pressure on the hydrant at time of arrival
    B. approximate number of pounds of pressure on the hydrant at time of leaving
    C. approximate time at which control valves of any automatic sprinkler system was closed
    D. approximate number of gallons of water supplied to water towers of other companies
    E. names of all members who responded to the alarm

6. The one of the following for which the Official Action Guide provides that a permit is required for storage, regardless of quantity and purpose, is

   A. shale oil
   B. heavy lubricating oil
   C. machine oil
   D. kerosene
   E. illuminating oil

7. The preliminary signal for special calling the Fire Patrol to a street box is

   A. 2-9
   B. 5-5-5
   C. 8
   D. 12
   E. none of these

8. The alarm 9-3635-72 is a special call for a(n) _____ Unit.

   A. Searchlight
   B. Airport Crash
   C. Smoke Ejector
   D. Bridge Chemical
   E. Air Compressor

9. Of the following, the MOST accurate statement concerning the signal 66-333-241-12-18 is that it is

   A. transmitted over the alarm system in Manhattan
   B. transmitted from a box in Brooklyn or Queens
   C. a notification signal in Richmond
   D. a notification signal in Brooklyn or Queens
   E. a notification signal in Manhattan or Bronx

10. The signal 77-box A-33-box B would MOST probably be transmitted

    A. from box A in Brooklyn or Queens
    B. from box B in Manhattan or Bronx
    C. over the alarm circuit in Manhattan and Bronx
    D. from box B in Brooklyn or Queens
    E. over the alarm circuit in Brooklyn and Queens

11. Of the following, which question would be MOST relevant for deciding whether a simultaneous call or a borough call would be MORE appropriate in a specific situation?

    A. Are land companies only required in response to the signal?
    B. Is a chief officer desired in response to the signal?
    C. Is a second or higher alarm assignment desired in response to the signal?
    D. Are the two boxes enumerated in the signal located in different boroughs?
    E. Are the two boxes enumerated in the signal part of the same telegraph unit?

12. Suppose that your company is returning from a fire. You note flames coming out of a factory window, and your company stops to extinguish this fire.
    According to General Order No. 1, you are NOT required to send any notification to the dispatcher unless

    A. a full first alarm assignment is needed
    B. more than one company has stopped to extinguish the fire
    C. your company was specially called to the first fire
    D. your company responded originally to a 5-7 signal
    E. the fire is small and can be readily extinguished by your company alone

13. According to General Order No. 1, a rescue company shall respond to a verbal alarm when

    A. a refrigerator leak is reported
    B. quartered with an engine company which is out of service
    C. the fire involves danger to life and property
    D. the fire is visible from quarters
    E. the verbal alarm is transmitted by the dispatcher

14. *Between the hours of 8 A.M. and 6 P.M., the last due land engine company, where three or more land engine companies are assigned to respond to a special building box, shall be relieved from responding. General Order No. 1 provides certain exceptions to this rule.*
    The one of the following which is NOT an exception is

    A. schools   B. hospitals   C. churches
    D. ferries   E. sports arenas

15. The signal 5-7-139 sent from the morse key in company quarters indicates that

    A. engine company number 139 is responding to a still alarm near box 7
    B. engine company number 139 is responding to a verbal alarm near box 7
    C. the engine company and truck company first due are responding to a verbal alarm of fire near box 139
    D. engine company 7 is responding to a verbal alarm near box 139
    E. the engine company and truck company first due at box 139 are out of service temporarily

16. Verbal alarms of refrigerant leaks are handled differently in the Borough of Richmond than in any other borough.
    The one of the following which states this difference MOST accurately is that, in Richmond,

    A. rescue companies do not respond to alarms involving household units
    B. the nearest available battalion chief responds to all such alarms, large or small
    C. if the nearest available battalion chief is not in his regular quarters, the dispatcher transmits a special call for the battalion chief on the primary circuits
    D. a 7-4 signal is transmitted whether the verbal alarm is received by an engine company or by a hook and ladder company
    E. the police emergency squad responds instead of the fire department rescue company

17. The Multiple Dwelling Law provides that, in every multiple dwelling erected after April 18, 1929, every stair, fire stair, and fire tower beyond a specified width shall be provided with a handrail on each side.
    This specified width is

    A. 3'2"   B. 3'8"   C. 4'2"   D. 4'10"   E. 5'6"

18. The one of the following listed by the Administrative Code as a substance made dangerous by contact with other substances is

    A. zinc dust   B. picric acid
    C. anhydrous acetic acid   D. ethyl aldehyde
    E. ethyl chloride

19. The one of the following listed by the Administrative Code as a non-volatile inflammable liquid is

    A. glycerine   B. acetone   C. benzole
    D. naphtha   E. methyl alcohol

20. The one of the following which is NOT included among the six categories in which all structures are classified by the Administrative Code with respect to type of construction is _____ structures.

    A. heavy timber   B. metal
    C. wood frame   D. fireproof
    E. fire-resistant

21. All storage tanks, comprising or forming a part of an oil storage plant, shall be buried so that the tops thereof shall be a distance below the grade level of AT LEAST

    A. 1'   B. 2'   C. 3'   D. 4'   E. 6'

22. According to the Administrative Code, a Class B refrigeration system is one

    A. capable of less than 15 tons capacity
    B. containing not more than 20 lbs. of refrigerant
    C. capable of less than 30 tons capacity
    D. containing 1000 pounds or over of refrigerant
    E. capable of 40 tons capacity or over

23. According to the Administrative Code, it shall be unlawful to transport or store guncotton EXCEPT in

    A. strong wooden cases lined with liquid-proof paper
    B. strong wooden cases
    C. carboys so tinted as to exclude light
    D. water-tight metal vessels
    E. aluminum or other non-tarnishing metal

24. According to the Administrative Code, a refrigerant is defined as the chemical agent used to produce refrigeration, other than

    A. brine
    B. a chemical of the hydrocarbon clan
    C. the compressor
    D. methyl bromide
    E. ammonia

25. The Administrative Code defines as a combustible mixture any substance which, when tested in a Tagliabue open cup tester, emits an inflammable vapor at temperatures

    A. below 100° F
    B. above 300° F
    C. between 100° F. and 300° F.
    D. below 125° F
    E. above 125° F

26. *Before attacking a fire in a closed building, it is necessary to determine whether ventilation is necessary and, if so, the method of ventilating.*
    The one of the following actions which would be of LEAST value in reaching such a decision is to

    A. observe the points at which smoke may be oozing out from the building
    B. feel the windows for heat
    C. observe the density of smoke through the windows
    D. feel the walls and roof for hot spots
    E. observe the color of the smoke

27. The number of threads per inch in National Standard 2 1/2" hose coupling is

    A. 4   B. 6 1/2   C. 7 1/4   D. 7 1/2   E. 8

28. In sizing up a fire, the first lieutenant to arrive at the scene of the fire should generally attach LEAST importance to

    A. determining the extent of the fire
    B. rescue requirements
    C. where to enter to extinguish the fire
    D. value of the property involved
    E. type and construction of the building

29. The proper nozzle size to be used on a 1,000 ft. line of 24" hose is GENERALLY considered to be

    A. 3/4"   B. 7/8"   C. 1"   D. 1 1/8"   E. 1 1/4"

30. When fighting a fire involving naphtha and paint in open containers in a small low-ceilinged room, usually it would be BEST for the fire lieutenant to order his men to use

    A. carbon tetrachloride extinguishers
    B. carbon dioxide extinguishers
    C. soda-acid extinguishers
    D. ordinary sand
    E. a hose stream with a small tip

31. The one of the following which is LEAST useful for extinguishing confined oil or grease fires is

    A. sand   B. ashes
    C. soda-acid extinguishers   D. foam-type extinguishers
    E. carbon dioxide extinguishers

32. The one of the following chemicals on which it is MOST dangerous to direct a hose stream is

    A. sulphuric acid   B. nitric acid
    C. hydrochloric acid   D. ethyl alcohol
    E. acetic acid

33. Smothering action or cutting off the air supply is LEAST effective in a fire involving

    A. nitrocellulose   B. magnesium   C. acetone
    D. sulphuric acid   E. camphor

34. Of the following, the CHIEF objection to allowing newly appointed firemen under your supervision to learn correct firefighting procedures solely on the basis of their own experience is that a fireman

    A. rarely forgets a lesson taught by experience
    B. remembers best what he learns first
    C. learns best when he is allowed to exercise originality
    D. learns more quickly when he is guided
    E. is likely to resent an excessively domineering officer

34.____

35. Assume that you have been appointed a lieutenant.
Of the following, the BEST justification for learning as much as possible about the men to be under your supervision from the captain commanding the company to which you are assigned is that

    A. no lieutenant can be effective in his assignment unless his attitude towards the company commander is one of cooperation
    B. best results in handling men are usually obtained by treating them equally without favor
    C. some firemen often function more efficiently under one supervisor than under another supervisor
    D. confidence of the men in their supervisor is increased when they know he is interested in impartial and fair supervision
    E. effective handling of men is often based upon knowledge of individual personality differences

35.____

36. *Newly appointed lieutenants will find that it is the older men in their companies who will be their greatest concern and problem.*
This statement assumes MOST directly that

    A. competence in fire fighting tends to increase with experience
    B. strict supervision may increase the tendency on the part of firemen to break minor regulations
    C. the need for supervision bears little relationship to the amount of experience
    D. newly appointed firemen are usually less well-acquainted with detailed regulations
    E. newly appointed firemen are so assigned that there are only one or two in any one company

36.____

37. In planning courses for a fireman's training program, it is MOST important to make the content of each lesson capable of being

    A. taught in one class meeting
    B. *tied* to something which the trainee already knows or can do
    C. spread over a number of class meetings
    D. fully learned by the trainees as something entirely new
    E. explained by the instructor in technical terms

37.____

38. If a fire lieutenant is to be an effective leader of those under him, he MUST

    A. utilize whatever motives for work he is able to discern in the men working under him
    B. avoid training by direct instruction lest his men be deprived of initiative
    C. delegate to each man under him an equal amount of responsibility

38.____

D. outline repeatedly and in great detail the work to be performed by each member of the group
E. develop the assets of the men and encourage them to work for the good of the organization as a whole

39. When instructing firemen under his supervision, the fire lieutenant should recognize the fact that

    A. learning should be uniform if instruction is the same for all
    B. persons differ in the amount they can learn in a given period of time
    C. after the age of 20 or so, a person is less capable of learning than before
    D. learning is seldom possible without much individual instruction
    E. learning should be essentially a passive procedure without active participation by the learner

40. Assume that you are a lieutenant. A fireman under your supervision attempts to conceal the fact that he has made an error.
    You should proceed on the assumption that

    A. the evasion indicates something wrong in the fundamental relationship between you and this fireman
    B. a desire for concealment indicates an anti-social attitude on the part of this fireman
    C. probably the fireman was merely ignorant of proper procedures and the entire matter is best dropped
    D. the evasion should be overlooked provided that the error occurred in a matter of no great importance
    E. the handling of this fireman should not be such as to discourage his independence of spirit

41. *A good measure of the efficiency of a fire department with respect to fire prevention is the number of fires which occur per 1,000 of population.*
    Of the following, the CHIEF limitation of this suggested index of fire department efficiency is that

    A. the more efficient the fire department with respect to fire prevention, the smaller the number of fires occurring in that area is likely to be
    B. the size of the total population in an area should be related to the total number of fires which occur, not the number which are prevented
    C. areas in which fires occur frequently may have a lower index of fire incidence than areas in which fires occur infrequently
    D. fire departments in areas which have a high rate of fire incidence may prevent a large number of fires
    E. the number of fires which occur varies inversely, and not directly, with the number of fires prevented

42. *In the fire department, it is the lieutenant who is the key man in the enforcement of discipline.*
    Of the following, the BEST justification for this statement is that

    A. the lieutenant was most recently a fireman himself, and so is more likely to view minor violations sympathetically
    B. the lieutenant, as compared with other supervisory officers has a more rounded view of the operation of the fire department as a whole

8 (#2)

C. the lieutenant, as compared with other supervisory officers, is in closer contact with the men on the job
D. if a fire department is to be well-balanced, there should be proportionately more lieutenants than other supervisory officers
E. the future chiefs and administrators in any fire department must necessarily be chosen from among the present lieutenants

43. The principle of administration that the responsibility of higher authority for the acts of subordinates MUST be absolute means that

   A. coordinate officers are responsible for the acts of each other
   B. the chief executive alone is not responsible for the acts of his own subordinates
   C. each subordinate is held responsible for his own acts
   D. discretionary authority should not be delegated
   E. each superior officer is held responsible for all the acts of his subordinates

43.____

44. The theoretical displacement of a four cylinder, double-acting piston pump having a 5" diameter cylinder, a 6" stroke, and a 1" diameter piston rod, when delivering at the rate of 275 revolutions per minute, is MOST NEARLY _____ gpm.

   A. 300   B. 500   C. 800   D. 1100   E. 1300

44.____

45. A pumper, at 350 lbs. pressure, is pumping through 200' of 2 1/2" hose equipped with 1 1/8" nozzle. The nozzle pressure is _____ lbs.

   A. 25   B. 30   C. 35   D. 40   E. 45

45.____

46. A pumper at 200 lbs. pressure is pumping through 300' of 24" rubber-lined hose into a standpipe. On the eleventh floor (ten stories above the engine), two lengths of 24" hose are taken with a 1 1/8" nozzle.
Assuming 12 feet per story and a 25 lb. friction loss for the standpipe, the effective pressure at the nozzle will be _____ lbs.

   A. 5   B. 15   C. 25   D. 35   E. 45

46.____

47. Suppose that the rated capacity of a pumper is 750 gallons per minute at a pressure of 120 lbs. per square inch. At a fire, it is necessary to flood a basement which measures 10' x 10' x 12', and estimated to be half full of stock. Two lines of 3" hose with open butt are used. With 25 lbs. pressure at each butt, how long will it take to flood the basement completely? _____ minutes.

   A. 4   B. 6   C. 8   D. 10   E. 12

47.____

48. A 2" nozzle has four times the nozzle reaction, or *kickback,* as a 1" nozzle, provided that

   A. engine pressure is the same
   B. friction loss is the same
   C. nozzle pressure is the same
   D. cross-sectional areas at the nozzle are in the ratio of 4 to 1
   E. friction loss in the line where engine pressure is the same, is in the ratio of 4 to 1

48.____

49. An engine is pumping through two parallel lines of 2½" hose, each 200 feet in length, to the Siamese connection of a water tower. The mast is extended so that the nozzle is 65' above the street. A 1 3/4" *nozzle* is employed, and 90 lbs. pressure is desired at the nozzle. (Note: Friction loss in the water tower is 15 lbs.; the factor for converting two 2 1/2" lines into one 2 1/2" is 3.6; the constant for 2 1/2" hose and 1 3/4" nozzle is .907.)
The minimum engine pressure required will be MOST NEARLY _____ lbs.

   A. 165   B. 180   C. 190   D. 195   E. 220

50. A 300' line of 2 1/2" hose, with a 1 1/8" nozzle, is stretched up a fire escape to a point 50 feet above street level. Engine pressure is 150 lbs. (Note: Constant for 2½" hose and 1 1/8" nozzle is .167.)
The pressure at the nozzle is MOST NEARLY _____ lbs.

   A. 40   B. 50   C. 60   D. 70   E. 80

KEY (CORRECT ANSWERS)

1. B	11. E	21. B	31. C	41. D
2. A	12. A	22. C	32. A	42. C
3. E	13. B	23. D	33. A	43. E
4. C	14. D	24. A	34. D	44. D
5. D	15. C	25. C	35. E	45. E
6. A	16. E	26. E	36. C	46. A
7. D	17. B	27. D	37. B	47. B
8. E	18. A	28. D	38. E	48. C
9. B	19. A	29. C	39. B	49. E
10. C	20. E	30. B	40. A	50. C

EXAMINATION SECTION
TEST 1

DIRECTIONS: Each question or incomplete statement is followed by several suggested answers or completions. Select the one that BEST answers the question or completes the statement. *PRINT THE LETTER OF THE CORRECT ANSWER IN THE SPACE AT THE RIGHT.*

1. While operating a department geiger counter, you notice that the pointer of the meter is fluctuating considerably. The one of the following statements which is MOST valid is that the instrument probably is functioning 1.____

    A. properly
    B. improperly because of defective batteries
    C. improperly because of failure to close the probe shield
    D. improperly because of contamination of the probe by radioactive material

Questions 2-3.

DIRECTIONS: Questions 2 and 3 are based upon the diagram of the control pedestal of the American La France Metal Aerial Ladder, which appears below.

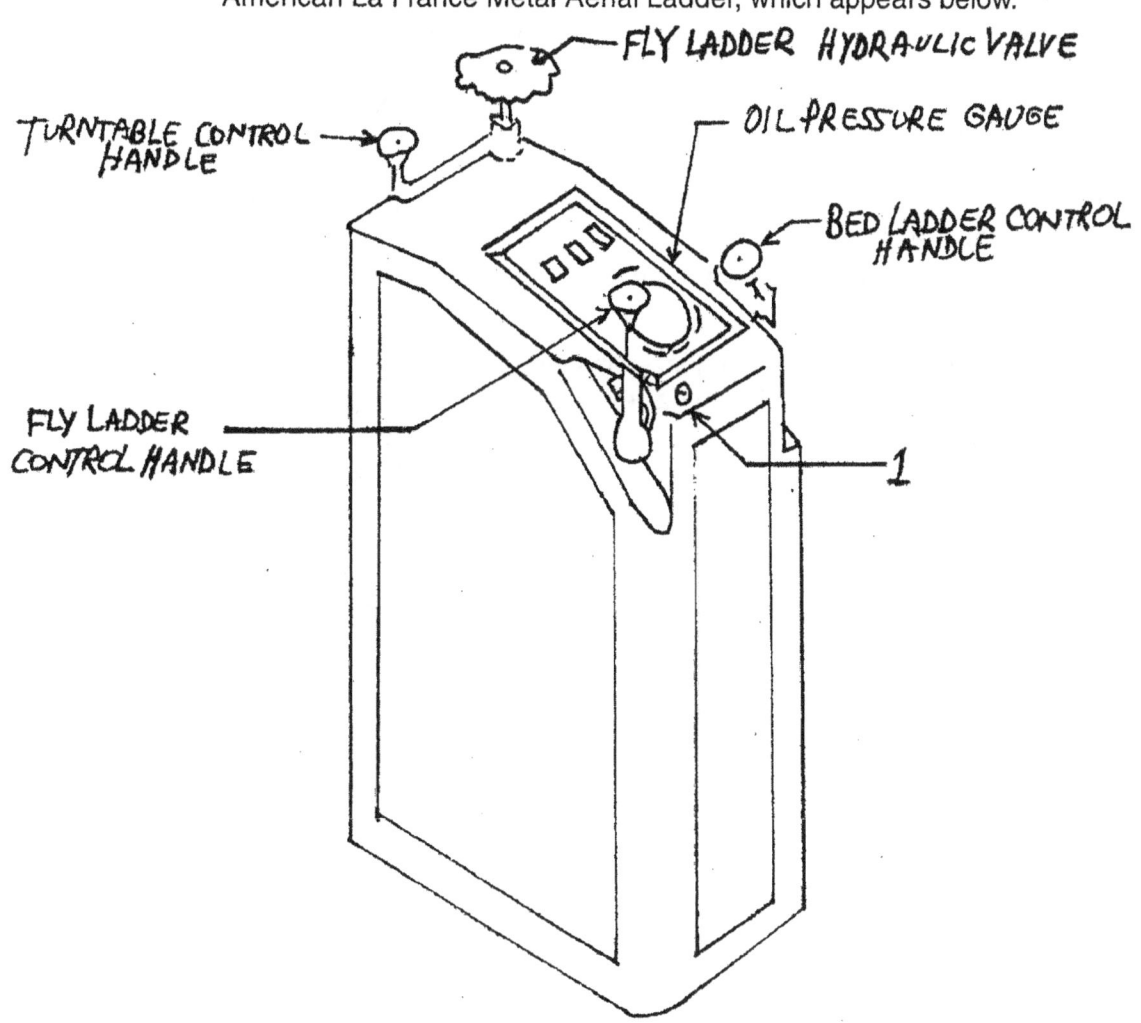

2. The one of the following parts that is INCORRECTLY labeled in the diagram is the one marked

   A. Turntable Control Handle
   B. Fly Ladder Hydraulic Lock Valve
   C. Bed Ladder Control Handle
   D. Oil Pressure Gauge

3. The control marked *1* is the _____ switch.

   A. panel light
   B. engine starter
   C. master throttle
   D. air brake

4. Assume that a Master Stream Fog Nozzle #700 is set at 90 and that the nozzle pressure is increased from 75 psi to 125 psi.
   The one of the following statements that is MOST accurate is that as the nozzle pressure increases,

   A. both the width of the fog pattern and the projection of the fog pattern increase
   B. the width of the fog pattern increases and the projection of the fog pattern decreases
   C. the width of the fog pattern decreases and the projection of the fog pattern increases
   D. the width of the fog pattern increases and the projection of the fog pattern remains constant

5. When an aerial ladder is used as a water tower, the ladder is subjected to back pressure from the hose stream.
   If various size nozzle tips are used at the same nozzle pressure, the amount of back pressure

   A. *increases* as the size of the nozzle tips increase
   B. *decreases* as the size of the nozzle tips increase
   C. remains constant as the size of the nozzle tips increase
   D. *increases* up to a critical point and then decreases as the size of the nozzle tips increases

6. When setting the relay relief valve, the control handle is put at a high setting initially and, with the nozzle opened, gradually lowered until water discharge to the ground indicates that the relay relief valve has opened. The *setting is then raised about* _____ *pounds above former intake* pressure.
   The number which belongs in the blank space above is

   A. 25   B. 20   C. 15   D. 10

7. The one of the following statements that is MOST accurate is that departmental electric wire cutters may be used safely to cut live electrical wires carrying

   A. a maximum of 1,000 volts
   B. a maximum of 8,000 volts
   C. a maximum of 30,000 volts
   D. any voltage presently in use

8. The fire extinguishers which are preferred for extinguishment of fires in mail boxes are _____ extinguishers.

   A. dry powder and carbon tetrachloride
   B. dry powder and carbon dioxide
   C. carbon tetrachloride and carbon dioxide
   D. dry powder, carbon tetrachloride, and carbon dioxide

9. When using an eductor for removal of water, the jet pressure recommended to cover MOST situations is _____ lbs.

   A. 150   B. 165   C. 180   D. 195

10. A pumper is supplying three 2 1/2" hose lines, each 100 feet long and equipped with 1 1/4" nozzles. One hose line requires a nozzle pressure of 50 psi, the second requires 40 psi, and the third requires 30 psi.
    The pumper should be operated at a pressure sufficient to supply the

    A. average of the nozzle pressures required (40 psi), with all discharge gates fully opened
    B. highest of the nozzle pressures required (50 psi), with the discharge gates of the second and third lines partially closed
    C. total of the nozzle pressures required (120 psi), with the discharge gates of all lines partially closed
    D. total of the nozzle pressures required (120 psi), with the discharge gates of the second and third lines partially closed

11. Don't open a nozzle on mere smoke. Wait until you actually see the fire.
    Of the following, the MAIN exception to this rule is where the smoke

    A. is super-heated
    B. is very dense and impairs visibility
    C. contains ammonia or other soluble detergents
    D. contains carbon disulfide or similar explosive vapors

12. Cherry red color of cheeks and lips is a symptom of

    A. heat exhaustion   B. electrical shock
    C. carbon monoxide poisoning   D. internal bleeding

13. At a training session, the instructor asked, *How should the officer in command of a fireboat counteract the drift of the boat caused by back pressure from operation of deck pipes?*
    The following suggestions were made by members of the class:
    I. Properly secure the fireboat
    II. Discharge half the deck pipes into the water in the direction of drift
    III. Operate the fireboat's engines at slow speed in the opposite direction
    The one of the following statements that is MOST acceptable is

    A. I *only*   B. I, II   C. I, III   D. I, II, III

14. Air in hose lines, usually caused by operating pumps under negative pressure, is objectionable CHIEFLY because the air imprisoned in the hose stream tends to

A. intensify the fire
B. break up the stream
C. reduce the quantity of water discharged
D. reduce nozzle pressure

15. In combatting a gasoline spill fire following the crash landing of a passenger plane, the first engine company to respond should use fog streams held

    A. at shoulder height and the stream pointed downward at the center of the fire
    B. at waist height and the stream pointed above the fire
    C. about three feet off the surface of the ground and the stream pointed at the edges of the spill
    D. about two feet off the surface of the ground and the stream pointed parallel to the ground

16. A crowded excursion boat catches fire about 15 minutes after leaving its pier. When the first fireboat arrives on the scene, heavy smoke and flames are seen pouring from the boat, many passengers are seen in the water, and many more are preparing to jump. In this situation, the method of rescue which SHOULD be employed is to

    A. board the excursion boat and assist in the lowering of life boats
    B. lower the punts of the fireboat and remove from the water as many persons as possible
    C. throw overboard life preservers, life rings, and buoyant materials to support persons in the water
    D. attempt to tow the excursion boat to shore

17. You are in command of the first engine company to respond to a fire involving a tank containing a highly volatile refined oil. Upon your arrival, you see a stream of vapor burning at the vent of the tank.
    In this situation, it is MOST important for you to consider the possibility of

    A. boil-over of the oil in the tank
    B. ignition of combustibles in the area
    C. explosion of combustible vapors in the surrounding atmosphere
    D. flashback of flames into the tank causing an explosion

18. When a stretch of more than 10 lengths of 2 1/2" hose is required, a Siamese should be placed between the

    A. first and second length from the nozzle
    B. third and fourth length from the nozzle
    C. fifth and sixth length from the nozzle
    D. two lengths in the mid-point of the stretch

19. The MAXIMUM distance which may be bridged safely by a 25-foot straight portable metal ladder is _____ feet.

    A. 15   B. 17   C. 19   D. 21

20. When using a lock puller to force entrance through an apartment exterior door secured by a cylinder lock, GENERALLY the lock puller

    A. alone is sufficient
    B. and key tool are required
    C. and flat head axe are required
    D. key tool and flat head axle are required

21. The one of the following statements that is MOST accurate is that a fireman testifying in court in an arson case may

    A. not refer to written notes to refresh his memory
    B. refer to written notes provided that the notes were made at the time and place of the fire occurrence
    C. refer to written notes provided that the signatures of persons mentioned in the notes were obtained at the time the notes were made
    D. refer to written notes provided that other persons were witnesses to the facts noted

22. Smoke at fires generally rises and is found on the floors above the fire.
    Of the following type of fires, the one that is MOST likely to be an exception to this generalization, one in which the smoke may be found on the floors below the fire rather than above, is a fire in a

    A. multi-story parking garage without walls
    B. cold storage plant
    C. grain storage warehouse with no windows
    D. building with many levels of sub-basements

23. At a fire in a lumber yard, the officer in command directed the lieutenant in charge of the third due engine company to hook up to a hydrant across railroad tracks. The lieutenant ordered the removal of ballast from between railroad ties and passing of the hose under the rails.
    The procedure employed in this situation was

    A. *good,* chiefly because the hose is protected from damage by passing trains
    B. *bad,* chiefly because the maneuverability of the hose line is reduced
    C. *good,* chiefly because interference with the operations of the railroad is reduced
    D. *bad,* chiefly because delay in getting water on the fire results

24. During an overhauling operation, a lieutenant observed members of his company performing the following operations:
    I. Tipping a drill sideways to make a hole larger than the drill bit diameter
    II. Using a pocketknife to pry a deeply embedded nail out of the heel of a boot
    III. Using pliers on the shank of a screwdriver
    The one of the following statements that is MOST acceptable is

    A. I *only*
    B. II *only*
    C. III *only*
    D. none of the above

25. When raising a metal aerial ladder in an emergency, when time is of the essence,

    A. all tormentors must be in position
    B. the placing of tormentors on the outboard side may be delayed temporarily

C. the placing of the tormentors on the inboard side may be delayed temporarily
D. the placing of all tormentors may be delayed temporarily

26. High pressure hose should be used when supplying standpipe systems of buildings more than _____ stories in height.

    A. 20 B. 22 C. 24 D. 25

27. When serving a summons for violation of the Building Code, it is most important that proper procedure be followed.
Of the following statements, the one that is MOST acceptable is that a summons may be

    A. mailed to the residence of the building's owner if he is not on the premises
    B. given to a superintendent to be forwarded to the owner if he is not on the premises
    C. placed on the desk or in the immediate vicinity of the owner if he refuses to accept it
    D. made out with the initials of the owner if the full name is not known

28. An unconscious civilian is discovered by two firemen at a fire with the following symptoms: he is not breathing, his pulse cannot be felt, and his pupils are wide and dilated. The one of the following courses of treatment which would be BEST under these circumstances would be to apply

    A. mouth-to-mouth resuscitation until breathing is restored and then cardiac massage
    B. cardiac massage until the pulse can be felt and then mouth-to-mouth breathing
    C. mouth-to-mouth resuscitation and cardiac massage alternately
    D. mouth-to-mouth resuscitation and cardiac massage simultaneously

29. The MOST effective of the following methods of reducing the amount of radiant heat energy passing through exposed glass windows is to use a

    A. solid stream water curtain
    B. fog stream water curtain
    C. solid stream water curtain alternating with a fog stream water curtain
    D. thin film of water over the window glass

30. The one of the following statements about transmission of heat that is INCORRECT is that

    A. dark materials absorb heat radiation more readily than light-colored materials
    B. rough surfaces absorb heat radiation more readily than smooth surfaces
    C. good conductors of heat ignite more readily than poor conductors
    D. a high rate of radiant heat transfer is more likely to ignite a substance than the same total amount of energy absorbed over a longer interval of time

31. The Stokes Navy Stretcher is to be used

    A. in preference to any other when available
    B. *only* if the standard Army Stretcher is not available
    C. interchangeably with the Army Stretcher
    D. *only* if the victim is to be raised from a pit or lowered from a height

32. Smoke is seen coming from several cornices of a row of buildings when the first due company arrives at the scene of an alarm.
    The MOST likely of the following conclusions to be drawn is that

    A. fire has involved all of the buildings
    B. more than one fire is burning
    C. fire stops are either absent or ineffective
    D. smoke is under high pressure

33. The MAIN fire hazard of sodium nitrate is that it

    A. releases oxygen when heated
    B. ignites readily when in contact with oxidizing chemicals
    C. heats spontaneously if in contact with moisture
    D. gives off flammable vapors when heated moderately

34. The use of water should be avoided when extinguishing a fire in

    A. acetone
    B. calcium carbide
    C. hydrochloric acid
    D. potassium chlorate

35. The chemical formula of the compound carbon monoxide is written

    A. CO
    B. CO_2
    C. CO_3
    D. C_2O

36. At a fire in an understreet installation, the manhole cover was removed, revealing the fact that the insulation of electrical wires was burning.
    Of the following, the BEST course of action to be taken by the officer in command is to order

    A. that the fire be permitted to burn itself out
    B. the replacement of the manhole cover to reduce the oxygen supply to the fire
    C. the application of a carbon dioxide extinguisher to the manhole
    D. the application of a carbon tetrachloride extinguisher to the manhole

37. At a very severe fire in a large loft building, the officer in charge had the alternative of using two large caliber streams or several small caliber streams capable of producing the same total volume of water as the heavy streams.
    In this situation, it GENERALLY is preferable to use the

    A. *small* caliber streams chiefly because greater maneuverability in hose placement results
    B. *large* caliber streams chiefly because they have a better chance of reaching the seat of the fire
    C. *small* caliber streams chiefly because less water damage results from the greater precision in directing the streams
    D. *large* caliber streams chiefly because less manpower is required to operate the streams

38. The one of the following statements concerning the stand-pipe systems of bridges that is MOST accurate is that normally

    A. all shut-off and control valves should be kept open
    B. the central control valves should be kept open and all other shut-off valves kept closed

C. the central control valves should be kept closed and all other shut-off valves kept open
D. all shut-off and control valves should be kept closed

39. Friction loss in a 24" hose, compared to friction loss in a 3" hose for the same discharge and under similar conditions, is APPROXIMATELY _____ times as much.

   A. 1 1/2 B. 2 1/2 C. 5 D. 7 1/2

40. The *Underwriters' formula* for calculating nozzle pressure in a rubber-lined hose 24" or greater in diameter and employing nozzles of 1" or greater in diameter is NP =

   A. EP x (1.1 + KL)
   B. EP x (1.1 x KL)
   C. EP/(1.1 + KL)
   D. D.EP/(1.1 x KL)

41. Two hose lines have identical nozzle pressures, lengths, and diameters, but the first has a 1 1/2" nozzle and the second a 1" nozzle.
   Comparing the engine pressures and reach of the two streams, we find that the FIRST line requires a _____ engine pressure and has a _____ reach.

   A. higher; longer
   B. higher; shorter
   C. lower; longer
   D. lower; shorter

42. The difference between the pressure at the nozzle and the pressure at the engine is the true loss due to friction *only* if the

   A. hose line is laid without bends or kinks
   B. velocity of flow is constant
   C. hose line has no washers protruding into the waterway
   D. hose line is laid horizontally

43. The nozzle pressure on a charged line when the nozzle is closed is

   A. zero
   B. substantially greater than the engine pressure
   C. approximately the same as the engine pressure
   D. substantially less than the engine pressure

Questions 44-46.

DIRECTIONS: Questions 44 through 46 are based upon the following paragraph.

When wood products are heated sufficiently under fire conditions, they undergo thermal decomposition and evolve various combustible gases or vapors which burn as the familiar flames. After these volatile decomposition products of the wood are driven off, the combustible residue is essentially carbon which, on further heating, undergoes surface combustion reactions with the oxygen of the air, producing considerable heat (glowing), but usually very little flame.

44. The one of the following explanations of thermal decomposition that is MOST accurate is that it is a process by which

   A. heat is transferred from solid substances to gaseous substances
   B. a substance is consumed during the course of a fire

C. a substance is broken down into component parts when subjected to heat
D. heat is generated until the ignition point of the substance is reached

45. The one of the following statements that is MOST accurate is that pure carbon has an ignition temperature which, compared to the combustible vapors of wood, is   45.____

   A. lower
   B. approximately the same
   C. higher
   D. higher or lower, depending upon the variety of wood involved

46. A substance which burns with a large amount of flames is one that   46.____

   A. contains a large amount of inorganic material
   B. produces during the burning process a large amount of pure carbon
   C. contains a large amount of calories per unit of combustibles
   D. produces during the burning process a large amount of combustible gases or vapors

Questions 47-50.

DIRECTIONS: Questions 47 through 50 are based upon the following paragraph.

For the five-year period 2006-2010, inclusive, the average annual fire loss in the United States amounted to approximately $1,354,830,000. Included in this estimate is $2,072,666,000 damage to buildings and contents, and $282,164,000 average annual loss in aircraft, motor vehicles, forest and other miscellaneous fires not involving buildings. Preliminary estimates indicate that the total United States fire loss in 2011 was $1,615,000,000. These are property damage fire losses only and do not include indirect losses resulting from fires which are just as real and sometimes far more serious than property damage losses. "But because evaluation of indirect monetary losses is usually very difficult, their importance in the national fire waste picture is often overlooked.

47. According to the data in the above paragraph, the BEST of the following estimates of the total direct fire loss in the United States for the six-year period 2006-2011, inclusive, is   47.____

   A. $1,400,000,000   B. $2,700,000,000
   C. $7,000,000,000   D. $8,400,000,000

48. The BEST example of an indirect fire loss, as that term is used in the above paragraph, is monetary loss due to   48.____

   A. smoke or water damage to exposures
   B. condemnation of foodstuffs following a fire
   C. interruption of business following a fire
   D. forcible entry by firemen operating at a fire

49. Suppose that during the period 2011-2015 the average annual fire loss to buildings and contents increases 10 percent, and the average annual loss due to fires not involving buildings decreases 10%.   49.____
   The MOST valid of the following conclusions is that the average annual fire loss for the 2011-2015 period, compared to the losses for the 2006-2010 period,

A. will increase
B. will decrease
C. will be unchanged
D. cannot be calculated from the information given

50. If a comparison is made between total annual direct and indirect fire losses on the basis of the information given in the above paragraph, the MOST valid of the following conclusions is that

    A. generally, direct losses are higher
    B. generally, indirect losses are higher
    C. generally, direct and indirect losses are approximately equal
    D. there is not sufficient information to determine which is higher or if they are approximately equal

KEY (CORRECT ANSWERS)

1. A	11. A	21. B	31. A	41. A
2. B	12. C	22. B	32. C	42. D
3. B	13. A	23. A	33. A	43. C
4. C	14. B	24. D	34. B	44. C
5. A	15. D	25. B	35. A	45. C
6. B	16. C	26. A	36. C	46. D
7. B	17. D	27. C	37. B	47. D
8. C	18. B	28. D	38. C	48. C
9. A	19. A	29. D	39. B	49. A
10. B	20. D	30. C	40. C	50. D

TEST 2

DIRECTIONS: Each question or incomplete statement is followed by several suggested answers or completions. Select the one that BEST answers the question or completes the statement. *PRINT THE LETTER OF THE CORRECT ANSWER IN THE SPACE AT THE RIGHT.*

1. In the equipment of Mask Service Unit #41, the connections between manifold stations and between manifolds and cylinders are made of rubber hose reinforced with wire braid, rather than of metal pipe.
   The MAIN reason for using hose instead of pipe is to reduce the possibility of

   A. transmission of vibrations from truck body to cylinders
   B. failure of the connections
   C. injury to members from flying pipe in the event of an accident
   D. rust or corrosion of the connections

   1.____

2. The one of the following statements about the inhalator as used by the Fire Department that is NOT accurate is that

   A. the rate of flow of oxygen is measured in liters
   B. manual artificial respiration must be applied at the same time
   C. alternating positive and negative pressure are maintained on the lungs
   D. it is effective on persons with respiratory diseases as well as on persons overcome by smoke

   2.____

3. When working at maximum capacity, the quantity of water discharged through the Mystery *nozzle* is

   A. *greater* in the fog spray position than in the solid stream position
   B. *greater* in the solid stream position than in the fog spray position
   C. *equal* in the fog spray and solid stream positions
   D. *greater* in the fog spray position at low pressure and greater in the solid stream position at high pressure

   3.____

4. Future department apparatus will be equipped with pressurized dry powder extinguishers in place of carbon tetra-chloride extinguishers.
   The one of the following statements comparing the two types of extinguishers that is MOST complete and accurate is that the dry powder extinguisher is superior because dry powder presents no hazard of

   A. noxious fumes
   B. noxious fumes and is superior as an extinguishing agent
   C. noxious fumes and the extinguisher has a longer range
   D. noxious fumes, is superior as an extinguishing agent, and the extinguisher has a longer range

   4.____

5. The one of the following statements that is MOST accurate and complete is that carbon monoxide is MOST likely to be a hazard in a relatively cool

   A. fire
   B. fire in a confined area

   5.____

C. fire in a confined area involving a substance that liberates oxygen
D. fire in a confined area involving a substance that liberates oxygen, and the presence of catalytic agents

6. The one of the following actions which may cause malfunctioning of the new type all-purpose educators is

   A. the removal of strainer before starting operation
   B. keeping intake end far below surface
   C. using fittings in the discharge line which first reduce, and then increase, the diameter of the waterway
   D. clearing a clogged strainer by shutting down at the source of supply and permitting the head of water in the supply and discharge lines to back flow

7. The fire extinguisher which would be MOST suitable for use in a machine shop containing electrical equipment and substantial amounts of flammable liquids is

   A. dry chemical
   B. foam
   C. loaded stream
   D. vaporizing liquid

8. The one of the following tools which would be MOST useful for breaking deadlights is a(n)

   A. rivet cutter
   B. heavy sledge
   C. acetylene torch
   D. punch and chisel

9. From the viewpoint of fire safety, the CHIEF advantage of a foam rubber mattress compared to a cotton mattress is that the foam rubber mattress

   A. is slower burning
   B. generates less heat when burning
   C. does not smolder
   D. is less subject to water damage

10. Of the following statements concerning the explosion hazard of dust, the one that is LEAST correct is that

    A. dust explosions frequently occur in pairs
    B. there are explosive limits beyond which an explosion cannot occur
    C. the likelihood of an explosion is affected by particle size and amount of impurities present
    D. the intensity of an explosion is affected by the duration of a source of ignition

11. The one of the following actions which is LIKELY to cause injury to a fireman lifting a heavy box is

    A. bending the knees outward and straddling the load
    B. distributing the load among the muscles of the arms, legs, and back
    C. keeping the box about 8 to 12 inches from the body while lifting
    D. placing the feet about 8 to 12 inches apart before starting to lift

12. The one of the following methods of storing large piles of coal which is undesirable because it increases the danger of spontaneous heating is

    A. making the pile compact by use of a roller
    B. storing the coal on smooth, solid ground
    C. covering the sides and top of the pile with road tar
    D. mixing coal of various sizes in one pile

13. When 1 1/2" hose is to be used, care should be taken to prevent pressures at the pump discharge from exceeding _____ pounds.

    A. 50   B. 75   C. 100   D. 125

14. The number of sprinkler heads which can be supplied by a 750 gallon pumper is APPROXIMATELY

    A. 35   B. 45   C. 55   D. 65

15. When operating at a fire and drafting salt water, connections may

    A. be made to a wet standpipe system but not to a dry standpipe system
    B. be made to a dry standpipe system but not to a wet standpipe system
    C. be made to either a wet or dry standpipe system
    D. not be made to either a wet or dry standpipe system

16. When radioactive materials are involved in hot fires, the radiation coming from the substance

    A. is not affected
    B. increases in rate and intensity
    C. decreases in rate and intensity
    D. increases in rate and decreases in intensity

17. The officer in command at a fire in a laboratory containing substantial quantities of radioactive material ordered his men to attack the fire with fog nozzle streams. This way of handling the fire was

    A. *bad;* the longer reach of solid streams is needed to protect the men
    B. *good;* disturbance of the radioactive material is minimized
    C. *bad;* solid streams offer greater resistance to penetration of radiation rays
    D. *good;* contamination of the water is reduced

18. Suppose that you are in command of an engine company first due at a fire involving the trailer of a trailer-truck carrying explosives. The truck is parked just off a well-traveled highway about 30 yards from a house. The fire evidently has been burning for some time and has resisted the driver's efforts to extinguish it.
    In this situation, the BEST course for you to follow is to

    A. have one man try to move the truck to a more remote spot if it appears that an explosion is not imminent
    B. keep apparatus at a distance and, with the fewest men possible, make a close attack on the fire
    C. stop traffic, evacuate the area, and prepare to protect exposures
    D. use high pressure stream and attack the fire from the greatest possible distance

19. Smother with sand or ashes. Use chemical streams. Avoid water except in the form of spray.
    The one of the following chemicals involved in fire for which this procedure would be the MOST appropriate is

    A. camphor
    B. naphthalene
    C. sodium sulfide
    D. zinc powder

20. While supervising the operation of a pumper drafting water from the harbor, you notice that the vacuum reading of the compound gauge of the pumper is slowly increasing and is reaching excessive amounts.
    The MOST likely cause of this condition is that the

    A. discharge gate of the pumper is closed
    B. inner lining of the suction connection is defective
    C. tide is dropping
    D. suction strainer is blocked

21. The one of the following gases which is NOT released by burning cellulose nitrate is

    A. hydrogen
    B. oxygen
    C. carbon monoxide
    D. nitrogen peroxide

22. Fireboats Weeks and Arthur are equipped with monitors fashioned into a 270 loop.
    The one of the following statements about the advantages of this monitor that is MOST complete and accurate is that it reduces friction

    A. loss
    B. loss and water turbulence
    C. loss and water turbulence and eliminates barrel whip
    D. loss and water turbulence, eliminates barrel whip, and permits the water to streamline itself before leaving the barrel

23. Avoid water unless necessary to use on other burning materials, in which case flood with water.
    The one of the following chemicals involved in fire for which this procedure would be MOST appropriate is

    A. calcium oxide
    B. aluminum dust
    C. phenol
    D. potassium cyanide

24. At company gas mask drills, members should be required to perform heavy work while wearing masks.
    The one of the following which is the MOST important reason for this practice is that the members will learn how to

    A. increase the air capacity of their lungs
    B. pace their activities at an optimum level
    C. adjust to the decrease in vision due to the facepiece
    D. become accustomed to the discomfort of sweating and the bulk of the mask

25. When your company arrives first at a fire in a large warehouse, you discover heavy smoke coming from one of the trailer trucks loaded and hooked up for the next day's deliveries.
Of the following, the BEST action for you to take FIRST is to

    A. attack the fire with hand lines
    B. open the trailer to find out what it contains
    C. apply small streams to the gasoline tank
    D. move the trailer away from the building

    25._____

26. If a deck pipe stream is needed to hit a fire on the third floor of an apartment house, the deck pipe should be placed,
street conditions permitting, APPROXIMATELY _____ feet from the building.

    A. 15   B. 30   C. 45   D. 60

    26._____

27. *Smother with dry sand, soda ash, or rook dust. Do not use water.*
The one of the following chemicals involved in fire for which this procedure would be MOST appropriate is

    A. bleaching powder   B. carbon disulfide
    C. potassium peroxide   D. sodium nitrate

    27._____

28. When opening bales of rags in order to examine the contents for smoldering fire, the BEST procedure is to cut the metal bands

    A. in the center first and the outside bands last
    B. alternating between center bands and outside bands
    C. on the outside first and the center bands last
    D. which are most accessible first and the less accessible bands last

    28._____

29. The one of the following procedures which is NOT proper in administering mouth-to-mouth resuscitation is

    A. placing the subject on his back with his head slightly higher than his body
    B. covering the subject's nose and mouth with a clean handkerchief
    C. holding closed either the nose or mouth of the subject
    D. keeping the subject warm

    29._____

30. In general, nozzles should not be used that are over one-half the diameter of the hose on which they are used.
An exception to this rule occurs when using

    A. 1 1/2" hose   B. fog streams
    C. pipeholders   D. foam streams

    30._____

31. Suppose that you are in command of the first due engine company at a fire in a pharmaceutical laboratory. The chief chemist informs you that the storeroom is on fire, giving off substantial amounts of carbon monoxide, sulfur dioxide, and hydrocyanic acid gases.
In this situation, you should realize that adequate protection to your men is afforded by

    A. a demand-type gas mask
    B. an oxygen rebreathing-type gas mask
    C. an all-purpose-type gas mask
    D. no gas mask now in use

    31._____

32. The one of the following substances with the LEAST tendency to spontaneous heating is

   A. fish meal
   B. lamp black
   C. scrap rubber
   D. soap powder

33. A ladder pipe being used as a water tower is fully extended and is using a large size nozzle tip.
   In this situation, the angle recommended for MAXIMUM stability of the apparatus is between

   A. 50°-60°   B. 60°-70°   C. 70°-80°   D. 80°-90°

34. Stretching a hose up the interior stairway to the fifth floor of an apartment house, compared to stretching a hose up the fire escape on the front of a building, requires APPROXIMATELY _____ additional length(s) of hose.

   A. 4   B. 3   C. 2   D. 1

35. *For proper protection of low flash point flammable liquid processes, automatic sprinkler protection with a strong water supply is essential.*
   The BEST justification of this statement is that

   A. a sprinkler system with a strong water supply will extinguish most fires involving such processes
   B. water from sprinklers will reduce the intensity of burning of the liquid and the danger to exposures
   C. although the sprinklers are ineffective on flammable liquid fires, they provide protection in the event of other types of fires
   D. water from the sprinklers will dilute the flammable liquid and make extinguishment easier

36. Suppose that you are in command of a truck company operating at a fire in a warehouse containing high piles of porcelain sinks, gas stoves, and washing machines. The hazard to which you should be particularly alert in this situation is that of

   A. falling objects
   B. building collapse
   C. toxic fumes
   D. blockage of sprinklers

37. Suppose that you are in charge of a ladder company overhauling at a fire in a loft building. After about one hour's operation, you discover at a point remote from the fire a bin containing bolts of silk which show slight scorching. There is no sign of smoke coming from the bin. Under these circumstances, you should

   A. assume that there is no fire in the bin and proceed to another bin
   B. remove all the contents of the bin and carefully inspect for signs of fire
   C. dampen the contents of the bin with a small amount of water
   D. remove a few items from the front, middle, and back of the bin and, if there is no sign of fire, proceed to another area

38. Suppose that after cutting a hole in the roof of a fire building, you find that only a small draft is set up. In this situation, the FIRST action that should be taken is to

   A. probe the hole with a pole for obstructions
   B. enlarge the opening

C. see whether the smoke is escaping from another opening
D. start a second opening at a spot some distance away

39. When filled with water, a 50-foot section of a 2 1/2" hose, assuming no expansion of the hose, contains water weighing MOST NEARLY _____ lbs.

    A. 75   B. 85   C. 95   D. 105

40. The friction loss in a 1 1/2" hose, compared to the friction loss in a 2 1/2" with the same amount of water flowing, is APPROXIMATELY _____ times greater.

    A. 3   B. 8   C. 13   D. 18

41. If the discharge from a 1 1/4" nozzle is 300 gallons per minute, the nozzle pressure is APPROXIMATELY _____ lbs.

    A. 35   B. 42   C. 49   D. 56

42. An engine is pumping water through 1200 feet of 2 1/2" rubber-lined hose equipped with a 1" nozzle (K=.105).
    If 60 lbs. of pressure is needed at the nozzle, the required engine pressure should be, in pounds per square inch, APPROXIMATELY

    A. 195   B. 215   C. 230   D. 260

43. A pumper, at 150 lbs. pressure, is pumping through two parallel lines of 2 1/2" rubber-lined hose each 500 feet in length, siamesed into a deluge set equipped with a 1 1/2" nozzle. (For these conditions, K = .135 and L = 10.) The pressure at the nozzle, in pounds per square inch, is MOST NEARLY

    A. 49   B. 55   C. 61   D. 67

Questions 44-47.

DIRECTIONS: Questions 44 through 47 relate to the paragraph below and are to be answered in accordance with the paragraph.

The unadjusted loss per $1000 valuation has only a very limited usefulness in evaluating the efficiency of a fire department, for it depends upon the assumption that other factors will remain constant from time to time and city to city. It might be expected that high fire department operation expenditures would tend to be associated with a low fire loss. A statistical study of the loss and cost data in more than 100 cities failed to reveal any such correlation. The lack of relationship, although to some extent due to failure to make the most efficacious expenditure of fire protection funds, must be attributed in part at least to the obscuring effect of variations in the natural, physical, and moral factors which affect fire risk.

44. One reason for the failure to obtain the expected relationship between fire department expenditures and fire loss data which is stated in the above paragraph is the

    A. changing dollar valuation of property
    B. unsettling effects of rapid technological innovations
    C. inefficiency of some fire department activities
    D. statistical errors made by the investigators

45. We may conclude that the *unadjusted loss per $1000* figure is useful in comparing the fire departments of two cities

    A. only if the cities are of comparable size
    B. only if adjustments are made for other factors which affect fire loss
    C. under no circumstances
    D. only if properly controlled experimental conditions can be obtained

46. The one of the following factors which affect fire risk that is MOST adequately reflected in the *unadjusted loss per $1000 valuation* index is

    A. fire department operation expenditures
    B. physical characteristics of the city
    C. type of structures most prevalent in the city
    D. total worth of property in the city

47. According to the above paragraph, cities which spend larger sums on their fire departments _____ cities which spend smaller sums on their fire departments.

    A. tend to have lower fire losses than
    B. do not tend to have lower fire losses than
    C. tend to have higher fire losses than
    D. do not tend to have the same total property valuation as

Questions 48-50.

DIRECTIONS: Questions 48 through 50 relate to the paragraph below and are to be answered in accordance with the paragraph.

Shafts extending into the top story, except those stair shafts where the stairs do not continue to the roof, shall be carried through and at least two feet above the roof. Every shaft extending above the roof, except open shafts and elevator shafts, shall be enclosed at the top with a roof of materials having a fire resistive rating of one hour and a metal skylight covering at least three-quarters of the area of the shaft in the top story, except that skylights over stair shafts shall have an area not less than one-tenth the area of the shaft in the top story, but shall be not less than fifteen square feet in area. Any shaft terminating below the top story of a structure and those stair shafts not required to extend through the roof shall have the top enclosed with materials having the same fire resistive rating as required for the shaft enclosure.

48. The above paragraph states that the elevator shafts which extend into the top story are

    A. not required to have a skylight but are required to extend at least two feet above the roof
    B. neither required to have a skylight nor to extend above the roof
    C. required to have a skylight covering at least three-quarters of the area of the shaft in the top story and to extend at least two feet above the roof
    D. required to have a skylight covering at least three-quarters of the area of the shaft in the top story but are not required to extend above the roof

49. The one of the following skylights which meets the requirements of the above paragraph is a skylight measuring

   A. 4' x 4' over a stair shaft which, on the top story, measures 20' x 9'
   B. 4 1/2' x 3 1/2' over a pipe shaft which, on the top story, measures 5' x 4'
   C. 2 1/2 x 1 1/2' over a dumbwaiter shaft which, on the top story, measures 2 1/2' x 2 1/2'
   D. 4' x 3' over a stair shaft which, on the top story, measures 15' x 6'

50. Suppose that in a Class I building, a shaft which does not go to the roof is required to have a three-hour fire resistive rating.
    In regard to the material enclosing the top of this shaft, the above paragraph

   A. states that a one-hour fire resistive rating is required
   B. states that a three-hour fire resistive rating is required
   C. implies that no fire resistive rating is required
   D. neither states nor implies anything about the fire resistive rating

KEY (CORRECT ANSWERS)

1. B	11. C	21. B	31. D	41. B
2. C	12. D	22. D	32. B	42. B
3. A	13. C	23. A	33. C	43. C
4. B	14. A	24. B	34. C	44. C
5. B	15. B	25. D	35. B	45. B
6. C	16. A	26. B	36. A	46. D
7. A	17. B	27. C	37. A	47. B
8. B	18. C	28. C	38. A	48. A
9. C	19. A	29. A	39. D	49. B
10. D	20. D	30. D	40. C	50. B

EXAMINATION SECTION
TEST 1

DIRECTIONS: Each question or incomplete statement is followed by several suggested answers or completions. Select the one that BEST answers the question or completes the statement. *PRINT THE LETTER OF THE CORRECT ANSWER IN THE SPACE AT THE RIGHT.*

1. According to the Regulations, officers on duty with ladder companies last to leave the scene of a fire shall have the responsibility to

    A. see that fire escape drop ladders remain extended to the ground
    B. make certain that hydrants are shut down and outlets properly capped
    C. make certain that no tools used by the companies operating at the fire are left in the fire building
    D. see that all openings made by operating companies are left with minimum hazard to salvage or other authorized persons
    E. make certain that counterbalanced stairways are placed in proper position

    1.____

2. According to the Regulations, the reason for continuously noting the rise and fall of the tide when a pumper is being used to draught water is to

    A. prevent foreign matter from being drawn into the pumps
    B. insure constant pump suction
    C. provide a proper balance between atmospheric pressure and pump suction
    D. avoid possible backflow conditions
    E. protect the suction pipe and inlet from injury from floating driftwood

    2.____

3. Officers on duty are required to see that all apparatus, department vehicles and equipment located in their quarters are properly cared for and protected.
   Of the following, the Regulations require that

    A. motor hoods be washed or cleaned after each run while the motor is hot
    B. manually operated stage valves of centrifugal pumpers be operated once each week to prevent sticking
    C. pumpers equipped with hydraulically operated stage valves be tested once a month
    D. crankcase oil in pumpers in active service be changed every total 24 hours of pumping operation
    E. gasoline tanks on apparatus in quarters be filled whenever half full

    3.____

4. The Regulations describe the method and precautions to be observed in using scaling ladders.
   The Regulations recommend that a scaling ladder should NOT be relied on if

    A. an ordinary ladder can reach within six feet of the trapped person
    B. an ordinary ladder cannot be used in conjunction with it
    C. the person to be rescued is unconscious
    D. the person to be rescued appears upset or extremely nervous
    E. the person to be rescued is of excessive weight

    4.____

5. According to the Regulations, the one of the following statements which is NOT given as a precaution to be taken before lowering or hoisting a person is

   A. make sure that the rope is long enough
   B. work away from obstructions such as fire escapes, copings, signs, etc.
   C. if possible, select a point for hoisting which is not directly in a vertical line with windows of the building
   D. a leather hand grip should be used by the man manipulating the rope
   E. make sure that the person to be hoisted or lowered is conscious and able to cooperate

6. The Verification of Detail Report Form is required, according to the Regulations, for members

   A. of the Band when performing duty with such units
   B. performing watch line duty
   C. attending one of the schools of the Fire College
   D. attending battalion drills
   E. assigned to theatre detail duty

7. Lieutenants on duty are required to submit reports on certain situations that develop or happen in their hours of duty.
   According to the Regulations, the one of the following reports that should be made by a lieutenant on duty concerns

   A. chimney fire violation
   B. inferior fuel
   C. burst or porous hose
   D. activities of departmental mechanics in quarters
   E. watch line

8. Of the following, the BEST method of fighting a fire involving flammable oils in an open tank is to use a

   A. foam generator, directing the foam stream against the oil surface
   B. foam generator, directing the foam stream against the inside plate above fire
   C. foam generator, directing the foam stream against the inside plate at fire level
   D. fog nozzle, directing fog against the burning oils so as to churn up surface of oil
   E. fog nozzle with high velocity fog on the oil surface to push heat away

9. The Regulations for the care of hose provide that

   A. couplings be greased regularly with heavy duty grease to prevent corrosion
   B. new hose shall be stored in original packing cases until required for use
   C. greasy hose shall be washed with gasoline or kerosene
   D. hose hung in towers shall be suspended by the male coupling
   E. hose be arranged neatly on the apparatus using the old bends to prevent wear

10. A written evolution mentions a definite source of water supply.
    When company officers are conducting drills on this evolution, they should, according to Regulations,

A. always order the evolution to be performed with the same water source
B. never permit the use of a low pressure hydrant if a high pressure hydrant is specified
C. never permit the use of a high pressure hydrant if a low pressure hydrant is specified
D. vary, if possible, the source of supply from the one specified in the evolution
E. make use of the pumper instead of a high pressure hydrant whenever possible

11. The signal 8-127 to indicate that pressure is no longer wanted at Box 127 and shall be shut down shall be OMITTED   11._____

    A. under no circumstances
    B. if signal 902 is sent from Box 127
    C. if signal 2-2-2-127 is sent from Box 127
    D. if signal 13-13 is transmitted from Box 127
    E. if signal 4-4-4 is sent from Box 127

12. The one of the following signals which indicates that Hook and Ladder Company 9 stopped at Box 163 to extinguish a fire is   12._____

    A. 2-2-2-163-7-9   B. 2-2-2-163-9-7   C. 2-2-2-9-163-7
    D. 2-2-2-7-163-9   E. 2-2-2-7-9-163

13. When received at a street box, signal 6-5 is an order to   13._____

    A. respond to a telephone call from dispatcher
    B. send a hose wagon to Box 5
    C. call the dispatcher on the telephone
    D. check the telephone
    E. turn on the radio

14. According to the Multiple Dwelling Law, a part of a building is *fire-retarded* if it is protected against fire in an approved manner with materials of fire-resistive ratings of AT LEAST _____ hour(s).   14._____

    A. one   B. two   C. three   D. four   E. five

15. The Multiple Dwelling Law permits the conduct of business in any multiple dwelling EXCEPT that   15._____

    A. no space in a non-fireproof multiple dwelling may be used for a bakery or business where fat is boiled under any condition
    B. the number of persons employed in manufacturing enterprises in multiple dwellings shall be limited to a maximum of seven persons
    C. exits of the dwelling portion and the business space may be common if the number of persons employed is limited to ten persons or less
    D. when the ground story of any non-fireproof multiple dwelling is extended for business purposes, the underside of the roof of such extension shall be fire-retarded if there are fire escapes above such extension
    E. there shall be no manufacturing business conducted above the second floor of any non-fireproof multiple dwelling

16. According to the Building Code, a sprinkler system is NOT required in

   A. garages in cellars of multiple dwellings if area is less than 5,000 square feet
   B. dressing rooms and stage of auditoriums of large public high schools where seating capacity is less than 1,500
   C. furnished rooms of converted non-fireproof multiple dwellings if the public hall has sprinkler protection
   D. non-fireproof lodging houses if equipped with an automatic, closed-circuit fire alarm system
   E. department stores if each floor does not exceed 10,000 square feet

17. The Building Code requires that in all newly constructed loft buildings used for mercantile purposes,

   A. 8 inch standpipe risers shall be installed in buildings 150 feet or more in height
   B. standpipes be installed if 75 feet in height or over
   C. the minimum size of standpipe riser in a building 100 feet high be at least 3 inches
   D. when a standpipe is required, no point on a floor be more than 75 feet from a riser
   E. multiple standpipe risers may not be cross-connected

18. The proscenium of a theatre is MOST closely associated with the

   A. stage
   B. special entrance for scenery
   C. street entrance and exit
   D. passageways to boxes
   E. balcony arch over the orchestra section

19. The MAXIMUM quantity of kerosene fuel oil that may be stored for heating and cooking use without a permit from the Fire Commissioner is _____ gallons.

   A. 10   B. 25   C. 50   D. 100   E. 150

20. An acceptable method of absorbing waste oils in a dry cleaning establishment is, according to the Fire Prevention Code,

   A. a quantity of sand spread on the floor
   B. use of thin asbestos fibre flooring
   C. non-combustible cloth on the floor
   D. diatomaceous earth or equivalent absorbent material spread on the floor
   E. woven glass fibre mats

21. According to the Fire Prevention Code, an ESSENTIAL oil is defined as an oil

   A. needed to provide the viscosity of a given grade of oil
   B. derived from animal life and not from mineral sources
   C. which has low volatility at room temperature
   D. used for flavoring or perfuming purposes
   E. required as the base of lubricating compounds

22. According to the Fire Prevention Code, it shall be UNLAWFUL to sell or deliver for use

   A. sticks or cartridges of explosives which are packed so as to lie on their sides
   B. any explosive except in original and unbroken packages

C. dynamite in cases of 25 and 50 lbs.
D. nitroglycerine in liquid form under any circumstances
E. any explosives packed in quantities in excess of 50 lbs.

23. The Fire Prevention Code requires that a storage garage containing more than four motor vehicles shall be continuously under the supervision of one or more persons, each holding a certificate of fitness.
    The MAXIMUM number of such certificated persons required for any garage shall be

    A. 7   B. 6   C. 5   D. 4   E. 3

24. The MINIMUM receiving pressure required to prevent the collapse of the soft supply hose to a Loftus Suction Collector is, according to Civil Defense directives, _____ lbs.

    A. 50   B. 10   C. 15   D. 20   E. 25

25. According to Civil Defense directives, when outdoor drills are held with Civil Defense pumpers, using deckpipes and handlines, the officer in charge of the auxiliaries should operate his streams so as to avoid injuries to persons or damage to property on the drill street.
    Deckpipe streams should be operated in a very narrow range from side to side AND _____ from the horizontal.

    A. between 50° and 75°
    B. not less than 70°
    C. between 60° and 70°
    D. not more than 50°
    E. between 50° and 60°

26. The greatest responsibility for sizing up a fire rests upon the first officer to arrive at the fire.
    In sizing up the fire, his FIRST step should be to

    A. determine the life hazard
    B. ascertain details of construction of the fire building
    C. note type of occupancy
    D. check exposures
    E. locate the fire

27. Suppose that after you have been newly assigned to a company, one of the men informs you that some of the men are resentful of your command and plan to make things difficult for you.
    You should

    A. discuss the matter with your company commander and suggest that the clique be broken up
    B. go out of your way to be pleasant and friendly with the other men to eliminate any objections to your command
    C. thank the man and then analyze your actions and the reactions of the men in your company

D. discuss the fancied or real grievances with other men of the company
E. advise the man that he should not inform on others and that you can handle anyone in the company

28. When an order which an officer knows will make heavy demands on his men is to be read to them, it is wise policy for him to preface the reading with some remarks.
Of the following, the comment which would be the MOST appropriate is:

   A. An explanation why the order is necessary at this time
   B. His reading of the regulation or regulations pertaining to the order
   C. His statement of his personal feelings about the fairness of the order
   D. A warning to the men to follow the order even if they feel put out about the extra work involved
   E. A suggestion that objections to such assignments be taken up through line organizations

29. Suppose that at a drill, a fireman asks you, his superior officer, a question which you are unable to answer at that moment.
Of the following, the MOST desirable action to take is to

   A. tell the fireman that the question is not important and to stop delaying the progress of the drill
   B. advise the man that you cannot answer the question at the moment but that you will answer it later
   C. avoid considering the question if it does not assist the men in understanding the function of the drill
   D. refuse to answer the question because your lack of knowledge may be embarrassing and reflect on your leadership
   E. tell the fireman that he should look up the answer and report his results at the next drill

30. An officer, in discussing regulations with his company members, commented, *We ought to recognize that our interests are mutual and that by working together, we can achieve our common objective.*
This approach is

   A. *good;* it recognizes the status of the individual and avoids favoritism
   B. *poor;* such an approach invites excessive criticism and bickering
   C. *good;* most of the men will come up with beneficial suggestions if so encouraged
   D. *good;* this attitude will promote cooperation between members and the officer
   E. *poor;* in appealing in this way to the men, the officer is inviting too much familiarity

31. In planning a lesson to be given to your men, the FIRST step should *usually* be to

   A. distribute a study outline of the subject in advance so that the men will be more attentive when the lesson is given
   B. determine the amount of information on the subject that can be effectively presented in that lesson
   C. prepare the materials and equipment so that everything is ready when the lesson is given
   D. determine how the subject matter is to be presented
   E. make certain that the men are interested and receptive to your choice of the subject to be taught

32. In training their men, officers have learned that it is rarely justifiable to stand before their company and merely lecture to them
Of the following, the MOST probable reason for this conclusion is that

    A. the number of persons who can be trained in this manner is severely limited
    B. most persons dislike being *talked to* constantly
    C. in order to learn, the learner must participate in the teaching process
    D. too much material is usually covered, making it difficult to memorize details
    E. this procedure overemphasizes the superiority of the officer

32.____

33. Fundamental to good supervision is the ability to realize and act effectively on the fact that employees' motivations, attitudes, and work output often are keyed to some aspect of their lives that is apart from their job. The officer who appreciates this

    A. expects the same performance from each man on all occasions
    B. considers the possibility of factors outside of the job influencing the poor performance of a fireman
    C. spends considerable time counseling his men on the various aspects of their personal lives
    D. refrains from consideration of the personal problems of a fireman that may affect his performance
    E. allows his men to *let off steam* whenever they appear to have the need to talk about some difficulties outside of their job

33.____

34. When disciplinary action in the form of an oral reprimand is to be administered to a newly appointed fireman, the officer should, at the same time,

    A. warn the fireman that he'd better read up on his regulations so as not to be at fault again
    B. advise the fireman that he is required to reprimand him, but that the fireman should not worry about it
    C. ask the older men to keep a sharp eye on the new man and to notify him if additional disciplining is needed
    D. discipline other men at the same time so that the fireman will not feel that he is being persecuted
    E. attempt to determine the reason for the fireman's error

34.____

35. *Environment is like the photographer's developing chemical. It creates nothing, but it can bring out what is on the film.* To the company officer, this means MOST nearly that

    A. individual capacity determines what should be taught, not the predetermined course content
    B. it is necessary to provide a good environment and understandable objectives in order to make the training process effective
    C. the individual with better educational background will learn more readily the elements of efficient fire fighting and fire prevention
    D. knowledge of the developing process of photography provides key points in a productive training program
    E. if an individual does not have the required mental capacity, he will be unable to benefit from training to the desired degree

35.____

36. The one of the following jobs for which a fireman is LEAST likely to use a claw tool is in   36.___

    A. prying up flooring   B. opening iron shutters
    C. shifting baled goods   D. breaking locks
    E. forcing windows

37. The one of the following door openers which operates on the ratchet principle is the   37.___

    A. Jimmy   B. Hale Door Opener
    C. Detroit Door Opener   D. Kelley tool
    E. Callahan Door Opener

38. *Their lesser weight, size, and ease of operation make them adaptable to such evolutions*   38.___
    as operating a line from a roof or a fire escape, etc., where other types might prove
    unwieldy or impractical.
    The pipe holder to which this description MOST probably refers is the

    A. Perfection   B. Eureka   C. Simplex
    D. Paradox   E. Mohaw

39. An all-purpose nozzle can be used effectively in attacking with water fog inside fires   39.___
    which emit much smoke and heat. To use it properly, the nozzle should be pointed
    upward,
    depending on ceiling height, at an angle of _____ degrees from the _____ .

    A. 20 to 30; vertical   B. 20 to 30; horizontal
    C. 30 to 45; horizontal   D. 30 to 45; vertical
    E. 40 to 60; horizontal

40. Of the following, the MOST important reason why all-purpose nozzles are not recom-   40.___
    mended for high voltage electrical fires is that

    A. fog streams from such nozzles are not safe at any effective distance for voltages
       about 7500 volts
    B. the poor spray patterns available from such nozzles limit their effectiveness
    C. they are all high pressure type and are difficult to handle at such fires
    D. fog streams tend to decompose when applied to high voltage fires
    E. there is danger of accidentally switching to a solid stream

41. The discharge line from a foam generator should be two hose lengths or 100 feet PRI-   41.___
    MARILY because

    A. foam requires some cooling after it is generated and before it is discharged
    B. usually two lengths are required from the pumper to the generator inlet
    C. the foam will become too thick and firm if the discharge line is more than 100 feet
    D. about 100 feet is required for firm stable foam to be formed
    E. the usual pressure at the inlet of the generator is 100 lbs.

42. The Hart cellar pipe covers an area which is APPROXIMATELY   42.___

    A. equal to that covered by the sub-cellar type
    B. equal to that covered by the Baker cellar type
    C. twice that covered by the Bresnan distributor
    D. one-fourth that covered by the Bresnan distributor
    E. one and one-third times that covered by the bent cellar pipe

43. In handling the O'Brien Rotary Cutter, a PROPER procedure is to   43._____
    A. take power from the buildings in the immediate area wherever possible rather than from street light poles
    B. avoid its use where the required cut is 8 inches or more
    C. drill two openings where a hole with a diameter greater than 4 inches is required
    D. remove any terrazzo with hand tool before making a cut through the floor
    E. make openings in doorways where possible so that vertical beams can be avoided

44. When hoisting a 25-foot ladder to a roof, the rope should be placed _____ rungs from   44._____
    the top.
    A. 6   B. 8   C. 10   D. 12   E. 14

45. No paint, varnish, or lacquer should be applied to the handles of any tools used for forc-   45._____
    ible entry or overhauling PRIMARILY because
    A. members' hands may become blistered and infected during such operations
    B. such applications are inflammable and reduce usefulness of the tools
    C. defects in the handles may be covered up by such applications
    D. handles so treated will tend to slip in the hands during the operations
    E. such coating quickly deteriorates during use

46. In driving an engine or ladder truck, it is GOOD practice to   46._____
    A. brake on wet road surfaces with the clutch engaged
    B. descend a steep grade in a lower gear range than that required to ascend it
    C. descend on steep grade in neutral gear if speed is not excessive
    D. cramp front wheels at a sharp angle when trying to pull the apparatus out of a soft sandy area
    E. use one-way streets against traffic with caution when returning from an alarm

47. It is advisable not to *gun* a gasoline engine before shutting down PRIMARILY because   47._____
    such action
    A. causes crankcase dilution with gasoline
    B. results in excessively fast starts the next time the motor is started
    C. encourages sludge formation
    D. wets spark plugs with gasoline
    E. results in vapor block in the carburetor

48. Packing glands of rotary gear pumps should be tightened so that   48._____
    A. they drip a little
    B. no water drips through the packing
    C. the packing is tightly compressed against revolving parts
    D. contained oil will fully lubricate revolving shafts
    E. pump slip is at a minimum

49. An evidence of manila rope that is badly worn is   49._____
    A. elastic reaction when bent   B. mildew inside rope
    C. extreme softness   D. change in color of surface fibers
    E. dry feel

50. Of the following, the MOST likely result of the failure to remove ashes daily from the ash-pit of low pressure boilers in company quarters is

    A. frequent adjustment of boiler safety valves to let off excess steam
    B. unburned coal in the ashpit
    C. priming and foaming in the boiler
    D. warped and burned-out grates
    E. excessive use of coal

KEY (CORRECT ANSWERS)

1. E	11. B	21. D	31. B	41. D
2. A	12. D	22. B	32. C	42. B
3. C	13. C	23. E	33. B	43. D
4. C	14. A	24. B	34. E	44. C
5. E	15. E	25. C	35. E	45. A
6. B	16. E	26. E	36. C	46. A
7. A	17. B	27. C	37. B	47. A
8. B	18. A	28. A	38. A	48. A
9. D	19. A	29. B	39. B	49. C
10. D	20. A	30. D	40. E	50. D

TEST 2

DIRECTIONS: Each question or incomplete statement is followed by several suggested answers or completions. Select the one that BEST answers the question or completes the statement. *PRINT THE LETTER OF THE CORRECT ANSWER IN THE SPACE AT THE RIGHT.*

1. Of the following statements concerning coal storage, the one that is ACCEPTABLE is   1._____

    A. coal for storage should preferably be deposited in horizontal layers
    B. alternate wetting and drying will prevent development of heat in the pile
    C. the desirable height of a properly stored coal pile is 25 to 30 feet
    D. storage of mixed sizes of coal together will reduce spontaneous ignition to a minimum
    E. standing timbers should be placed in coal piles to provide air access and circulation

2. *It is well known that hydrogen gas is produced when water comes in contact with highly heated or molten iron. But hydrogen explosions from the decomposition of water under ordinary fire conditions are unlikely.*   2._____
The MAIN reason for this is that

    A. the volume of water used will inhibit the formation of an explosive mixture
    B. the oxygen supply will not be sufficient for both the burning material and the hydrogen
    C. oxygen is liberated at the same time causing the hydrogen to burn
    D. hydrogen-air mixtures burn only at temperatures above that of an ordinary flame
    E. the explosive range of hydrogen is very wide

3. Of the following, the substance which has the HIGHEST ignition temperature is   3._____

    A. wood alcohol   B. kerosene   C. gasoline
    D. wood   E. sulphur

4. If possible, the BEST method of handling liquified petroleum gas fires is to   4._____

    A. apply foam to escaping gas and shut off or reduce gas flow at source
    B. allow escaped gas to burn while attempting to shut off gas at the source
    C. use foam on both the cylinder or tank and the escaping gas
    D. apply a fine water spray on both the source and the escaping gas
    E. apply a stream of dry chemical on both the source and the escaping gas

5. When fighting a smoky fire, it is often useful to detect the characteristic smoke of various burning materials by the color.   5._____
Of the following, the burning material MOST likely indicated by a *black* smoke is

    A. magnesium   B. chlorine   C. phosphorus
    D. rubber   E. nitrous oxide

6. A toxic gas which is USUALLY non-combustible is   6._____

    A. hydrogen sulfide   B. ammonia   C. ethyl chloride
    D. chlorine   E. carbon monoxide

7. *The tendency of this substance to spontaneous heating is very slight. It is usually shipped in bulk. This substance should be kept dry, and storing or loading in hot wet piles should be avoided.*
   This description applies MOST closely to

   A. metal powder   B. soft coal   C. charcoal
   D. scrap film   E. jute

8. Of the following refrigerants, the one which has the LOWEST life hazard is

   A. sulphur dioxide   B. methyl bromide   C. carbon dioxide
   D. ammonia   E. ethyl bromide

9. Fuel oils which usually require preheating before they are admitted into an oil burner are Grade

   A. 0   B. 2   C. 4   D. 6   E. 8

10. *It is liquid at room temperature, giving off poisonous suffocating fumes at ordinary temperature. It is corrosive, has an oxidizing effect, and is stored in glass bottles or earthen jugs.*
    This description fits MOST NEARLY the hazardous chemical

    A. sulfuric acid   B. bromine   C. phenol
    D. picric acid   E. naphthalene

11. A fire has been smoldering in a building. When the fire is attacked, an explosion of pent-up, heated combustible gases occurs.
    The PROBABLE cause of the explosion is the

    A. mushrooming of the fire due to lack of proper ventilation
    B. admission of fresh air into the building
    C. rise of the gases to the flashpoint of one of the gases
    D. excessive pressure level of the pent-up gases
    E. introduction of flame into the body of the gas

12. *The rule to the effect that the first engine company to arrive at a fire takes the front stairway is not true under all conditions.*
    An example of a situation where this rule does NOT hold is where fire

    A. and smoke break out through the front windows of the upper floor of a two-story multiple dwelling and can be reached by outside hose lines
    B. is coming out of cellar windows, cutting off entrance or exit and exposing adjoining buildings
    C. is evident on an upper floor and it is quite certain that occupants are out of the building
    D. shows on the first floor, starts to spread via the stairway to the second floor, and back up to the rear building
    E. is found to be confined to a rear bedroom and shows no sign of extension

13. *The weather plays a more important part in lateral and cross ventilation than it does in overhead and vertical venting.*
    An example of the kind of weather in which lateral ventilation is MORE dangerous than overhead is

A. cool with brisk changeable winds
B. hot and humid without wind
C. cold with heavy rain
D. cold with low humidity and some snow
E. fair with some clouds

14. *The raising of the aerial ladder to the roof in order to ventilate, except under unusual conditions, is unnecessary.*
Of the following, the MOST important reason why raising the aerial ladder for this purpose is sometimes not desirable is that

    A. the ladder company is generally needed for other more important duties
    B. use of the aerial ladder is more hazardous than other means
    C. the primary purpose of the aerial ladder is to remove trapped persons
    D. it blocks the street and may make placement of needed apparatus difficult
    E. access to the roof by this means usually takes more time than by other means

15. *Partitions, ceilings, floors, and the like should not be op-ened unnecessarily.*
From the practical operating viewpoint, the BEST guide in determining where to open floors or partitions is

    A. A. observation of the spread of fire above and below the officer's location
    B. use of sensitive thermo-detection instruments available
    C. detection of heat by the hand
    D. smoke issuing through floors and partitions
    E. the smell of smoke and gases of combustion

16. *When setting up a hose line to attack a fire, leave most of the slack hose near the fire rather than near the hydrant or other source of water.*
The procedure advocated in this statement is, in general,

    A. *desirable;* it reduces the possibility of accidents
    B. *undesirable;* it increases the possibility of accidents
    C. *desirable;* the fireman will be able to advance quickly into the fire if necessary
    D. *undesirable;* it will be difficult for the fireman to surround the fire when necessary
    E. *desirable;* standardization of procedures makes for better operation

17. Generally, a good rule for estimating the quantity of hose required in a line (fire building with moderate floor area per floor) is

    A. one length per story plus one
    B. one length per story plus two
    C. two lengths per story plus one
    D. two lengths per story plus two
    E. two lengths per story

18. *In a smoky sub-basement fire, it is desirable to simultaneously operate hose lines in as many directions as possible.*
This statement is

    A. *incorrect;* this would tend to hold the heat, smoke, and gases in the cellar area
    B. *correct;* this would tend to drive the heat, smoke, and gases from the cellar area
    C. *incorrect;* this would tend to create a water hazard for the firefighting force
    D. *correct;* this may create atmospheric turbulence which would be equivalent to venting
    E. *incorrect;* no hose lines should be put into operation until ventilation is possible

19. A fire has been in progress for some time. Tremendous heat is generated which causes the collapse of windows on the fire floor.
The officer in charge at this point is LEAST concerned with the

   A. danger to members on the fire floor
   B. production of gaseous combustibles by the intense heat
   C. danger of a backdraft occurring
   D. need for large volumes of water to check the fire
   E. possible spread of fire to exposures

20. Where the public hall of an old-law tenement is involved by fire, a line should be advanced up the stairs, extinguishing the fire in the first flight; the stream shut down and the line advanced to the second flight, the fire extinguished, etc.
The one of the following which is the MAIN reason for shutting down the stream when advancing the line is to

   A. avoid excessive use of water when the stream is not actually directed at the fire
   B. avoid unnecessary water damage and weakening of the stair support
   C. make it possible to totally extinguish the fire on each flight of stairs without excessive pressure loss
   D. permit advancing the line very rapidly
   E. make the task of getting the line upstairs less difficult

21. You are in command of the first due ladder company. When you arrive at the fire building, you find that fire has involved the interior stairs of a Class B multiple dwelling. The MAJOR problem that confronts you is

   A. quick spread of fire to upper floors
   B. smoke spread into upper floor rooms
   C. smoky fire from panelled walls and carpeted flooring
   D. no second way of egress for occupants
   E. delay in reaching roof to ventilate

22. Suppose that smoke is found on the floor below the fire in a cold storage plant.
The PROBABLE cause is that

   A. fire has spread to lower floors
   B. down pressure results from failure to ventilate
   C. extensive crossdrafts have been created on the fire floor
   D. cooled combustion gases are heavier than air
   E. downdraft is caused by ventilation

23. A gasoline tank truck spills the major part of its contents near a large department store. The gasoline is ignited. The one of the following actions which will help prevent the large plate glass windows from cracking, with the least time taken from other duties, is

   A. set up a curtain with the deck pipe
   B. wet down the windows with a fog nozzle
   C. apply foam to the windows
   D. cover the windows with dry chemical
   E. frost the windows with carbon dioxide

24. Automobile fires are caused MOST frequently by 24.____

   A. overheating of the motor
   B. gasoline explosion
   C. defective carburetor
   D. defective or overheated brakes
   E. faulty ignition wiring

25. The PRINCIPAL fire hazard in connection with heating equipment in mercantile buildings comes from 25.____

   A. failure to operate and clean equipment properly
   B. insufficient clearance from combustible material
   C. use of improper types or grades of fuel
   D. defective flues
   E. exposed wiring in heating controls

26. Supermarket fires have in common the fact that MOST fires occur in the 26.____

   A. utility area
   B. sales area
   C. basement storage area
   D. check-out and packaging area
   E. shelves containing paper products

27. *Regardless of the type of construction, the presence of an air conditioning system in a building introduces added hazards for extension of fire.* 27.____
   The FIRST step in overhauling in a fire building that has an air conditioning system is to

   A. examine all falsework enclosing duct construction
   B. check ducts for cleanout openings which can be used for further inspection of exposures
   C. shut off the blower fan if it is operating
   D. determine the extent of the air conditioned area
   E. introduce a heavy water stream in ducts to eliminate fire extension by sparks and heat

28. When a fire in a television set is to be extinguished, the officer should caution his men to 28.____

   A. avoid any contact of the cooling agent with the picture tube
   B. attack the fire from the back of the set rather than from the sides
   C. cool the picture tube immediately to prevent explosion hazard
   D. let the fire burn itself out, but protect exposures
   E. cool the protective glass front before attacking the fire itself

29. On arrival at a fire on the stage of a theatre during a performance, the first due officer finds the audience moving out by way of the exits. 29.____
   His FIRST action should be to

   A. search the stage for trapped persons
   B. lower the protective curtain between the stage and auditorium
   C. see that the ventilators over the stage are in operation
   D. hasten the orderly exit of the audience by urging them to keep moving
   E. take one line into the auditorium to prevent fire spread

30. A fire occurs in a row of stores in a taxpayer. Because of smoke, it is difficult to locate the exact place of origin.
    Of the following, the BEST method of locating the origin immediately upon your arrival at the fire is to

    A. check the store from which the greatest volume of smoke is emitted
    B. inspect the area which seems to have the hottest fire
    C. cut a hole in the roof where the heat seems concentrated
    D. ventilate and then check the place of origin
    E. observe if one of the store front windows is discolored from the heat

Questions 31-35.

DIRECTIONS: Column I lists five properties of fire extinguishers. Column II lists various types of fire extinguishers. For each property in Column I, select the fire extinguisher from Column II having that property and place the letter next to the extinguisher in the properly numbered spce.

COLUMN I	COLUMN II
31. Contains aluminum sulphate in solution	A. Water gas cartridge expelled
32. Water in extinguishing agent will cause corrosion of container	B. Antifreeze (water mixed with antifreeze chemical)
33. Usually contains calcium chloride	C. Carbon dioxide
34. Produces a mass of bubbles filled with CO_2 gas	D. Foam
	E. Carbon tetrachloride
35. Inspection check by weighing extinguisher only	

36. The MOST effective type of extinguishing agent to use on The MOST effective type of extinguishing agent to use on fires involving sodium or potassium metals is

    A. carbon dioxide   B. dry chemicals
    C. foam   D. water
    E. carbon tetrachloride

37. According to the annual report statistics for the last two years, the floor of multiple dwellings where fires started MOST frequently was the

    A. cellar   B. 1st floor   C. 2nd floor
    D. 3rd floor   E. roof

38. A fireman incurs a severe head injury and appears to be in a state of shock. After medical help has been summoned, a PROPER step in handling the injured fireman is to

    A. make the fireman lie down, cover him, and have his head level or slightly raised
    B. make the fireman lie down, cover him, and keep his head lower than his body
    C. wrap the prone fireman in blankets so that the perspires heavily and keep the head low
    D. keep the prone fireman's head level, wrap him warmly, and give him stimulants
    E. avoid all conversation with the prone fireman after wrapping him warmly and keeping his head slightly lower than horizontal

39. To the fire officer, the word *salamander* USUALLY refers to a

    A. method of connection of hose
    B. horizontal spread of fire
    C. vent piping in fuel storage
    D. building water supply line for fire protection
    E. heating device in building construction

40. In the collapse of buildings in an atomic or other extensive disaster, the MOST effective of the following methods of locating trapped persons is ordinarily to

    A. sound all horns and bells on apparatus to give warning to trapped persons
    B. remove all debris on stairways and exits which may block the path of trapped persons
    C. use the controlled silence period when members of the team can listen for signs of life
    D. locate voids in areas most likely to be sought by victims
    E. have all members of a rescue team make a loud noise simultaneously in the *controlled noise* method

41. If about 400 gallons per minute is desired from a 1 1/2" nozzle, the required nozzle pressure is

    A. 24   B. 30   C. 36   D. 42   E. 48

42. The engine pressure of a pumper is 265 lbs. 600 ft. of 3" hose with a 1 1/2" nozzle is being used (K = .192). The nozzle pressure, in pounds, is MOST NEARLY

    A. 40   B. 50   C. 60   D. 70   E. 80

43. A pumper, operating at 180 pounds engine pressure, is pumping water through 400 feet of 2 1/2" hose equipped with a 1 1/8" nozzle (K = .167) to a point 40 feet below the pumper.
    The nozzle pressure, in pounds, is MOST NEARLY

    A. 74   B. 81   C. 88   D. 95   E. 102

44. *The angle at which a maximum horizontal range of a fire stream is theoretically obtained differs considerably from that found in actual practice.*
    Under actual conditions, the MAXIMUM horizontal range of a fire stream is obtained when the angle it makes with the level of the earth is MOST NEARLY

    A. 56°   B. 50°   C. 44°   D. 38°   E. 32°

45. The effective vertical reach of a fire stream at nozzle pressure of 60 pounds from a 1 1/4" nozzle is MOST NEARLY _____ feet.

    A. 75   B. 84   C. 93   D. 102   E. 111

46. If the *kickback* of a 1 1/4" nozzle is 117 lbs., the nozzle pressure is MOST NEARLY _____ pounds.

    A. 35   B. 40   C. 45   D. 50   E. 55

47. An engine is pumping through a 300 ft. stretch of 24" hose into a Siamese connection of a standpipe. A 50 ft. line of 24" hose is stretched from the outlet on the eighth floor, 80 ft. above engine, and a 1 1/8" nozzle is used (K = .167). In order to obtain a nozzle pressure of 60 lbs., the engine pressure, in pounds, should be MOST NEARLY

   A. 150   B. 170   C. 190   D. 210   E. 230

48. An engine pumps at 250 pounds pressure through a 1,000 ft. line of 2 1/4" hose equipped with a 1 1/8" nozzle. Nozzle pressure is about 56 pounds.
   If the engine pressure remains the same, but the nozzle is changed to a 1" diameter (K = .105), the change in nozzle pressure will be MOST NEARLY _____ pounds.

   A. 16   B. 22   C. 28   D. 34   E. 40

49. An engine pumps water through two parallel lines of 2 1/2" hose, each 400 feet in length, to a deck pipe which has a 1 3/4" nozzle (K = .907 for a single 24" line and 1 3/4" nozzle). If 80 lbs. pressure is desired at the nozzle, the required engine pressure, in pounds, will be MOST NEARLY

   A. 150   B. 200   C. 250   D. 300   E. 350

50. A fire causes 55 sprinkler heads to open.
   If the total discharge from the heads is 1870 gallons per minute, the pressure at the heads, in pounds per square inch, is MOST NEARLY

   A. 26   B. 29   C. 32   D. 35   E. 48

KEY (CORRECT ANSWERS)

1. A	11. B	21. A	31. D	41. C
2. C	12. B	22. D	32. E	42. E
3. A	13. A	23. A	33. B	43. B
4. B	14. D	24. E	34. D	44. E
5. D	15. C	25. B	35. C	45. B
6. D	16. C	26. A	36. B	46. D
7. E	17. A	27. C	37. A	47. C
8. C	18. A	28. A	38. A	48. B
9. D	19. C	29. B	39. E	49. C
10. B	20. D	30. E	40. C	50. D

EXAMINATION SECTION
TEST 1

DIRECTIONS: Each question or incomplete statement is followed by several suggested answers or completions. Select the one that BEST answers the question or completes the statement. *PRINT THE LETTER OF THE CORRECT ANSWER IN THE SPACE AT THE RIGHT.*

1. A fire at the front windows of the second story of an apartment house is discernible from the street. It is apparent that the fire originated close to these windows and that a small portion of the floor is involved.
   The action which should be taken by the lieutenant of the first company to arrive is to get his line set up and
   A. strike at the fire from the street
   B. wait for the first due chief to arrive
   C. attack the fire from the inside, drawing the line up the stairs
   D. attack the fire from the window, drawing the line up the fire escape or the ladder is no fire escape is available

   1.____

2. The one of the following which should NOT be done when manning a life net with the minimum number of men is to
   A. hold the net so that the ring is about even with the necks of the holders
   B. hold the net by grasping the hand holds with both hands
   C. have the men stand with the left foot advanced in front of the right
   D. span the hinged joints

   2.____

3. When working from ladders, it is frequently necessary to have both hands free. When safety devices are not available, it is necessary to take a leglock.
   The one of the following which is characteristic of a PROPER leglock is that
   A. it should be on the side of the ladder opposite the side on which the work is being done
   B. the ball of the foot on which the weight is carried should rest on the rung near the beam
   C. the toe of the leg which is locked should be placed around the rung
   D. the arch of the foot on which the weight is carried should rest in the middle of the rung

   3.____

4. Where fire has involved flow from a liquefied petroleum gas storage tank and the flow cannot be checked, it is generally considered SAFEST practice to
   A. fight the fire with foam   B. use explosives in small quantities
   C. fight the fire with sand   D. permit the fire to burn itself out

   4.____

5. The one of the following hazards which should be specifically taken into consideration in a fire involving an old non-fireproof hotel (Class B Multiple Dwelling) is the
   A. possibility that the floors, when subjected to fire and flooded with water, will collapse
   B. presence in almost all cases of barred windows at the rear of the basement and the main story
   C. possibility of spread of the fire to lower floors
   D. presence of narrow courts between buildings of this type

6. The one of the following which is a serious hazard often encountered when fighting a fire in Class A Multiple Dwelling – fireproof apartment is
   A. an unusually large undivided space in the cockloft covering the entire area of the structure
   B. large quantities of paint stored in the cellar
   C. poorly constructed fire-stopped columns made of iron channel rails
   D. the presence of dumbwaiter shafts

7. You are in charge of an interior line stretched to the sixth floor of a new-law tenement. The fire is in a seven room apartment. Upon opening the door to the apartment, you are faced by a long narrow hall which is smoke-filled. The chief in command orders truckmen to ventilate by means of the fire escape window.
   When ventilation is effected, you should
   A. wait a few minutes before advancing the line in order to permit the smoke to dissipate
   B. advance into the apartment at once
   C. advance with the nozzle open in order to give added protection to the pipeman
   D. stretch your line through the apartment directly underneath the fire up the fire escape and operate through the windows on the fire

8. The officer in charge of the first engine company to arrive at a fire in the cellar of an old-law tenement takes a line of hose into the main hallway, first floor, and then down into the cellar to attack the fire.
   This procedure is
   A. *desirable*; the primary objective is to put the fire out before it can get out of hand
   B. *undesirable*; his first action should have been to break the basement windows and use a cellar pipe to flood the basement
   C. *desirable*; moving in on the fire will prevent excessive water damage and permit the building to be emptied with a minimum of danger
   D. *undesirable*; his objective should be to protect the first floor and to prevent the extension of the fire

9. Oil-filled transformers and switch gear which are located outdoors should be   9.____
   protected by an approved
   A. fine water spray system
   B. carbon dioxide system
   C. foam-type fire extinguisher
   D. soda and acid-type fire extinguisher

10. The one of the following which describes a procedure which should generally   10.____
    be followed when ventilating a building fully charged with smoke is to
    A. make openings in the roof close to flashings
    B. open all doors and windows
    C. cut such holes as are necessary in the most accessible passageways
    D. make one large opening in the roof rather than several small ones

Questions 11-16.

DIRECTIONS: Column I lists six properties of fire extinguishers. Column II lists seven types of fire extinguishers. For each property in Column I, select the fire extinguisher from Column II having that property and place the letter next to the extinguisher in the properly numbered space.

COLUMN I

11. Extinguishing effect is both blanketing and cooling

12. May contain potassium carbonate

13. Is considered effective on Class A and Class B fires

14. Produces a dispersed sodium bicarbonate blanket

15. Maximum effective range of discharge is 4 ft. to 10 ft.

16. Extinguishes by means of a gas produced by the vaporization of the extinguisher liquid

COLUMN II

A. Water, gas cartridge expelled
B. Antifreeze (water mixed with an antifreeze chemical)
C. Foam
D. Chemical solution (soda and acid)
E. Dry chemical
F. Carbon tetrachloride
G. Carbon dioxide

11.____
12.____
13.____
14.____
15.____
16.____

17. When large quantities of the substance are involved in the fire, the substance   17.____
    may fuse or melt in which condition application of water may result in extensive
    scattering of the molten material and, therefore, care should be taken in
    applying water to the material after fire has been burning for some time.
    The chemical referred to is
    A. ammonium perchlorate   B. potassium chlorate
    C. potassium nitrate   D. sodium chlorite

18. The one of the following chemicals to which the storage instructions: *Safeguard containers against mechanical injury. Keep away from oxidizing agents, particularly nitric acid and chlorates. Avoid contact by leakage or otherwise with all common metals*, would BEST apply is
    A. hydrochloric acid
    B. hydrogen peroxide
    C. calcium chloride
    D. potassium peroxide

19. It is NOT desirable to use water in a fire involving large quantities of
    A. sodium chlorite
    B. potassium peroxide
    C. potassium perchlorate
    D. hydrochloric acid

20. The statement, *Does not burn or explode per se but mixtures of this substance and combustible substances are explosive and ignite easily even by friction*, describes
    A. potassium peroxide
    B. ammonium perchlorate
    C. hydrochloric acid
    D. phosphorous pentasulphide

21. A strong oxidizing material which when raised to 347°F decomposed with the evolution of heat is
    A. bleaching powder
    B. sodium chlorite
    C. phosphorous pentasulphide
    D. potassium nitrate

22. A flammable liquid which is Class II (flashpoint between 25°F and 70°F) is
    A. carbon disulphide
    B. toluol
    C. turpentine
    D. benzol

23. The one of the following combustible substances which is LEAST likely to produce a quick-spreading flash fire is
    A. excelsior
    B. jute bagging folded and baled
    C. kapok
    D. print paper in rolls

24. The hazard which is generally presented by a transformer stems from the
    A. use of rotating electrical equipment
    B. use of high potentials
    C. location in which it is usually placed
    D. starting equipment which produces arcs

Questions 25-28.

DIRECTIONS: In order to detect arson, it is important that firemen be able to identify odors or residues left by materials used by arsonists. Column I lists four materials used by arsonists. Column II lists eight identifying odors or residues. For each material in Column I, select the characteristic from Column II by means of which it may be identified.

COLUMN I	COLUMN II	
25. Sulphur candle	A. No residue, odor of peach pits	25.____
26. Celluloid	B. No residue, odor of rotten cabbage	26.____
27. Phosphorous	C. A grey-yellow residue	27.____
28. Carbon bisulphide	D. A fibrous residue	28.____
	E. A coal black glistening molten residue	
	F. No residue, sweet perfumed odor	
	G. Brownish-red residue containing many bubbles	
	H. No residue, odor of ammonia	

29. Fire extinguishers whose extinguishing effect is the result of smothering are usually LEAST effective on fires involving
    A. rubbish
    B. alcohol
    C. paint
    D. electrical equipment

30. The breaking strength of 1 inch new manila rope is, in pounds, MOST NEARLY
    A. 2450   B. 4000   C. 4900   D. 8200

31. When testing a pump by means of a dry test, the MAXIMUM time that a pump should be operated dry is
    A. 30 seconds   B. 1 minute   C. 2 minutes   D. 5 minutes

32. If you wish to determine whether or not any fire has penetrated walls or partitions which have been exposed to fire, and an electric or gas fixture is present, you should
    A. remove the fixture
    B. remove a small area of laths and plaster from around the fixture
    C. check the fixture for smoke stain
    D. punch a small hole in the plaster above and below the fixture

33. After a fire in a grain elevator, you are assigned to do overhauling work. During this work, you should pay special attention to
    A. all overhead pulleys, belts, motors, and flat surfaces
    B. the middle of the floor as this is the weakest point and must be relieved first
    C. concealed spaces in bins
    D. the point at which the fire started

34. The time of day when the GREATEST number of fires occur is from
    A. midnight to 6 A.M.
    B. 6 A.M. to 12 noon
    C. 12 noon to 6 P.M.
    D. 6 P.M. to midnight

35. Of the following types of industrial organizations, the one in which the GREATEST number of fires occur is
    A. newspaper and printing shops
    B. carpet and rug factories
    C. foundries, metal works, and machine shops
    D. paint, oil, and varnish factories

36. In order for the top of a 55-foot ladder to reach a point 54 feet above the ground, the distance between the base of the building and the foot of the ladder should be MOST NEARLY _____ feet.
    A. 1.6
    B. 3.4
    C. 7.6
    D. 10.4

37. When checking a battery with a hydrometer, the rubber nozzle is placed into the battery vent opening, and electrolyte is drawn into the barrel
    A. as far as it will go
    B. until the float rides freely
    C. until the electrolyte level is even with the marker
    D. until the pointer stops moving

38. Failure to operate the motor of automotive apparatus for a sufficiently long period every day will cause
    A. sludge to form in the crankcase
    B. rust to accumulate in the radiator
    C. the head gasket to rot
    D. valves to stick

39. Upon inspecting a fire truck, you find that the starter will start the engine although the electrolytic solution in the battery is so far down it can't be seen. You should
    A. do nothing as the motor can be started
    B. replace the battery; it may go at any time
    C. fill the battery by adding water in small quantities
    D. fill the battery with water at once

40. The clutch should be adjusted so that the free play in the foot pedal is MOST NEARLY _____ inch(es).
    A. 1/8
    B. 1 1/8
    C. 5/8
    D. 1 5/8

41. If the friction loss in 450 ft. of 2½" hose is 36 pounds, the flow, in gallons per minute, is MOST NEARLY
    A. 150
    B. 175
    C. 200
    D. 225

42. The *kickback* of a 1 1/8" nozzle delivering water at 40 pounds pressure is MOST NEARLY _____.
    A. 66
    B. 71
    C. 76
    D. 81

43. If an engine pumps water at 150 pounds per square inch engine pressure through 800 ft. of 2½" hose equipped with a 1¼" nozzle (K = .248), the nozzle pressure will be MOST NEARLY _____ pounds.
    A. 30   B. 35   C. 40   D. 45

44. If an engine pumps water through 700 ft. of 2½" hose equipped with a 1¼" nozzle so that the nozzle pressure is 60 pounds, the engine pressure, in pounds is MOST NEARLY
    A. 265   B. 270   C. 285   D. 290

45. If a pumper with engine pressure at 175 pounds delivers water through two parallel lines of 2½" hose, each 500 ft. long, siamesed into a deluge set equipped with a 1½" nozzle (K = .06 for two 2½" lines siamesed), then the nozzle pressure, in pounds, will be MOST NEARLY
    A. 90   B. 100   C. 110   D. 120

46. If it is required that an engine deliver water at a nozzle pressure of 65 pounds, through two parallel lines of 2½" hose, each 400 feet in length, siamesed into a deluge set equipped with a 1 ³⁄₈" nozzle (K = .096 for two 2½" lines siamesed), then it is necessary for the engine pressure to be MOST NEARLY
    A. 116   B. 141   C. 126   D. 131

47. A line of 2½" hose equipped with a 1 ⅛" nozzle is stretched from a pumper down an incline to a point 50 feet below the pumper. If the line is 500 feet long, which of the following engine pressures will result in a nozzle pressure CLOSEST to 50 pounds (K = .167)? _____ pounds.
    A. 107   B. 112   C. 117   D. 122

48. Using an angle of stream of about 70, a nozzle pressure of 70 pounds and a 1 ⅛" tip, the MAXIMUM effective vertical reach of a fire stream will be MOST NEARLY _____ ft.
    A. 87   B. 92   C. 97   D. 102

49. An engine at 300 pounds per square inch pressure delivers water through a 900 foot line of 2½" hose equipped with a 1 ⅛" nozzle.
    If the nozzle is closed for a few minutes and then suddenly opened, the nozzle pressure at the moment the nozzle is opened will be MOST NEARLY _____ PSI.
    A. 50   B. 150   C. 225   D. 300

50. A sprinkler system covering an area 90 ft. x 120 ft. has one ½" diameter outlet sprinkler per 80 square feet. The number of gallons of water per minute which will have to be supplied to maintain a sprinkler head pressure of 20 pounds per square inch is MOST NEARLY
    A. 1875   B. 2375   C. 2875   D. 3375

KEY (CORRECT ANSWERS)

1. C	11. C	21. B	31. B	41. B
2. D	12. B	22. B	32. D	42. C
3. A	13. C	23. D	33. A	43. A
4. D	14. E	24. B	34. C	44. B
5. A	15. G	25. E	35. C	45. B
6. B	16. F	26. D	36. D	46. A
7. B	17. C	27. G	37. B	47. C
8. D	18. A	28. B	38. A	48. A
9. A	19. B	29. A	39. C	49. D
10. D	20. A	30. D	40. B	50. D

TEST 2

DIRECTIONS: Each question or incomplete statement is followed by several suggested answers or completions. Select the one that BEST answers the question or completes the statement. *PRINT THE LETTER OF THE CORRECT ANSWER IN THE SPACE AT THE RIGHT.*

1. The discharge, in gallons per minute, from a 3" outlet on a hydrant when the pressure at the outlet is 25 lbs. per square inch is MOST NEARLY
   A. 400 B. 600 C. 800 D. 1000 E. 1200

   1.____

2. A pumper is to deliver water through 400 feet of 2 ½" hose equipped with a 1 ⅛" nozzle (K = .167). A pressure of 60 lbs. is desired at the nozzle. Of the following, the MINIMUM engine pressure required is
   A. 130 B. 140 C. 150 D. 160 E. 170

   2.____

3. An engine at 150 lbs. is pumping through a single line of 2 ½" hose equipped with a 1 ⅛" nozzle.
   The discharge from the nozzle is MOST NEARLY _____ gpm.
   A. 200 B. 220 C. 240 D. 260 E. 280

   3.____

4. The friction loss in a 200" line of 2 ½" hose discharging 220 gallons per minute is 24 lbs.
   With the discharge rate remaining the same, what would be the APPROXIMATE friction loss if the length of the line is increased to 700'?
   _____ pounds
   A. 60 B. 72 C. 84 D. 90 E. 108

   4.____

5. Two nozzles are discharging at the same pressure. One of the nozzles is 1"; the other is 1 ¼".
   How much GREATER will be the reach of the stream from the 1 ¼" nozzle?
   A. 5" B. 10 C. 15" D. 20" E. 25"

   5.____

6. The number of gallons being discharged per minute at 60 lbs. pressure from a hose line is 290.
   The diameter of the nozzle is MOST NEARLY
   A. 7/8" B. 1" C. 1 ⅛" D. 1 ¼" E. 1 ¾"

   6.____

7. When two engines are operating in relay in a single line of 2 ½" hose at a pump pressure of 200 lbs., the length of the line from the second engine to the nozzle should be what fraction of the length of the line from the first to the second engine?
   A. ½ B. ⅖ C. ⅔ D. ¾ E. ⅚

   7.____

8. *Experienced firefighters learn to identify gases and chemicals present at a fire by odor.*
   The one of the following which has the odor of bitter almonds is
   A. hydrocyanic acid   B. hydrogen sulphide   C. phosphorus
   D. methyl bromide   E. phosgene

   8.____

115

9. Naphtha has a flashpoint of about
   A. 100°F   B. 125°F   C. 150°F   D. 175°F   E. 200°F

   9.____

10. Turpentine has a flashpoint APPROXIMATELY equal to
    A. 45°F   B. 65°F   C. 95°F   D. 115°F   E. 135°F

    10.____

11. The one of the following plastics which is *thermosetting* rather than *thermoplastic* is
    A. koroseal
    B. celluloid
    C. lucite
    D. nylon
    E. bakelite

    11.____

12. Of the following, the plastic with the LOWEST relative flammability is
    A. lucite
    B. bakelite
    C. celluloid
    D. lustron
    E. ethocel

    12.____

13. Of the following, the MOST accurate statement of a difference between the thermoplastic category of plastics and the thermosetting category is that plastics in the first group
    A. have less flexural strength
    B. are more durable
    C. have greater pliability
    D. are less elastic
    E. are harder

    13.____

14. The toxic gas produced by the burning of carbon disulphide is
    A. bromine
    B. chlorine
    C. hydrocyanic acid
    D. sulphur dioxide
    E. hydrogen sulphide

    14.____

15. The reason that a small stream is often of little value in fighting very hot fires is that the
    A. water from such stream is broken up quickly into hydrogen and oxygen which in turn ignite and increase the heat of the fire
    B. amount of heat drawn from the fire in breaking up the small stream into hydrogen and oxygen may be greater than the heat generated by these gases when they burn
    C. the heat absorbing power of water is greatly reduced when the water is in the form of fog or fine droplets
    D. amount of heat drawn from the fire in breaking up a small stream into hydrogen and oxygen is less than the heat generated by these gases when they burn
    E. the small stream may vaporize or become steam and pass off before reaching the seat of the fire

    15.____

16. The *specific heat* of a substance is BEST defined as the
    A. temperature at which the substance will ignite
    B. rate at which the substance will absorb heat as compared to water
    C. number of BTU's of heat produced by the combustion of one pound of the substance
    D. heat resistive quality of the substance as compared to asbestos
    E. amount of heat required to raise the temperature of a pound of the substance one degree Fahrenheit

    16.____

17. The occurrence of unusual percentages of carbon monoxide at both smoldering fires and in fast burning fires such as furniture factories would probably be due PRIMARILY to
    A. unusually high temperatures
    B. the similarity of materials in most cases
    C. oxygen deficiency
    D. unusually low temperatures
    E. the characteristic use of large volumes of water at such fires

18. When water is thrown on burning magnesium dust, the gas which is liberated is
    A. hydrogen   B. oxygen   C. helium
    D. manganese dioxide   E. calcium carbide

19. The one of the following which has the LOWEST ignition point is
    A. butane   B. carbon disulphide   C. gasoline
    D. naphthalene   E. propane

20. Wood normally ignites at a temperature of about
    A. 212°F   B. 500°F   C. 750°F   D. 1000°F   E. 1200°F

Questions 21-30.

DIRECTIONS: Column I below lists ten emergencies or complaints that may be reported by telephone to the dispatcher. Column II lists five possible actions that may be taken by the dispatcher. For each of the emergencies or complaints in Column I, on the correspondingly numbered line at the right, print the letter preceding the BEST description of the dispatcher's CORRECT ACTION in Column II.

Column I
21. Steam pipe burst
22. Water leak in street
23. Cave-in at excavation
24. Building collapse – no fire
25. Automobile collision in street – no fire – persons trapped
26. Overcrowded theater
27. Unserviceable sprinkler
28. Gasoline stored in building
29. Flooded cellar due to burst water main
30. Obstructed fire escape

COLUMN II
A. Notify commanding officer of company in whose district the situation exists
B. Notify the battalion chief
C. Notify nearest hook and ladder company
D. Transmit 5-7 signal
E. Notify some city department other than the fire department

Questions 31-40.

DIRECTIONS: Questions 31 through 40 are steps or procedures taken from the following five evolutions:

    A. Stretching hose line to roof, via outside of building
    B. Stretching hose line, via fire escape
    C. Siamesing two lines to develop heavy stream
    D. Relaying water from one pumping engine to another
    E. Supplying water to standpipe system through standpipe hose outlet valve inside of building

For each of the steps or procedures numbered 31 through 40, in the correspondingly numbered space at the right, print the letter preceding the one of the five evolutions listed above in which such step or procedure occurs.

31. Connect female butt of 3" hose to H.P. hydrant gauge.   31.____

32. Connect six lengths of 2 ½" hose in one line.   32.____

33. Connect reducers (3" x 2 ½") to H.P. hydrant gauge and H.P. hydrant outlet.   33.____

34. Connect 3 lengths of 2 ½" hose in one line.   34.____

35. Tie a clove hitch with binder knot around hose butt of 3" hose and double female swivel reducer.   35.____

36. Tie end of rope around the hose (using clove hitch and binder knot) two feet from male butt.   36.____

37. Connect 4 ½" suction to 4 ½" outlet on L.P. hydrant.   37.____

38. Connect 2 ½" double female swivel connection to 2 ½" end of reducer.   38.____

39. Connect double female swivel connection (4 ½" x 4 ½") to male butt of suction.   39.____

40. Tie rolling hitch (four times around the hoses with a half-hitch over all and a binder) beneath coupling.   40.____

Questions 41-50.

DIRECTIONS: Questions 41 through 50 are actions which are required by the Rules and Regulations. The frequency with which each action is required to be taken is BEST described by one of the following:

    A. Daily
    B. Weekly
    C. Monthly
    D. Yearly
    E. No specified period, but frequently

For each of the actions numbered 41 through 50, in the correspondingly numbered space at the right, print the letter preceding the one of the five alternatives listed above which BEST describes the frequency with which such action is required by the Rules and Regulations.

41. Inspection of Company Building Inspection Records by battalion chief.   41.____

42. Testing of all key slots of gas shut-off and ammonia valve boxes.   42.____

43. Gate valves worked.   43.____

44. Sediment bulb and gas lines cleaned to remove dirt.   44.____

45. Operate A and B valves of Mack centrifugal pumping engines.   45.____

46. Examination of cables on hook and ladder trucks.   46.____

47. Examination of rear wheels of apparatus equipped with tractors.   47.____

48. Life nets brushed, dried, and aired.   48.____

49. Rope life nets tar oiled.   49.____

50. Radiator and cooling system of all apparatus flushed.   50.____

KEY (CORRECT ANSWERS)

1.	E	11.	E	21.	C	31.	E	41.	B
2.	C	12.	B	22.	E	32.	A	42.	C
3.	D	13.	C	23.	C	33.	C	43.	A
4.	C	14.	D	24.	D	34.	B	44.	E
5.	B	15.	E	25.	D	35.	E	45.	A
6.	C	16.	B	26.	B	36.	A	46.	E
7.	D	17.	C	27.	A	37.	D	47.	E
8.	A	18.	A	28.	A	38.	E	48.	C
9.	A	19.	B	29.	B	39.	D	49.	D
10.	C	20.	B	30.	A	40.	A	50.	C

EXAMINATION SECTION
TEST 1

DIRECTIONS: Each question or incomplete statement is followed by several suggested answers or completions. Select the one that BEST answers the question or completes the statement. *PRINT THE LETTER OF THE CORRECT ANSWER IN THE SPACE AT THE RIGHT.*

1. A lieutenant of a tower ladder is responsible for overhauling on the upper floors of a vacant building. The lieutenant orders that a full length of hose be connected directly to the tower ladder pipe and subsequently orders members to enter the rooms from the basket to perform extinguishment and overhauling operations.
The lieutenant's orders are

   A. *inappropriate,* mainly because this procedure is not permitted since it would restrict other uses of the tower ladder
   B. *appropriate,* mainly because this procedure often eliminates the need for repositioning the tower ladder
   C. *inappropriate,* mainly because the special 10 foot length of hose should be used in this case and members should remain in the basket
   D. *appropriate,* mainly because this procedure will afford members greater access to weakened stairs and fire escapes

1.____

2. A lieutenant supervising a company drill on safety and overhauling procedures in occupied buildings would be CORRECT in making which one of the following statements?

   A. In freezing weather, nozzles should be shut down to prevent creating an ice hazard.
   B. Hydraulic overhauling is an accepted practice in most building fires.
   C. Scorched bedding or clothing should not be used to absorb excess water on floors.
   D. Standpipe lines must be drained before disconnecting from the floor outlet valves.

2.____

3. A lieutenant is supervising the only unit present at an emergency where an unconscious victim is discovered. A quick check discloses a medic alert emblem on the victim's neck. The rear of the emblem has the inscriptions *epilepsy* and *asthma.*
In directing members to administer first aid, it would be MOST appropriate for the lieutenant to

   A. give oxygen to the victim
   B. clear airway and prevent victim from biting tongue
   C. give the victim concentrated sugar solution
   D. elevate the victim's feet

3.____

4. A lieutenant supervising rescue operations at the scene of an automobile accident notes that there is a victim whose left hand has been completely severed at the wrist and who is bleeding profusely from this wound.
Of the following, the lieutenant should order firefighters to apply

   A. direct pressure to the wound, seal the severed hand in a clean plastic bag, and place the bag in water containing ice
   B. a tourniquet above the elbow and pack the severed hand in ice
   C. direct pressure to the wound and pack the severed hand in ice

4.____

121

D. a tourniquet above the elbow, seal the severed hand in a clean plastic bag, and place the bag in water containing ice

5. A lieutenant is ordered to hoist a portable ladder to a roof for the purpose of rescue and escape from a remote area of the roof.
Which one of the following procedures would be the MOST appropriate for this operation?

   A. A ladder roller placed on the ledge of the roof is centered, if possible, between the line of windows.
   B. A rope is inserted between the center rung and the first rung above the center rung.
   C. As the ladder is raised by rope, the ladder tip must be between the rope and the building.
   D. A large loop bowline on a bight is tied 9 feet from the end of the rope, with a one foot end tail.

5.___

6. A lieutenant arrives at a heavy fire situation in a 4-story tenement and finds the front fire escape crowded with many people.
After members have properly placed the first portable ladder, the lieutenant should order a second portable ladder placed on the building wall alongside the fire escape at the _____ balcony, with the tip _____ above the fire escape railing and the base of the ladder placed so that the angle of the ladder is between _____ degrees.

   A. first; slightly; 50 to 60
   B. second; slightly; 65 to 75
   C. first; one to three feet; 65 to 75
   D. second; one to three feet; 50 to 60

6.___

7. A ladder company lieutenant responds to a fire where ventilation of windows on upper floors must be accomplished by a member operating from a portable ladder. The lieutenant should order that the ladder be placed on the _____ side of the window with the tip of the ladder _____.

   A. windward; level with the top of the window
   B. leeward; level with the sill
   C. windward; level with the center of the window
   D. leeward; higher than the tip of the window

7.___

8. A lieutenant supervising the cutting of a trench on the roof of an H type multiple dwelling with heavy fire in the cockloft should order members to cut the trench

   A. about 10 feet from the main or initial vent hole
   B. at the widest available roof section to protect the largest portion of the roof
   C. from wall to wall or to another firestop such as a main roof girder, bulkhead, or skylight
   D. at least 3 feet wide between parallel cuts

8.___

9. The lieutenant of the first arriving engine company discovers a fire in a small quantity of magnesium chips in a storage yard. This fire is exposing a nearby combustible building. Which one of the following substances should the lieutenant order members to use to extinguish the fire?

9.___

A. Halon
B. Dry sodium chloride
C. Sodium bicarbonate
D. Carbon dioxide

10. A lieutenant operating at a fire in an old law tenement is ordered to check exposure 4 for fire extension. Because these buildings have party wall balcony fire escapes in the rear, the lieutenant can use these fire escapes to

    A. travel from building to building
    B. gain access to the roof via the gooseneck
    C. get to the rear yard via drop ladder or counterbalanced stair
    D. get from one floor to another

11. A lieutenant is instructing a member in the proper placement and operation of fire department pumpers.
    Which one of the following statements would be an APPROPRIATE instruction for the lieutenant to give?

    A. Avoid using *air lock hydrants* if possible
    B. Use the *pressure* position when pumping more than one-half of the pump capacity
    C. Use the *volume* position while priming the pumps during a drafting operation
    D. Hook up the hydrant connection to the pumper before hooking up to the hydrant

12. The lieutenant of the first arriving engine company at the scene of a structural fire allows a ladder company to enter the block first. The engine must be positioned behind the rear of the ladder because the street on which the fire is located is narrow.
    In this situation, the lieutenant should remind the engine company chauffeur that the MINIMUM acceptable distance between the rear of the ladder apparatus and the front of the engine apparatus is _____ feet.

    A. 15   B. 20   C. 25   D. 30

13. During a snow emergency, the following teleprinter response message was received in the quarters of Engine Company 99 and Ladder Company 99 which is without a dividing wall:
    PHONE - 1ST ALARM - RESIDENTIAL
    E099 L099
    BOX 0145 40 NORTH ST
    9 AVE 10 AVE
    E=MULT DWELL A 3 STORY FIRE ON TOP FLOOR
    HEAVY SNOW ACCUMULATION ON NORTH ST
    INCIDENT #17
    1/5/   130552
    In this situation, what is the MOST appropriate response procedure for the units to follow?

    A. Ladder Company 99 should leave quarters first and direct Engine Company 99 to enter North Street first
    B. Ladder Company 99 should leave quarters first and enter North Street first
    C. Engine Company 99 should leave quarters first and enter North Street first
    D. Engine Company 99 should leave quarters first and direct Ladder Company 99 to enter North Street first

14. At a multi-unit drill, a lieutenant is supervising firefighters on the proper placement of aerial ladders for rescue or removal of victims.
    During the drill, the lieutenant should remind firefighters to make sure that, at fire scenes,

    A. ladder rung locks are always engaged before climbing an extended ladder
    B. the inboard side of the apparatus is placed not more than 35 feet from the building line
    C. when the ladder is placed at a window, the tip is less than 6 inches above the window sill
    D. when the ladder is placed to the roof, the tip is extended from one to three feet above the point where the ladder contacts the building

15. A lieutenant is ordered to position the tower ladder apparatus in front of a fire building for the purpose of overhauling a cornice.
    After ascending in the tower ladder basket with two members equipped with the proper tools and equipment, which one of the following instructions should the lieutenant give?

    A. Use the basket to lower large sections of the cornice to the street.
    B. Rest the basket firmly against the building wall for additional stability, and use 6-foot hooks and ropes to hold the cornice while pieces of it are being removed.
    C. If fire conditions permit, make openings at the ends of the cornice to preserve the integrity of the cornice.
    D. Cut metal hangers of the cornice first, using a power saw or bolt cutter.

16. The lieutenant of a tower ladder unit whose basket has double-acting swinging gates responds to a fire scene where the apparatus must be properly placed for rescue and removal.
    Which one of the following would be an APPROPRIATE action for the lieutenant to direct members to take?

    A. Place the basket initially so that the floor of the basket is level with the window sill.
    B. Place the apparatus parallel with the objective so that the basket is in line with the window.
    C. Place the basket directly on any roof which has no parapet, unless ice conditions are encountered.
    D. Use the platform's *dead man* trigger handle to perform all delicate positioning operations.

17. At a taxpayer fire where the metal security door is locked, a ladder company lieutenant must create an opening to provide adequate ventilation and space for the advancement of lines. The lieutenant orders members to use the portable power saw with an abrasive disc blade to cut a triangular opening in the security door.
    To perform this operation, the lieutenant should instruct members to use the

    A. yellow painted disc and cut below the center of the door
    B. unpainted disc and cut below the center of the door
    C. yellow painted disc and cut as high and as large as possible
    D. unpainted disc and cut as high and as large as possible

18. A ladder company is special called to an elevator emergency where a civilian is trapped in a stalled elevator at the lobby level. An examination of the hoistway door reveals that it is of the sliding type.
After making certain that the electrical power is off and that it will remain off, the lieutenant should order the firefighters to open the hoistway door by inserting the

    A. G.A.L. key and jiggling the door while depressing the spring latch
    B. escutcheon drop key and turning it away from the leading edge of the door
    C. half moon key and turning it until it stops
    D. Z key and applying downward pressure on the first obstruction encountered

18.____

19. A ladder company lieutenant is ordered by a battalion chief to force entry into a fast food restaurant during early morning hours in order to make an attack on a heavy body of fire. The door, which must be opened quickly, is a narrow stile aluminum and glass door and the only locking device on it is a pivoting deadbolt, mortise lock. In this situation, which one of the following is the LEAST appropriate method for the lieutenant to order the forcible entry team to use?

    A. Remove the lock cylinder and then insert the cam end of a key tool to depress the deadlock mechanism.
    B. Break the door glass to lessen damage to the door frame.
    C. Use conventional forcible entry tools to pry the aluminum stile from the door jamb.
    D. *Loid* the lock by slipping a piece of celluloid or a shove knife between the door and the jamb.

19.____

20. A ladder company lieutenant is operating on the fire floor at a fire in a class 3 multiple dwelling. The lieutenant immediately orders members to ventilate the glass windows. This action is

    A. *correct,* mainly because this type of ventilation should be accomplished immediately
    B. *incorrect,* mainly because the lieutenant must obtain permission from the chief in command before ordering lateral ventilation
    C. *correct,* provided the lieutenant has notified members and civilians in the street below
    D. *incorrect,* mainly because the lieutenant should wait until a charged line is in place before venting

20.____

21. A lieutenant of a tower ladder company is operating at a vacant building fire where all the windows have been sealed with plywood by the Department of Housing and Urban Development. The lieutenant orders the tower ladder raised to a second floor window in front of the building. He then orders members to ventilate this window from the tower ladder using the power saw. During the operation, the lieutenant insures that a safety zone is maintained below the work area and instructs the cutting member to use all available protective clothing and equipment.
In this situation, the actions of the lieutenant are

    A. *correct,* provided that the proper saw blade is used and the blade guard is moved and secured to protect the operator
    B. *incorrect,* mainly because this operation involves a degree of danger tha.t is not acceptable for a vacant building

21.____

C. *correct,* mainly because this procedure is the most efficient method of venting these windows
D. *incorrect,* mainly because a halligan tool should be used to vent these windows from the exterior

22. The engine company lieutenant in command of the first unit to arrive at a fire in a mobile home is informed by the dispatcher that the battalion chief will be delayed. The second arriving unit, a tower ladder, is also commanded by a lieutenant and arrives moments after the engine company.
The engine company lieutenant would be following the preferred procedure if he ordered the ladder company to perform roof ventilation from _____, and the engine company to use _____ for fire attack.

   A. the tower ladder; 2 1/2 inch hose with straight stream
   B. portable ladders; 2 1/2 inch hose with straight stream
   C. the tower ladder; 1 3/4 inch hose with fog stream
   D. portable ladders; 1 3/4 inch hose with fog stream

23. A lieutenant arrives at the scene of a fire in an oil burner which uses #2 fuel oil. An inspection of the area reveals fire in the chamber and in the pit around the burner where some oil had apparently spilled. The lieutenant decides at this point that the fire in the pit and in the chamber must be extinguished because of exposure to structural elements of the building.
After ordering the power and oil supply shut down, which would be the APPROPRIATE extinguishing agent for the lieutenant to order members to use? _____ in the chamber and _____ in the pit.

   A. Fog; foam   B. Foam; fog
   C. Foam; foam   D. Fog; fog

24. While an engine company is out of quarters, the lieutenant is ordered via department radio to provide explosive escort duty for a non-federal shipment of electric blasting caps. Upon arriving at the rendezvous point, the lieutenant notices that there is a carrier car present but no police car.
In planning the formation of the explosive escort and after examining the bill of lading, the lieutenant should insure that the maximum number of electric blasting caps does NOT exceed _____ caps and should order the _____ to precede the explosive shipment.

   A. 1000; pumper   B. 1000; carrier car
   C. 5000; carrier car   D. 5000; pumper

25. An engine company lieutenant has been ordered by the chief in command at a large oil fire to set up and operate the foam cannon.
Of the following, which action would be MOST appropriate for the lieutenant to take?

   A. Position the portable foam reservoir at least 12 feet from the cannon.
   B. Direct members to lay hose so that the supply is balanced and not likely to create a side force which could make the cannon unstable.
   C. After properly positioning the cannon and locking its legs, secure the cannon with a slip-over clove hitch.
   D. After a controlling nozzle has been secured to the top of the reservoir, have one member remain to manually control the supply of foam concentrate.

26. The lieutenant of the first arriving engine company finds a vacant building in the middle of a row of occupied frame buildings. The second floor of the vacant building is fully involved with fire from front to rear.
    After transmitting signal 10-84, it would be MOST appropriate for the lieutenant to transmit a

    A. second alarm and order two lines; one 3 1/2 inch line to supply the tower ladder and one hand line to enter the fire building
    B. 10-75 signal and order two lines; one 3 1/2 inch line to supply the tower ladder and one hand line to the most severe exposure
    C. second alarm and order two hand lines; one line to exposure 2 and one line to exposure 4
    D. 10-75 signal and order two hand lines; one line into the fire building and the other line into the most severe exposure

27. The lieutenant of the first engine company to arrive at a cellar fire in a sprinklered taxpayer building would be CORRECT to order the first line stretched

    A. into the occupancy above the fire
    B. to feed the sprinkler system
    C. into the cellar via the outside entrance
    D. to the most severely exposed adjacent store

28. An engine company lieutenant is the first officer to arrive at a fire in a storage building which has adequate ventilation. Upon arrival, the lieutenant is unable to determine the size or extent of the fire or of the fire area, but orders the unit to stretch the first line, equipped with an FT-2 tip, into the fire area.
    In this situation, the lieutenant should direct members to initially use a

    A. 1 3/4 inch line with a fog stream pattern slightly wider than the area through which it is being directed
    B. 2 1/2 inch line with a fog stream pattern slightly wider than the area through which it is being directed
    C. 1 3/4 inch line with a straight stream pattern
    D. 2 1/2 inch line with a straight stream pattern

29. An engine company lieutenant is at the scene of a heavy fire situation in a 5-story tenement building. It is necessary to operate the stream as the line is being advanced down the hallway to reach the main body of fire. While the line is being advanced, the lieutenant should instruct the nozzleman to direct the stream INITIALLY

    A. at the main body of fire using a side to side motion
    B. slightly forward and, upward at the ceiling using a side to side motion
    C. at the main body of fire using a clockwise motion
    D. slightly forward and. upward at the ceiling using a counterclockwise motion

30. A lieutenant, arriving at the scene of a fire on the fourth floor of a 6-story building, is ordered by the chief in charge to stretch a line to protect an elevator containing people which is stalled at the fire floor.
To cool and protect the elevator car, the lieutenant should order the firefighters to operate a _____ from the floor _____, between the car and hoistway door.

   A. solid stream; above
   B. 30 fog line; below
   C. solid stream; below
   D. 30 fog line; above

KEY (CORRECT ANSWERS)

1.	B	16.	B
2.	D	17.	D
3.	B	18.	B
4.	A	19.	D
5.	A	20.	D
6.	B	21.	A
7.	A	22.	C
8.	D	23.	A
9.	B	24.	C
10.	A	25.	B
11.	C	26.	B
12.	B	27.	A
13.	C	28.	D
14.	C	29.	B
15.	C	30.	B

TEST 2

DIRECTIONS: Each question or incomplete statement is followed by several suggested answers or completions. Select the one that BEST answers the question or completes the statement. *PRINT THE LETTER OF THE CORRECT ANSWER IN THE SPACE AT THE RIGHT.*

1. An engine company lieutenant arrives at a high-rise office building where there is fire on the 35th floor. A high pressure pumping operation is being implemented and the lieutenant is ordered to supply the building's standpipe Siamese.
   The lieutenant issues the following orders:
   I. Connect the first line supplying the Siamese to the pumper on the side opposite the control panel and secure it with utility ropes at the pumper and at the Siamese
   II. Connect the first line supplying the Siamese to the discharge gate of the pumper, avoiding any discharge gate that is equipped with flow gauges
   III. Connect special red 2 1/2 inch hose to feed the stand-pipe Siamese
   Which of the above orders are APPROPRIATE?

   A. I, II
   B. I, III
   C. II, III
   D. I, II, III

   1.____

2. At a 6-story *H* type apartment building with fire on the third floor, the lieutenant of the second arriving ladder company is operating on the floor above the fire. The lieutenant learns that there is fire in a void containing a vertical channel rail and notifies the officer in command of this fact.
   At this point, which one of the following actions should the lieutenant IMMEDIATELY take?

   A. Go to the basement to examine the base of the shaft
   B. Go to the top floor to examine the termination point of the void
   C. Check for the presence of other voids on this floor
   D. Call for a line and order members to open the void from floor to ceiling

   2.____

3. You are the lieutenant of the third arriving ladder company at a fire on the 23rd floor of a 50-story office building.
   According to Fire Department standard operating procedures, you should expect to operate on the _____ using the handie-talkie on the _____ tactical channel.

   A. 24th floor; secondary
   B. roof; secondary
   C. 24th floor; primary
   D. roof; primary

   3.____

4. While members of the second arriving ladder company are ascending to the floor above the fire in an occupied old law tenement, the lieutenant is alerted that the fire is extending upward via the enclosed shaft between the fire building and exposure 2.
   At this point, the lieutenant would be CORRECT to order the

   A. outside vent man to close the windows on the shaft
   B. chauffeur to bring the saw to the roof of the fire building
   C. can man to operate at the base of the shaft
   D. roof man to operate on the roof of exposure 2 and then assist the first arriving roof man if necessary

   4.____

5. A lieutenant is conducting a drill on various situations in which an engine company and a ladder company in the same quarters can make themselves available in quarters (AQ) simultaneously on the teleprinter selector panel. Which one of the following situations should the lieutenant include in the drill as a CORRECT example of such a situation?

   A. One of the units is a relocated unit and the other a regularly assigned unit.
   B. Both units are relocated units as a result of the same incident.
   C. One of the regularly assigned units did not go 10-8 before returning to quarters.
   D. Both regularly assigned units responded to the same incident at different times.

6. A lieutenant is instructing members in the proper method of warning motorists and pedestrians when the apparatus is entering or leaving quarters.
   Of the following, which instruction should the lieutenant give to members?

   A. The housewatchman is responsible for proper opening, closing, and securing of apparatus doors.
   B. Members positioned on the sidewalk apron should face oncoming pedestrians and physically stop those pedestrians who are aware of and ignore warnings.
   C. A member may be in a lane of traffic between an approaching vehicle and the apparatus only when the vehicle is stopped and the member is boarding or dismounting the apparatus.
   D. Once vehicles are stopped, one member should take a position in front of the lane of traffic and be alert to take refuge if motorists begin to move.

7. A civilian enters quarters and informs the lieutenant that there is a structural fire in progress three blocks north of the firehouse. The computer assisted dispatch system is operational.
   After ordering the unit to turn out, which one of the following actions would be MOST appropriate for the lieutenant to take?

   A. Notify the dispatcher by department telephone giving available details
   B. Notify the dispatcher by radio giving available details
   C. Order the firefighter on housewatch to notify the dispatcher via the teleprinter by pressing the buttons labelled UNIT, VERBAL, SEND, followed by radio report
   D. Order the firefighter on housewatch to notify the dispatcher via the teleprinter by pressing the buttons labelled UNIT, 10-8, SEND, followed by radio report

8. A lieutenant is in command of the first ladder company to arrive at a 4-story brownstone building with fire on the third floor. The roofman reports from his position on the roof that there is a person trapped at a top floor rear window and that there is no rear fire escape.
   In this situation, the lieutenant should instruct the roofman to

   A. assure the victim that help is on the way
   B. initiate single slide and rescue pickup using the lifesaving rope
   C. delay roof ventilation since such ventilation may intensify the fire
   D. notify the chauffeur, by calling over the front of the roof, to bring a portable ladder to the rear of the building

9. While responding to a telephone alarm for a fire in a public school, the lieutenant of the second due engine company receives a 10-20 signal for the box to which the unit is responding. The lieutenant instructs the chauffeur to proceed to the box location at reduced speed.
   To comply with department policy, it would also be appropriate for the lieutenant to order the chauffeur to

   A. turn on warning lights and come to a full stop before proceeding through a,n intersection against a red light
   B. slow down and turn off warning devices when approaching an intersection against a red light, and then proceed only if traffic permits
   C. turn off the warning lights and come to a full stop against red lights, and proceed through the intersection only when the light turns green
   D. make a full stop and turn warning lights on before entering a one-way street against traffic

9.____

10. A ladder company lieutenant is supervising the only unit on the scene of a sprinkler alarm in a public assembly building which is not in his administrative district. The chauffeur tells the lieutenant via handie-talkie that he has shut down one of the sprinkler control valves in the basement. The chauffeur states further that there is no fire and that the alarm was transmitted because freezing temperatures had caused the sprinkler riser to burst. Upon investigation, the lieutenant concludes that the system is only partially out of service and it can still be supplied. In order to comply with fire department regulations, the lieutenant should notify _____ and instruct members to place a _____ disc on the Siamese connection.

    A. Fire Salvage; blue
    B. the administrative battalion chief to report to the scene; blue
    C. the administrative battalion chief to report to the scene; white
    D. Fire Salvage; white

10.____

11. An engine company lieutenant responding to a multiple alarm is informed by the dispatcher that his unit has been designated as a field communications satellite unit and is to assist in the deployment of the *Figaro communications system.*
    The lieutenant, in briefing members on this system, should inform them that the Figaro system is a communications aid that utilizes

    A. voice-powered phone and reels of cable with headsets and is to be used where handie-talkies are ineffective
    B. a band frequency repeater system which increases transmission wattage and high rise communications capability
    C. a base station with portable units operating on a special frequency to enhance underground communications
    D. a multi-channel recorder/playback system to monitor and record vital handie-talkie transmissions

11.____

12. A ladder company lieutenant at a fire in a high-rise office building is ordered to search the 27th floor.
    To perform this assignment, the unit must use an elevator car that has been placed on *Fireman Service*.
    Which one of the following statements should serve as a guideline to the lieutenant regarding the activation of the *emergency stop* button if operation of the elevator becomes erratic and members must exit from the car at the nearest safe floor?
    The emergency stop button will

    A. operate in the recall phase
    B. operate in both the operational phase and the recall phase
    C. operate in the operational phase
    D. not operate in either the operational phase or the recall phase

13. A lieutenant is supervising the interior operations of a ladder company at a fire in a vacant tenement building. In this situation, which one of the following actions should the lieutenant take?

    A. Order members searching above the fire to use masks and to move quickly in order to reduce exposure time
    B. Assign two members to search all floors below the fire and assure that one of these members is equipped with a handie-talkie
    C. Order members to operate with extreme caution on the roof if the stability of the roof is in question
    D. When tower ladder streams are being operated, exercise close supervision over members working on floors below the tower ladder stream operation

14. A lieutenant is in command of the second arriving ladder company at a fire on the 30th floor of a 50-story class E high-rise building. The operations post and the search and evacuation post have been established. The lieutenant would be correct, in the absence of other orders, to instruct members to conduct primary search on the _____ floor and report conditions to the _____ post.

    A. 30th; operations
    B. 30th; lobby command
    C. 31st; operations
    D. 31st; lobby command

15. A lieutenant holds a critique after a serious fire in an old law tenement with railroad flats that involved difficult search procedures.
    Which one of the following statements would be APPROPRIATE for the lieutenant to make during the critique?

    A. The normal entrance to an apartment with two doors is the front door and this door should generally be used to facilitate entrance for a primary search.
    B. When all known residents have been accounted for, the secondary search may be concluded.
    C. Cellars and basements not directly exposed to heat and flame generally do not require a secondary search.
    D. The preferred method for conducting the primary search in the apartment above the fire is to start the search immediately upon entering the apartment.

16. A lieutenant who is responding first due to a serious vehicular accident is requested to provide a 10-12. Upon arrival, the lieutenant finds an overturned truck with the placard shown at the right displayed. As part of the preliminary report, the lieutenant should inform the dispatcher that the material involved is a(n)

    A. gas
    B. liquid
    C. solid
    D. oxidizer

17. At a fire where a member is reported missing, a lieutenant whose company is equipped with MX-330 handie-talkies is ordered to implement feedback assisted rescue.
    The lieutenant should order the member producing the feedback tone to

    A. replace the handie-talkie battery if the light on top of the transmitting radio goes on
    B. release the transmitting button momentarily every 30 seconds
    C. reduce the squelch control to a position just beyond the point of quieting
    D. place both handie-talkies on the new primary tactical channel

18. A lieutenant is conducting a drill on handie-talkie usage. Of the following messages mentioned by members, which one is an example of a proper *urgent* transmission?

    A. Urgent-urgent, firefighter cardiac, possible heart attack, 3rd floor rear apartment
    B. Urgent-urgent, collapse, 3rd floor rear and roof
    C. Urgent-urgent, line burst 2nd floor, firefighters operating above endangered
    D. Urgent-urgent, firefighter unconscious, 3rd floor rear apartment, cause unknown

19. A newly promoted lieutenant covering a tour in a lower Manhattan ladder company is assigned to respond, as part of the primary high-rise roof team (HRRT), to a third alarm high-rise fire in midtown. The lieutenant, while airborne in a police department helicopter in the vicinity of the fire building, receives information from the high-rise roof chief that the HRRT will be landing on the roof of the fire building.
    Upon arrival on the roof, the lieutenant would be CORRECT to

    A. be the first member to leave the helicopter and then supervise unloading of the helicopter
    B. position himself in front of the helicopter to supervise the unloading operation within the pilot's field of vision
    C. have members place tools alongside rubber pontoons during the unloading of the helicopter
    D. initiate vertical ventilation of the interior stairs by opening bulkhead doors

20. As long as immediate rescue and removal are not necessary, the lieutenant of the second arriving ladder company would be operating in the CORRECT area of responsibility in which one of the following situations?
    At a

A. top floor fire in an old law tenement, the lieutenant initially supervises firefighters venting the roof of the fire building with a power saw
B. top floor and cockloft fire in a row frame, the lieutenant initially conducts search and examination on the top floor of the most seriously exposed building
C. top floor fire in a brownstone, the lieutenant initially assists in search and entry on the top floor
D. cockloft fire in a taxpayer, the lieutenant initially supervises ventilation and ceiling removal in the store below the fire's origin

21. A lieutenant of an engine company arrives at a small outside fire with no life hazard or exposure problem and is ordered by the officer in command to stretch a booster line to the fire. During size-up, the lieutenant sees that a high chainlink fence topped with barbed wire is blocking the path of the line. Further investigation reveals that there is no entry way immediately available through the fence.
Of the following, it would be MOST appropriate for the lieutenant to order members to

    A. bridge the fence by using a 16 foot extension ladder and a 12 foot hook ladder and stretching the line over a hose roller
    B. cut the fence using a bolt cutter and stretch the line through the opening
    C. breach the fence by covering it with a coat or a ladder or any strong; pliable object and stretch the line through the fence
    D. cut only the lower portion of the fence, lift the chain links from the ground with hand tools, and stretch the line under the fence

22. You are the first officer to arrive at a building fire where no extension is likely and where exposure 3 is a rear yard. The chief officer, who will be delayed responding, requests a preliminary report.
Of the following, your preliminary report transmission describing exposure 3 need NOT include any buildings which are more than _____ feet distant from the fire building.

    A. 15   B. 20   C. 25   D. 30

23. After arriving at the scene of a fire in the hold of a ship in dry dock, a ladder company lieutenant learns from the engine company lieutenant on the scene that the ship's master has secured the hold in which the fire is located and has activated the CO_2 flooding system prior to the arrival of the fire department units.
Since these two companies are the only units presently on the scene, the ladder company officer would be CORRECT to take which one of the following actions while awaiting the arrival of a chief officer?

    A. Order members to search flooded hold areas while using mandatory masks and life lines
    B. Enter hold areas once a charged line has been placed in position
    C. See that hold areas remain sealed and flooded with CO_2
    D. Stretch precautionary hose lines into adjacent hold areas

24. You are the lieutenant of the first engine company to arrive at a brownstone building where fire is in control of the cellar and the first floor.
In this situation, as the first line, you should order a 1 3/4" handline stretched to the

    A. parlor floor by way of the outside stairs
    B. first floor by way of the first floor entrance

C. parlor floor by way of the interior stairs
D. cellar by way of the interior cellar stairs

25. A lieutenant, the first officer to arrive at a subway station, finds a light smoke condition in a tunnel with many excited and disoriented civilians exiting the tunnel from the tracks. After assuring power removal by proper use of the power removal box and emergency telephone, in addition to requesting that power be turned off through the fire department dispatcher, the lieutenant should order members operating under his command to

   A. direct civilians to areas of refuge which are designated by diagonal red and white stripes
   B. operate only from the station platform and the catwalks until the fire department dispatcher confirms that the power has been turned off
   C. expedite removal from the track area by directing civilians towards the blue light which indicates an emergency exit location
   D. remove civilians via, the roadbed instead of via the catwalks

25.____

26. The lieutenant arriving first at a compactor fire in a 15-story multiple dwelling sizes up the situation and determines that the blockage and the fire are in the compactor chute between the 4th and 5th floors.
Of the following, the lieiutenant should order the

   A. forcible entry man to the compactor room to shut off the electric power to the compactor
   B. outside vent man to operate on the 4th floor to try to free the blockage;
   C. roofman to drop a heavy object down the chute from the roof to free the; blockage
   D. chauffeur to operate with the engine company to free the blockage

26.____

27. The lieutenant of the first arriving ladder company at a high-rise building is met in the lobby by the building engineer who immediately takes the lieutenant to the basement where light smoke is coming from a transformer vault. The lieutenant determines that all of the transformers on the premises use air as a coolant. The engineer then directs the lieutenant to the switch that will deactivate the involved transformers.
In this situation, it would be APPROPRIATE for the lieutenant to assume that the transformers are

   A. PCB contaminated and instruct members not to deactivate them
   B. not PCB contaminated and instruct members not to deactivate them
   C. PCB contaminated and order members to deactivate them in accordance with procedures provided by the building engineer
   D. not PCB contaminated and order members to deactivate them in accordance with procedures provided by the building engineer

27.____

28. An engine company lieutenant is supervising the advance of a hose line equipped with an FT-2 tip on a heavy body of fire in a building. The lieutenant observes that the stream appears to be adequate, that it is reaching the seat of the fire, and that the nozzleman is easily handling the nozzle without the aid of the backup man. In this situation, of the following, the lieutenant should order the

   A. nozzleman to change the stream pattern to increase the water flow
   B. backup man to leave the hose line and assist the ladder company with ventilation

28.____

C. chauffeur to increase engine pressure
D. doorman to feed more hose line into the fire area

29. A ladder company lieutenant is in command of the first unit to arrive at a high-rise building where a fire has been reported on the 18th floor. The lieutenant takes the elevator to the 16th floor and then confirms that there is a fire on the 18th floor.
After safe access to the fire stairs is assured, which one of the following actions would be MOST appropriate for the lieutenant to take?

A. Hold the elevator for possible use by the company members.
B. Assign a handie-talkie equipped firefighter to return the elevator to the lobby.
C. Return the elevator unmanned to the lobby.
D. Assign a handie-talkie equipped firefighter to remain with the elevator on the 16th floor until primary search is completed.

30. During operations, a lieutenant orders two firefighters to go to the staging area to obtain one can of fluoroprotein foam concentrate and one can of alcohol foam concentrate. The lieutenant should inform the firefighters that the fluoroprotein can is color coded _____ and the alcohol can is color coded _____.

A. brown; blue
B. blue; yellow
C. brown; green
D. green; blue

KEY (CORRECT ANSWERS)

1. B
2. B
3. C
4. A
5. D

6. C
7. B
8. A
9. C
10. B

11. C
12. C
13. B
14. A
15. D

16. B
17. B
18. C
19. A
20. B

21. A
22. D
23. C
24. A
25. D

26. A
27. B
28. C
29. B
30. C

TEST 3

DIRECTIONS: Each question or incomplete statement is followed by several suggested answers or completions. Select the one that BEST answers the question or completes the statement. *PRINT THE LETTER OF THE CORRECT ANSWER IN THE SPACE AT THE RIGHT.*

1. Ladder Company 708 responds to an alarm after receiving the following teleprinter transmission: 1.____

    PHONE - 1ST ALARM - COMMERCIAL E503 E501 L708 L715 B22

    BOX 0004 - 1201 HYLAND BLVD

    MAPLE AVE   ELM ST
    COMM WHSE 1 STY 100x200 CLIE
    METAL BAR JOIST RF
    HVY AC-TRANS ON RF
    INCIDENT #20

    1/5/   150003

    Upon arrival, the lieutenant finds a heavy volume of fire, with high heat and visible flaming. Of the following, the lieutenant should INITIALLY order

    A. the simultaneous cutting of a main vertical ventilation hole over the fire along with a trench cut
    B. that two saws be brought to the roof to begin immediate ventilation over the fire
    C. the cutting of a trench in conjunction with horizontal ventilation via doors and windows
    D. horizontal ventilation of windows and doors, in advance of hoselines

2. A lieutenant is in command of a unit responding to a multiple alarm fire in a complex of multiple dwellings which are in various stages of renovation. 2.____
Which one of the following is the MOST appropriate instruction for the lieutenant to give members in this situation?
When a building is in the

    A. gutted stage, stairways should not be used for rapid hose stretching
    B. closed frame stage, the lath and plaster walls and ceilings will tend to inhibit fire spread
    C. closed frame stage, the vertical voids between apartments are the most serious of the new voids created
    D. gutted stage, collapse is not likely because the amount of combustible material remaining in the structure is limited

3. You are the lieutenant of a tower ladder company which is the first unit to arrive at a fire in a small 75' x 75' church. Upon arrival, you note that the building is full of smoke and that the roof is steep and is covered with slate shingles. 3.____
To properly ventilate this building, you would be CORRECT to order members to

    A. take out the stained glass windows before venting the roof
    B. locate the scuttle to the attic and ventilate the roof from the interior

C. place the tower ladder bucket into the plane of the roof and make an opening as high as possible
D. make an opening near the steeple's bell tower or gable ends from the tower ladder bucket

4. A lieutenant is the first officer to arrive at the scene of a suspicious fire in an occupied Amtrak train that is above ground. The fire is confined to a single car and is extinguished by a hand extinguisher prior to the arrival of the additional units.
In this situation, the lieutenant should transmit a signal 10-84, and also signals 10-19, 10-28 Code _____ above ground, 10-41 Code _____.

   A. 2; 1   B. 1; 3   C. 1; 1   D. 2; 3

5. You are the lieutenant of the first engine company to arrive at a reported fire in an *ABR in process* school while classes are in session. Upon your request, the principal hands you a copy of each student's individualized safety plan (ISP).
You should expect to find each of the following items of information listed in each ISP EXCEPT the

   A. type of disability suffered by the student
   B. location of the student within the building
   C. name of the staff member designated to evacuate the student
   D. name of the back-up staff member designated to evacuate the student

6. A ladder company lieutenant is in command of the first unit to arrive at a fire in a tightly sealed taxpayer which shows signs of backdraft potential.
At this point, the lieutenant would be CORRECT to order members to

   A. give the fire a chance to *blow* before starting ventilation, entry, and search
   B. force entry at doors and show windows for maximum ventilation
   C. vent the roof by removing skylights and scuttle covers
   D. await the arrival of a chief officer before making any openings

7. A lieutenant is in command of the first arriving unit at a manhole fire where smoke is issuing under pressure from two manhole covers.
In this situation, the lieutenant would be CORRECT to order

   A. the chauffeur to transmit radio signal 10-25, code orange
   B. members to look away from the manhole covers if they blow
   C. two members to cut the building service wires under the lieutenant's supervision
   D. a member to let water pour into the manhole only when so requested by Con Edison

8. After the responding fire company has returned to quarters from a mattress fire in a multiple dwelling a few blocks away from the firehouse, the occupant of the fire apartment enters quarters and reports that $300 in cash is missing from her bedroom.
In this situation, the lieutenant should IMMEDIATELY notify the

   A. office of the Inspector General
   B. fire marshal
   C. battalion responsible for the fire report
   D. police precinct responsible for the area where the fire building is located

9. A lieutenant on hydrant inspection duty finds an illegally opened hydrant which is defective and which must be shut down at the street control box.
The lieutenant would be CORRECT to inform the member who will be shutting down the hydrant that the operating nut is usually found off center at the _____ side of the chamber, and that to shut the hydrant, the operating nut must be turned _____.

   A. curb; clockwise
   B. street; counterclockwise
   C. curb; counterclockwise
   D. street; clockwise

9.____

10. During a holiday inspection, a lieutenant discovers a number of natural pine and balsam Christmas trees being stored and sold inside a building. Further investigation reveals that these are neither Halvorsan or Kirk trees and that the building is fully sprinklered. At this point, of the following, the lieutenant should

   A. order the immediate removal of the trees to a location outside the building
   B. serve a summons and then notify the bureau of fire prevention enforcement unit
   C. notify the deputy chief for consideration of a vacate order
   D. order the vendor to attach fire safety tags to the trees to make their storage legal

10.____

11. A civilian enters quarters to complain that a smoke detector that had been installed in her apartment in 1982 has not been operational for the past 6 months. The lieutenant, after checking unit records, determines that the premises is a class A multiple dwelling without sprinklers.
With respect to this situation, which one of the following actions should the lieutenant take?

   A. Inspect the premises and, if the situation is confirmed, issue a violation order to the owner of the building to repair the smoke detector.
   B. Advise the civilian making the complaint that maintenance and repairs to the smoke detector are her responsibility and refer her to the Department of Housing Preservation and Development for any further information.
   C. Inspect the premises and, if the situation is confirmed, forward an A-8A to the Bureau of Fire Prevention marked in the upper righthand corner *For Priority Transmittal*.
   D. Advise the civilian making the complaint that maintenance and repairs are the responsibility of the owner and refer her to the Department of Buildings for any further information.

11.____

12. A lieutenant, while out of quarters with the unit, observes an individual on the roof of a tall building who is threatening to jump. The lieutenant immediately notifies the dispatcher to transmit a request for a priority police response and to order the response of the nearest battalion chief.
While awaiting their arrival, it would be CORRECT for the lieutenant to order members to

   A. make no attempt to calm or soothe the distraught person as this effort may cause the individual to jump
   B. make the safety of fire department personnel and the distraught person their primary concern, and the safety of people using the sidewalks and streets their secondary concern
   C. take no actions, either physical or verbal, under any circumstances, until the arrival of the police or the battalion chief

12.____

D. make no attempt to forcibly restrain the distraught person unless there is a real threat of physical harm to fire department members

13. A lieutenant is conducting a drill on the preparation and service of summonses. Of the following statements, which one would be the MOST appropriate for the lieutenant to make?

   A. For a parking violation at a fire hydrant, the box entitled *Hydrant* should be marked with an X and the feet from the hydrant should be indicated.
   B. A member serving a personal service summons should issue the summons first and then explain the offense committed to the violator.
   C. A personal service summons may be issued in the name of a corporation as long as the person receiving the summons is an officer of that corporation.
   D. When more than one charge is listed on a summons, an X must be placed in the multiple charges box on the face of the summons.

14. A lieutenant supervising the inspection of Scott 4.5 masks would be CORRECT to point out that

   A. cylinders should be changed when the cylinder gauge needle falls below the green area
   B. both the purge valve and cylinder valve should be in the off position in order to check for leaks in the regulator or facepiece
   C. facepiece *E* clips should snap on or off by hand, and should face toward the demand regulator opening
   D. nylon *O* rings should be checked or replaced if leaks continue at the high pressure coupling after the coupling connection has been gently tightened with
   E. a wrench

15. During interior operations at a structural fire, a firefighter asks the lieutenant what action to take regarding his personal alert safety system (PASS) which is emitting a non-fluctuating low tone.
The lieutenant should instruct the firefighter to

   A. move either his body or the PASS itself and continue to operate
   B. turn the unit off and leave the area
   C. switch the unit to the ON position, then back to ARM
   D. turn the unit off and continue to operate with a partner

16. A firefighter is inspecting a construction site where detached, sprinklered, one-family private dwellings are being built. Plans for this construction have recently been approved by the Department of Buildings. The firefighter asks the lieutenant if smoke detecting devices will be required by law in these occupancies.
Of the following, the lieutenant should answer _____ and direct the firefighter to the Fire Prevention _____.

   A. *yes;* Code
   B. *no;* Code
   C. *yes;* Directives
   D. *no;* Directives

17. A ladder company lieutenant is operating at an elevator emergency in a high-rise building. Prior critical information dispatch system (CIDS) information has alerted the lieutenant that this elevator is in a single car blind shaft and has the required access doors. The lieutenant, in ordering members to open these access doors, should inform the members that the doors can be found in the hoistway

   A. on each story
   B. every 36 feet
   C. every four stories
   D. every 50 feet

18. A lieutenant responds to an alarm where CIDS information indicates the presence of a Halon 1301 extinguisher system. Upon arrival, the lieutenant is informed that the system has *dumped* and that the protected area is 75 feet x 100 feet.
    In briefing members prior to beginning operations, which one of the following statements would the lieutenant be CORRECT in making?

   A. The discharge of the extinguishing agent will continue at a steady rate for 30 minutes.
   B. The presence of the Halon 1301 agent will greatly reduce visibility.
   C. Emergency forced ventilation may consist of a series of portable electric fans.
   D. The system's alarm will cease after the agent is completely expelled.

19. At the scene of a suspicious fire, a civilian approaches a lieutenant and claims to be a witness to a crime of arson. The civilian is eager to talk to the lieutenant and makes a statement in which she incriminates herself. At this point, the lieutenant should

   A. allow the witness to continue to speak freely so as to obtain as much information from her as possible
   B. tell the witness not to give any further information until the arrival of the fire marshal
   C. interrogate the witness about the fire while she is still willing to talk
   D. advise the witness of his suspicions and advise her of her rights before allowing her to continue speaking

20. A lieutenant of a ladder company, conducting a primary search at a fire which had been quickly extinguished by aggressive engine tactics, discovers a victim classified as a 10-45 Code 1.
    Which one of the following conditions would MOST likely cause the lieutenant to suspect that arson may have been committed to conceal that the victim had been murdered prior to the fire?

   A. There is lividity present in the body.
   B. The victim is found in a pugilistic position.
   C. The victim is found in an unburned area.
   D. There is soot in and around the mouth of the victim.

21. During an inspection, a lieutenant discovers that the roof of a building has been recently covered with 1/8 inch steel plates. Further investigation reveals that a permit for this alteration has not been obtained, nor have architects or engineers submitted applications. The building is not sprinklered, and there are signs displayed indicating the presence of steel plates.
    In this situation, it would be APPROPRIATE for the lieutenant to

   A. prepare an A-234 form for lack of an alteration permit
   B. forward an A-8 form for absence of architects' or engineers' plans

C. submit a sprinkler recommendation
D. serve an immediate summons for improper alteration

22. While your unit is returning to quarters from a 10-92 at 1600 hours, you observe that there is a large accumulation of combustible rubbish at a building which is in the process of being demolished. Your inspection reveals that there is an accumulation of between 16 to 18 cubic yards of combustible debris that has been left for several days in an open area outside of this building.
In this situation, you would be CORRECT to have a violation order issued requiring compliance

   A. in 5 days, as indicated in the standard form of orders
   B. before the close of the day's work, as indicated in the standard form of orders
   C. in 5 days, as indicated in fire prevention directives
   D. before the close of the day's work, as indicated in fire prevention directives

23. A lieutenant of a tower ladder is discussing apparatus maintenance with a newly qualified chauffeur.
Which one of the following should the lieutenant instruct the chauffeur to do on a weekly basis? Check the

   A. transmission for fluid level
   B. basket gates and locks for cracks in welds
   C. hydraulic lines to the main reservoir for signs of possible failure
   D. suspension of leaf springs for broken sections

24. The company commander has delegated to a lieutenant the task of organizing a maintenance schedule for the unit's Seagrave rear mount aerial ladder.
In accordance with fire department procedures, the schedule the lieutenant should establish for the non-emergency operational test of the aerial ladder is once a _____ for a period of _____ seconds.

   A. month; not more than 30
   B. month; at least 60
   C. week; not more than 30
   D. week; at least 60

25. While conducting a drill on the operation of the Akron New Yorker Multiversal Nozzle, a lieutenant would be CORRECT to

   A. insure that members neither release the elevation safety stop nor operate below 35 above horizontal when in the portable mode
   B. prevent the backward movement of the Multiversal Nozzle by having members secure it with either a utility rope or the safety chain when in the portable mode
   C. inform members that horizontal rotation of 360 is possible without repositioning the nozzle when in the truck mount mode
   D. order members to sharpen or replace the spikes after each use if the flats on the ends of the spikes exceed 1/16" in diameter

KEY (CORRECT ANSWERS)

1.	D	11.	B
2.	A	12.	D
3.	C	13.	A
4.	A	14.	B
5.	A	15.	A
6.	C	16.	D
7.	D	17.	B
8.	C	18.	C
9.	B	19.	D
10.	A	20.	A

21. C
22. D
23. A
24. C
25. D

PHILOSOPHY, PRINCIPLES, PRACTICES, AND TECHNICS
OF
SUPERVISION, ADMINISTRATION, MANAGEMENT, AND ORGANIZATION

TABLE OF CONTENTS

	Page
MEANING OF SUPERVISION	1
THE OLD AND THE NEW SUPERVISION	1
THE EIGHT (8) BASIC PRINCIPLES OF THE NEW SUPERVISION	1
I. Principle of Responsibility	1
II. Principle of Authority	2
III. Principle of Self-Growth	2
IV. Principle of Individual Worth	2
V. Principle of Creative Leadership	2
VI. Principle of Success and Failure	2
VII. Principle of Science	3
VIII. Principle of Cooperation	3
WHAT IS ADMINISTRATION?	3
I. Practices Commonly Classed as "Supervisory"	3
II. Practices Commonly Classed as "Administrative"	3
III. Practices Commonly Classed as Both "Supervisory" and "Administrative"	4
RESPONSIBILITIES OF THE SUPERVISOR	4
COMPETENCIES OF THE SUPERVISOR	4
THE PROFESSIONAL SUPERVISOR-EMPLOYEE RELATIONSHIP	4
MINI-TEXT IN SUPERVISION, ADMINISTRATION, MANAGEMENT, AND ORGANIZATION	5
I. Brief Highlights	5
A. Levels of Management	6
B. What the Supervisor Must Learn	6
C. A Definition of Supervision	6
D. Elements of the Team Concept	6
E. Principles of Organization	6
F. The Four Important Parts of Every Job	7
G. Principles of Delegation	7
H. Principles of Effective Communications	7
I. Principles of Work Improvement	7
J. Areas of Job Improvement	7
K. Seven Key Points in Making Improvements	8

	L.	Corrective Techniques for Job Improvement	8
	M.	A Planning Checklist	8
	N.	Five Characteristics of Good Directions	9
	O.	Types of Directions	9
	P.	Controls	9
	Q.	Orienting the New Employee	9
	R.	Checklist for Orienting New Employees	9
	S.	Principles of Learning	10
	T.	Causes of Poor Performance	10
	U.	Four Major Steps in On-the-Job Instructions	10
	V.	Employees Want Five Things	10
	W.	Some Don'ts in Regard to Praise	11
	X.	How to Gain Your Workers' Confidence	11
	Y.	Sources of Employee Problems	11
	Z.	The Supervisor's Key to Discipline	11
	AA.	Five Important Processes of Management	12
	BB.	When the Supervisor Fails to Plan	12
	CC.	Fourteen General Principles of Management	12
	DD.	Change	12
II.	Brief Topical Summaries		13
	A.	Who/What is the Supervisor?	13
	B.	The Sociology of Work	13
	C.	Principles and Practices of Supervision	14
	D.	Dynamic Leadership	14
	E.	Processes for Solving Problems	15
	F.	Training for Results	15
	G.	Health, Safety, and Accident Prevention	16
	H.	Equal Employment Opportunity	16
	I.	Improving Communications	16
	J.	Self-Development	17
	K.	Teaching and Training	17
		1. The Teaching Process	17
		a. Preparation	17
		b. Presentation	18
		c. Summary	18
		d. Application	18
		e. Evaluation	18
		2. Teaching Methods	18
		a. Lecture	18
		b. Discussion	18
		c. Demonstration	19
		d. Performance	19
		e. Which Method to Use	19

PHILOSOPHY, PRINCIPLES, PRACTICES, AND TECHNICS
OF
SUPERVISION, ADMINISTRATION, MANAGEMENT, AND ORGANIZATION

MEANING OF SUPERVISION

The extension of the democratic philosophy has been accompanied by an extension in the scope of supervision. Modern leaders and supervisors no longer think of supervision in the narrow sense of being confined chiefly to visiting employees, supplying materials, or rating the staff. They regard supervision as being intimately related to all the concerned agencies of society, they speak of the supervisor's function in terms of "growth," rather than the "improvement" of employees.

This modern concept of supervision may be defined as follows: Supervision is leadership and the development of leadership within groups which are cooperatively engaged in inspection, research, training, guidance, and evaluation.

THE OLD AND THE NEW SUPERVISION

TRADITIONAL
1. Inspection
2. Focused on the employee
3. Visitation
4. Random and haphazard
5. Imposed and authoritarian
6. One person usually

MODERN
1. Study and analysis
2. Focused on aims, materials, methods, supervisors, employees, environment
3. Demonstrations, intervisitation, workshops, directed reading, bulletins, etc.
4. Definitely organized and planned (scientific)
5. Cooperative and democratic
6. Many persons involved (creative)

THE EIGHT (8) BASIC PRINCIPLES OF THE NEW SUPERVISION

I. Principle of Responsibility
    Authority to act and responsibility for acting must be joined.
    A. If you give responsibility, give authority.
    B. Define employee duties clearly.
    C. Protect employees from criticism by others.
    D. Recognize the rights as well as obligations of employees.
    E. Achieve the aims of a democratic society insofar as it is possible within the area of your work.
    F. Establish a situation favorable to training and learning.
    G. Accept ultimate responsibility for everything done in your section, unit, office, division, department.
    H. Good administration and good supervision are inseparable.

II. Principle of Authority
The success of the supervisor is measured by the extent to which the power of authority is not used.
   A. Exercise simplicity and informality in supervision
   B. Use the simplest machinery of supervision
   C. If it is good for the organization as a whole, it is probably justified.
   D. Seldom be arbitrary or authoritative.
   E. Do not base your work on the power of position or of personality.
   F. Permit and encourage the free expression of opinions.

III. Principle of Self-Growth
The success of the supervisor is measured by the extent to which, and the speed with which, he is no longer needed.
   A. Base criticism on principles, not on specifics.
   B. Point out higher activities to employees.
   C. Train for self-thinking by employees to meet new situations.
   D. Stimulate initiative, self-reliance, and individual responsibility
   E. Concentrate on stimulating the growth of employees rather than on removing defects.

IV. Principle of Individual Worth
Respect for the individual is a paramount consideration in supervision.
   A. Be human and sympathetic in dealing with employees.
   B. Don't nag about things to be done.
   C. Recognize the individual differences among employees and seek opportunities to permit best expression of each personality.

V. Principle of Creative Leadership
The best supervision is that which is not apparent to the employee.
   A. Stimulate, don't drive employees to creative action.
   B. Emphasize doing good things.
   C. Encourage employees to do what they do best.
   D. Do not be too greatly concerned with details of subject or method.
   E. Do not be concerned exclusively with immediate problems and activities.
   F. Reveal higher activities and make them both desired and maximally possible.
   G. Determine procedures in the light of each situation but see that these are derived from a sound basic philosophy.
   H. Aid, inspire, and lead so as to liberate the creative spirit latent in all good employees.

VI. Principle of Success and Failure
There are no unsuccessful employees, only unsuccessful supervisors who have failed to give proper leadership.
   A. Adapt suggestions to the capacities, attitudes, and prejudices of employees.
   B. Be gradual, be progressive, be persistent.
   C. Help the employee find the general principle; have the employee apply his own problem to the general principle.
   D. Give adequate appreciation for good work and honest effort.
   E. Anticipate employee difficulties and help to prevent them.
   F. Encourage employees to do the desirable things they will do anyway.
   G. Judge your supervision by the results it secures.

VII. Principle of Science
Successful supervision is scientific, objective, and experimental. It is based on facts, not on prejudices.
   A. Be cumulative in results.
   B. Never divorce your suggestions from the goals of training.
   C. Don't be impatient of results.
   D. Keep all matters on a professional, not a personal, level.
   E. Do not be concerned exclusively with immediate problems and activities.
   F. Use objective means of determining achievement and rating where possible.

VIII. Principle of Cooperation
Supervision is a cooperative enterprise between supervisor and employee.
   A. Begin with conditions as they are.
   B. Ask opinions of all involved when formulating policies.
   C. Organization is as good as its weakest link.
   D. Let employees help to determine policies and department programs.
   E. Be approachable and accessible—physically and mentally.
   F. Develop pleasant social relationships.

WHAT IS ADMINISTRATION

Administration is concerned with providing the environment, the material facilities, and the operational procedures that will promote the maximum growth and development of supervisors and employees. (Organization is an aspect and a concomitant of administration.)

There is no sharp line of demarcation between supervision and administration; these functions are intimately interrelated and, often, overlapping. They are complementary activities.

I. Practices Commonly Classed as "Supervisory"
   A. Conducting employees' conferences
   B. Visiting sections, units, offices, divisions, departments
   C. Arranging for demonstrations
   D. Examining plans
   E. Suggesting professional reading
   F. Interpreting bulletins
   G. Recommending in-service training courses
   H. Encouraging experimentation
   I. Appraising employee morale
   J. Providing for intervisitation

II. Practices Commonly Classified as "Administrative"
   A. Management of the office
   B. Arrangement of schedules for extra duties
   C. Assignment of rooms or areas
   D. Distribution of supplies
   E. Keeping records and reports
   F. Care of audio-visual materials
   G. Keeping inventory records
   H. Checking record cards and books

  I. Programming special activities
  J. Checking on the attendance and punctuality of employees

III. Practices Commonly Classified as Both "Supervisory" and "Administrative"
  A. Program construction
  B. Testing or evaluating outcomes
  C. Personnel accounting
  D. Ordering instructional materials

RESPONSIBILITIES OF THE SUPERVISOR

A person employed in a supervisory capacity must constantly be able to improve his own efficiency and ability. He represent the employer to the employees and only continuous self-examination can make him a capable supervisor.

Leadership and training are the supervisor's responsibility. An efficient working unit is one in which the employees work with the supervisor. It is his job to bring out the best in his employees. He must always be relaxed, courteous, and calm in his association with his employees. Their feelings are important, and a harsh attitude does not develop the most efficient employees.

COMPETENCES OF THE SUPERVISOR

  I. Complete knowledge of the duties and responsibilities of his position.
  II. To be able to organize a job, plan ahead, and carry through.
  III. To have self-confidence and initiative.
  IV. To be able to handle the unexpected situation and make quick decisions.
  V. To be able to properly train subordinates in the positions they are best suited for.
  VI. To be able to keep good human relations among his subordinates.
  VII. To be able to keep good human relations between his subordinates and himself and to earn their respect and trust.

THE PROFESSIONAL SUPERVISOR-EMPLOYEE RELATIONSHIP

There are two kinds of efficiency: one kind is only apparent and is produced in organizations through the exercise of mere discipline; this is but a simulation of the second, or true, efficiency which springs from spontaneous cooperation. If you are a manager, no matter how great or small your responsibility, it is your job, in the final analysis, to create and develop this involuntary cooperation among the people whom you supervise. For, no matter how powerful a combination of money, machines, and materials a company may have, this is a dead and sterile thing without a team of willing, thinking, and articulate people to guide it.

The following 21 points are presented as indicative of the exemplary basic relationship that should exist between supervisor and employee:

1. Each person wants to be liked and respected by his fellow employee and wants to be treated with consideration and respect by his superior.
2. The most competent employee will make an error. However, in a unit where good relations exist between the supervisor and his employees, tenseness and fear do not exist. Thus, errors are not hidden or covered up, and the efficiency of a unit is not impaired.

3. Subordinates resent rules, regulations, or orders that are unreasonable or unexplained.
4. Subordinates are quick to resent unfairness, harshness, injustices, and favoritism.
5. An employee will accept responsibility if he knows that he will be complimented for a job well done, and not too harshly chastised for failure; that his supervisor will check the cause of the failure, and, if it was the supervisor's fault, he will assume the blame therefore. If it was the employee's fault, his supervisor will explain the correct method or means of handling the responsibility.
6. An employee wants to receive credit for a suggestion he has made, that is used. If a suggestion cannot be used, the employee is entitled to an explanation. The supervisor should not say "no" and close the subject.
7. Fear and worry slow up a worker's ability. Poor working environment can impair his physical and mental health. A good supervisor avoids forceful methods, threats, and arguments to get a job done.
8. A forceful supervisor is able to train his employees individually and as a team, and is able to motivate them in the proper channels.
9. A mature supervisor is able to properly evaluate his subordinates and to keep them happy and satisfied.
10. A sensitive supervisor will never patronize his subordinates.
11. A worthy supervisor will respect his employees' confidences.
12. Definite and clear-cut responsibilities should be assigned to each executive.
13. Responsibility should always be coupled with corresponding authority.
14. No change should be made in the scope or responsibilities of a position without a definite understanding to that effect on the part of all persons concerned.
15. No executive or employee, occupying a single position in the organization, should be subject to definite orders from more than one source.
16. Orders should never be given to subordinates over the head of a responsible executive. Rather than do this, the officer in question should be supplanted.
17. Criticisms of subordinates should, whoever possible, be made privately, and in no case should a subordinate be criticized in the presence of executives or employees of equal or lower rank.
18. No dispute or difference between executives or employees as to authority or responsibilities should be considered too trivial for prompt and careful adjudication.
19. Promotions, wage changes, and disciplinary action should always be approved by the executive immediately superior to the one directly responsible.
20. No executive or employee should ever be required, or expected, to be at the same time an assistant to, and critic of, another.
21. Any executive whose work is subject to regular inspection should, wherever practicable, be given the assistance and facilities necessary to enable him to maintain an independent check of the quality of his work.

MINI-TEXT IN SUPERVISION, ADMINISTRATION, MANAGEMENT, AND ORGANIZATION

I. Brief Highlights

Listed concisely and sequentially are major headings and important data in the field for quick recall and review.

A. Levels of Management
Any organization of some size has several levels of management. In terms of a ladder, the levels are:

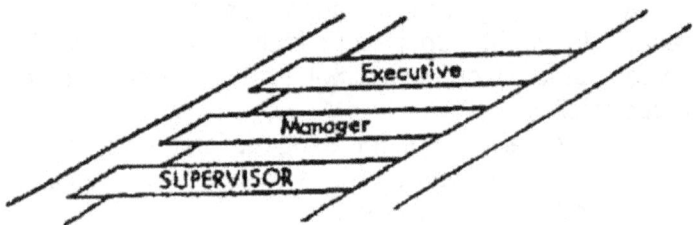

The first level is very important because it is the beginning point of management leadership.

B. What the Supervisor Must Learn
A supervisor must learn to:
1. Deal with people and their differences
2. Get the job done through people
3. Recognize the problems when they exist
4. Overcome obstacles to good performance
5. Evaluate the performance of people
6. Check his own performance in terms of accomplishment

C. A Definition of Supervisor
The term supervisor means any individual having authority, in the interests of the employer, to hire, transfer, suspend, lay-off, recall, promote, discharge, assign, reward, or discipline other employees or responsibility to direct them, or to adjust their grievances, or effectively to recommend such action, if, in connection with the foregoing, exercise of such authority is not of a merely routine or clerical nature but requires the use of independent judgment.

D. Elements of the Team Concept
What is involved in teamwork? The component parts are:
1. Members
2. A leader
3. Goals
4. Plans
5. Cooperation
6. Spirit

E. Principles of Organization
1. A team member must know what his job is.
2. Be sure that the nature and scope of a job are understood.
3. Authority and responsibility should be carefully spelled out.
4. A supervisor should be permitted to make the maximum number of decisions affecting his employees.
5. Employees should report to only one supervisor.
6. A supervisor should direct only as many employees as he can handle effectively.
7. An organization plan should be flexible.

8. Inspection and performance of work should be separate.
9. Organizational problems should receive immediate attention.
10. Assign work in line with ability and experience.

F. The Four Important Parts of Every Job
1. Inherent in every job is the *accountability* for results.
2. A second set of factors in every job is *responsibilities*.
3. Along with duties and responsibilities one must have the *authority* to act within certain limits without obtaining permission to proceed.
4. No job exists in a vacuum. The supervisor is surrounded by key *relationships*.

G. Principles of Delegation
Where work is delegated for the first time, the supervisor should think in terms of these questions:
1. Who is best qualified to do this?
2. Can an employee improve his abilities by doing this?
3. How long should an employee spend on this?
4. Are there any special problems for which he will need guidance?
5. How broad a delegation can I make?

H. Principles of Effective Communications
1. Determine the media.
2. To whom directed?
3. Identification and source authority.
4. Is communication understood?

I. Principles of Work Improvement
1. Most people usually do only the work which is assigned to them.
2. Workers are likely to fit assigned work into the time available to perform it.
3. A good workload usually stimulates output.
4. People usually do their best work when they know that results will be reviewed or inspected.
5. Employees usually feel that someone else is responsible for conditions of work, workplace layout, job methods, type of tools/equipment, and other such factors.
6. Employees are usually defensive about their job security.
7. Employees have natural resistance to change.
8. Employees can support or destroy a supervisor.
9. A supervisor usually earns the respect of his people through his personal example of diligence and efficiency.

J. Areas of Job Improvement
The areas of job improvement are quite numerous, but the most common ones which a supervisor can identify and utilize are:
1. Departmental layout
2. Flow of work
3. Workplace layout
4. Utilization of manpower
5. Work methods
6. Materials handling

7. Utilization
8. Motion economy

K. Seven Key Points in Making Improvements
1. Select the job to be improved
2. Study how it is being done now
3. Question the present method
4. Determine actions to be taken
5. Chart proposed method
6. Get approval and apply
7. Solicit worker participation

l. Corrective Techniques of Job Improvement
Specific Problems
1. Size of workload
2. Inability to meet schedules
3. Strain and fatigue
4. Improper use of men and skills
5. Waste, poor quality, unsafe conditions
6. Bottleneck conditions that hinder output
7. Poor utilization of equipment and machine
8. Efficiency and productivity of labor

General Improvement
1. Departmental layout
2. Flow of work
3. Work plan layout
4. Utilization of manpower
5. Work methods
6. Materials handling
7. Utilization of equipment
8. Motion economy

Corrective Techniques
1. Study with scale model
2. Flow chart study
3. Motion analysis
4. Comparison of units produced to standard allowance
5. Methods analysis
6. Flow chart and equipment study
7. Down time vs. running time
8. Motion analysis

M. A Planning Checklist
1. Objectives
2. Controls
3. Delegations
4. Communications
5. Resources
6. Manpower

7. Equipment
8. Supplies and materials
9. Utilization of time
10. Safety
11. Money
12. Work
13. Timing of improvements

N. Five Characteristics of Good Directions
In order to get results, directions must be:
1. Possible of accomplishment
2. Agreeable with worker interests
3. Related to mission
4. Planned and complete
5. Unmistakably clear

O. Types of Directions
1. Demands or direct orders
2. Requests
3. Suggestion or implication
4. volunteering

P. Controls
A typical listing of the overall areas in which the supervisor should establish controls might be:
1. Manpower
2. Materials
3. Quality of work
4. Quantity of work
5. Time
6. Space
7. Money
8. Methods

Q. Orienting the New Employee
1. Prepare for him
2. Welcome the new employee
3. Orientation for the job
4. Follow-up

R. Checklist for Orienting New Employees   Yes No
1. Do you appreciate the feelings of new employees when they first report for work? ___ ___
2. Are you aware of the fact that the new employee must make a big adjustment to his job? ___ ___
3. Have you given him good reasons for liking the job and the organization? ___ ___
4. Have you prepared for his first day on the job? ___ ___
5. Did you welcome him cordially and make him feel needed? ___ ___

		Yes	No

6. Did you establish rapport with him so that he feels free to talk and discuss matters with you? ___ ___
7. Did you explain his job to him and his relationship to you? ___ ___
8. Does he know that his work will be evaluated periodically on a basis that is fair and objective? ___ ___
9. Did you introduce him to his fellow workers in such a way that they are likely to accept him? ___ ___
10. Does he know what employee benefits he will receive? ___ ___
11. Does he understand the importance of being on the job and what to do if he must leave his duty station? ___ ___
12. Has he been impressed with the importance of accident prevention and safe practice? ___ ___
13. Does he generally know his way around the department? ___ ___
14. Is he under the guidance of a sponsor who will teach the right way of doing things? ___ ___
15. Do you plan to follow-up so that he will continue to adjust successfully to his job? ___ ___

S. Principles of Learning
  1. Motivation
  2. Demonstration or explanation
  3. Practice

T. Causes of Poor Performance
  1. Improper training for job
  2. Wrong tools
  3. Inadequate directions
  4. Lack of supervisory follow-up
  5. Poor communications
  6. Lack of standards of performance
  7. Wrong work habits
  8. Low morale
  9. Other

U. Four Major Steps in On-The-Job Instruction
  1. Prepare the worker
  2. Present the operation
  3. Tryout performance
  4. Follow-up

V. Employees Want Five Things
  1. Security
  2. Opportunity
  3. Recognition
  4. Inclusion
  5. Expression

W. Some Don'ts in Regard to Praise
1. Don't praise a person for something he hasn't done.
2. Don't praise a person unless you can be sincere.
3. Don't be sparing in praise just because your superior withholds it from you.
4. Don't let too much time elapse between good performance and recognition of it

X. How to Gain Your Workers' Confidence
Methods of developing confidence include such things as:
1. Knowing the interests, habits, hobbies of employees
2. Admitting your own inadequacies
3. Sharing and telling of confidence in others
4. Supporting people when they are in trouble
5. Delegating matters that can be well handled
6. Being frank and straightforward about problems and working conditions
7. Encouraging others to bring their problems to you
8. Taking action on problems which impede worker progress

Y. Sources of Employee Problems
On-the-job causes might be such things as:
1. A feeling that favoritism is exercised in assignments
2. Assignment of overtime
3. An undue amount of supervision
4. Changing methods or systems
5. Stealing of ideas or trade secrets
6. Lack of interest in job
7. Threat of reduction in force
8. Ignorance or lack of communications
9. Poor equipment
10. Lack of knowing how supervisor feels toward employee
11. Shift assignments

Off-the-job problems might have to do with:
1. Health
2. Finances
3. Housing
4. Family

Z. The Supervisor's Key to Discipline
There are several key points about discipline which the supervisor should keep in mind:
1. Job discipline is one of the disciplines of life and is directed by the supervisor.
2. It is more important to correct an employee fault than to fix blame for it.
3. Employee performance is affected by problems both on the job and off.
4. Sudden or abrupt changes in behavior can be indications of important employee problems.
5. Problems should be dealt with as soon as possible after they are identified.
6. The attitude of the supervisor may have more to do with solving problems than the techniques of problem solving.
7. Correction of employee behavior should be resorted to only after the supervisor is sure that training or counseling will not be helpful.

8. Be sure to document your disciplinary actions.
9. Make sure that you are disciplining on the basis of facts rather than personal feelings.
10. Take each disciplinary step in order, being careful not to make snap judgments, or decisions based on impatience.

AA. Five Important Processes of Management
1. Planning
2. Organizing
3. Scheduling
4. Controlling
5. Motivating

BB. When the Supervisor Fails to Plan
1. Supervisor creates impression of not knowing his job
2. May lead to excessive overtime
3. Job runs itself—supervisor lacks control
4. Deadlines and appointments missed
5. Parts of the work go undone
6. Work interrupted by emergencies
7. Sets a bad example
8. Uneven workload creates peaks and valleys
9. Too much time on minor details at expense of more important tasks

CC. Fourteen General Principles of Management
1. Division of work
2. Authority and responsibility
3. Discipline
4. Unity of command
5. Unity of direction
6. Subordination of individual interest to general interest
7. Remuneration of personnel
8. Centralization
9. Scalar chain
10. Order
11. Equity
12. Stability of tenure of personnel
13. Initiative
14. Esprit de corps

DD. Change

Bringing about change is perhaps attempted more often, and yet less well understood, than anything else the supervisor does. How do people generally react to change? (People tend to resist change that is imposed upon them by other individuals or circumstances.

Change is characteristic of every situation. It is a part of every real endeavor where the efforts of people are concerned.

1. Why do people resist change?
   People may resist change because of:
   a. Fear of the unknown
   b. Implied criticism
   c. Unpleasant experiences in the past
   d. Fear of loss of status
   e. Threat to the ego
   f. Fear of loss of economic stability

2. How can we best overcome the resistance to change?
   In initiating change, take these steps:
   a. Get ready to sell
   b. Identify sources of help
   c. Anticipate objections
   d. Sell benefits
   e. Listen in depth
   f. Follow up

II. Brief Topical Summaries

   A. Who/What is the Supervisor?
   1. The supervisor is often called the "highest level employee and the lowest level manager."
   2. A supervisor is a member of both management and the work group. He acts as a bridge between the two.
   3. Most problems in supervision are in the area of human relations, or people problems.
   4. Employees expect: Respect, opportunity to learn and to advance, and a sense of belonging, and so forth.
   5. Supervisors are responsible for directing people and organizing work. Planning is of paramount importance.
   6. A position description is a set of duties and responsibilities inherent to a given position.
   7. It is important to keep the position description up-to-date and to provide each employee with his own copy.

   B. The Sociology of Work
   1. People are alike in many ways; however, each individual is unique.
   2. The supervisor is challenged in getting to know employee differences. Acquiring skills in evaluating individuals is an asset.
   3. Maintaining meaningful working relationships in the organization is of great importance.
   4. The supervisor has an obligation to help individuals to develop to their fullest potential.
   5. Job rotation on a planned basis helps to build versatility and to maintain interest and enthusiasm in work groups.
   6. Cross training (job rotation) provides backup skills.

7. The supervisor can help reduce tension by maintaining a sense of humor, providing guidance to employees, and by making reasonable and timely decisions. Employees respond favorably to working under reasonably predictable circumstances.
8. Change is characteristic of all managerial behavior. The supervisor must adjust to changes in procedures, new methods, technological changes, and to a number of new and sometimes challenging situations.
9. To overcome the natural tendency for people to resist change, the supervisor should become more skillful in initiating change.

C. Principles and Practices of Supervision
1. Employees should be required to answer to only one superior.
2. A supervisor can effectively direct only a limited number of employees, depending upon the complexity, variety, and proximity of the jobs involved.
3. The organizational chart presents the organization in graphic form. It reflects lines of authority and responsibility as well as interrelationships of units within the organization.
4. Distribution of work can be improved through an analysis using the "Work Distribution Chart."
5. The "Work Distribution Chart" reflects the division of work within a unit in understandable form.
6. When related tasks are given to an employee, he has a better chance of increasing his skills through training.
7. The individual who is given the responsibility for tasks must also be given the appropriate authority to insure adequate results.
8. The supervisor should delegate repetitive, routine work. Preparation of recurring reports, maintaining leave and attendance records are some examples.
9. Good discipline is essential to good task performance. Discipline is reflected in the actions of employees on the job in the absence of supervision.
10. Disciplinary action may have to be taken when the positive aspects of discipline have failed. Reprimand, warning, and suspension are examples of disciplinary action.
11. If a situation calls for a reprimand, be sure it is deserved and remember it is to be done in private.

D. Dynamic Leadership
1. A style is a personal method or manner of exerting influence.
2. Authoritarian leaders often see themselves as the source of power and authority.
3. The democratic leader often perceives the group as the source of authority and power.
4. Supervisors tend to do better when using the pattern of leadership that is most natural for them.
5. Social scientists suggest that the effective supervisor use the leadership style that best fits the problem or circumstances involved.
6. All four styles—telling, selling, consulting, joining—have their place. Using one does not preclude using the other at another time.

7. The theory X point of view assumes that the average person dislikes work, will avoid it whenever possible, and must be coerced to achieve organizational objectives.
8. The theory Y point of view assumes that the average person considers work to be a natural as play, and, when the individual is committed, he requires little supervision or direction to accomplish desired objectives.
9. The leader's basic assumptions concerning human behavior and human nature affect his actions, decisions, and other managerial practices.
10. Dissatisfaction among employees is often present, but difficult to isolate. The supervisor should seek to weaken dissatisfaction by keeping promises, being sincere and considerate, keeping employees informed, and so forth.
11. Constructive suggestions should be encouraged during the natural progress of the work.

E. Processes for Solving Problems
1. People find their daily tasks more meaningful and satisfying when they can improve them.
2. The causes of problems, or the key factors, are often hidden in the background. Ability to solve problems often involves the ability to isolate them from their backgrounds. There is some substance to the cliché that some persons "can't see the forest for the trees."
3. New procedures are often developed from old ones. Problems should be broken down into manageable parts. New ideas can be adapted from old one.
4. People think differently in problem-solving situations. Using a logical, patterned approach is often useful. One approach found to be useful includes these steps:
   a. Define the problem
   b. Establish objectives
   c. Get the facts
   d. Weigh and decide
   e. Take action
   f. Evaluate action

F. Training for Results
1. Participants respond best when they feel training is important to them.
2. The supervisor has responsibility for the training and development of those who report to him.
3. When training is delegated to others, great care must be exercised to insure the trainer has knowledge, aptitude, and interest for his work as a trainer.
4. Training (learning) of some type goes on continually. The most successful supervisor makes certain the learning contributes in a productive manner to operational goals.
5. New employees are particularly susceptible to training. Older employees facing new job situations require specific training, as well as having need for development and growth opportunities.
6. Training needs require continuous monitoring.
7. The training officer of an agency is a professional with a responsibility to assist supervisors in solving training problems.

8. Many of the self-development steps important to the supervisor's own growth are equally important to the development of peers and subordinates. Knowledge of these is important when the supervisor consults with others on development and growth opportunities.

G. Health, Safety, and Accident Prevention
1. Management-minded supervisors take appropriate measures to assist employees in maintaining health and in assuring safe practices in the work environment.
2. Effective safety training and practices help to avoid injury and accidents.
3. Safety should be a management goal. All infractions of safety which are observed should be corrected without exception.
4. Employees' safety attitude, training and instruction, provision of safe tools and equipment, supervision, and leadership are considered highly important factors which contribute to safety and which can be influenced directly by supervisors.
5. When accidents do occur, they should be investigated promptly for very important reasons, including the fact that information which is gained can be used to prevent accidents in the future.

H. Equal Employment Opportunity
1. The supervisor should endeavor to treat all employees fairly, without regard to religion, race, sex, or national origin.
2. Groups tend to reflect the attitude of the leader. Prejudice can be detected even in very subtle form. Supervisors must strive to create a feeling of mutual respect and confidence in every employee.
3. Complete utilization of all human resources is a national goal. Equitable consideration should be accorded women in the work force, minority-group members, the physically and mentally handicapped, and the older employee. The important question is: "Who can do the job?"
4. Training opportunities, recognition for performance, overtime assignments, promotional opportunities, and all other personnel actions are to be handled on an equitable basis.

I. Improving Communications
1. Communications is achieving understanding between the sender and the receiver of a message. It also means sharing information—the creation of understanding.
2. Communication is basic to all human activity. Words are means of conveying meanings; however, real meanings are in people.
3. There are very practical differences in the effectiveness of one-way, impersonal, and two-way communications. Words spoken face-to-face are better understood. Telephone conversations are effective, but lack the rapport of person-to-person exchanges. The whole person communicates.
4. Cooperation and communication in an organization go hand in hand. When there is a mutual respect between people, spelling out rules and procedures for communicating is unnecessary.
5. There are several barriers to effective communications. These include failure to listen with respect and understanding, lack of skill in feedback, and misinterpreting the meanings of words used by the speaker. It is also common

practice to listen to what we want to hear, and tune out things we do not want to hear.
6. Communication is management's chief problem. The supervisor should accept the challenge to communicate more effectively and to improve interagency and intra-agency communications.
7. The supervisor may often plan for and conduct meetings. The planning phase is critical and may determine the success or the failure of a meeting.
8. Speaking before groups usually requires extra effort. Stage fright may never disappear completely, but it can be controlled.

J. Self-Development
1. Every employee is responsible for his own self-development.
2. Toastmaster and toastmistress clubs offer opportunities to improve skills in oral communications.
3. Planning for one's own self-development is of vital importance. Supervisors know their own strengths and limitations better than anyone else.
4. Many opportunities are open to aid the supervisor in his developmental efforts, including job assignments; training opportunities, both governmental and non-governmental—to include universities and professional conferences and seminars.
5. Programmed instruction offers a means of studying at one's own rate.
6. Where difficulties may arise from a supervisor's being away from his work for training, he may participate in televised home study or correspondence courses to meet his self-development needs.

K. Teaching and Training
1. The Teaching Process
Teaching is encouraging and guiding the learning activities of students toward established goals. In most cases this process consists of five steps: preparation, presentation, summarization, evaluation, and application.

   a. Preparation
   Preparation is two-fold in nature; that of the supervisor and the employee. Preparation by the supervisor is absolutely essential to success. He must know what, when, where, how, and whom he will teach. Some of the factors that should be considered are:
   1) The objectives
   2) The materials needed
   3) The methods to be used
   4) Employee participation
   5) Employee interest
   6) Training aids
   7) Evaluation
   8) Summarization

   Employee preparation consists in preparing the employee to receive the material. Probably the most important single factor in the preparation of the employee is arousing and maintaining his interest. He must know the objectives of the training, why he is there, how the material can be used, and its importance to him.

b. Presentation
   In presentation, have a carefully designed plan and follow it. The plan should be accurate and complete, yet flexible enough to meet situations as they arise. The method of presentation will be determined by the particular situation and objectives.

c. Summary
   A summary should be made at the end of every training unit and program. In addition, there may be internal summaries depending on the nature of the material being taught. The important thing is that the trainee must always be able to understand how each part of the new material relates to the whole.

d. Application
   The supervisor must arrange work so the employee will be given a chance to apply new knowledge or skills while the material is still clear in his mind and interest is high. The trainee does not really know whether he has learned the material until he has been given a chance to apply it. If the material is not applied, it loses most of its value.

e. Evaluation
   The purpose of all training is to promote learning. To determine whether the training has been a success or failure, the supervisor must evaluate this learning.
   In the broadest sense, evaluation includes all the devices, methods, skills, and techniques used by the supervisor to keep himself and the employees informed as to their progress toward the objectives they are pursuing. The extent to which the employee has mastered the knowledge, skills, and abilities, or changed his attitudes, as determined by the program objectives, is the extent to which instruction has succeeded or failed.
   Evaluation should not be confined to the end of the lesson, day, or program but should be used continuously. We shall note later the way this relates to the rest of the teaching process.

2. Teaching Methods
   A teaching method is a pattern of identifiable student and instructor activity used in presenting training material.
   All supervisors are faced with the problem of deciding which method should be used at a given time.

   a. Lecture
      The lecture is direct oral presentation of material by the supervisor. The present trend is to place less emphasis on the trainer's activity and more on that of the trainee.

   b. Discussion
      Teaching by discussion or conference involves using questions and other techniques to arouse interest and focus attention upon certain areas, and by doing so creating a learning situation. This can be one of the most

valuable methods because it gives the employees an opportunity to express their ideas and pool their knowledge.

    c. Demonstration
The demonstration is used to teach how something works or how to do something. It can be used to show a principle or what the results of a series of actions will be. A well-staged demonstration is particularly effective because it shows proper methods of performance in a realistic manner.

    d. Performance
Performance is one of the most fundamental of all learning techniques or teaching methods. The trainee may be able to tell how a specific operation should be performed but he cannot be sure he knows how to perform the operation until he has done so.
As with all methods, there are certain advantages and disadvantages to each method.

    e. Which Method to Use
Moreover, there are other methods and techniques of teaching. It is difficult to use any method without other methods entering into it. In any learning situation, a combination of methods is usually more effective than any one method alone.

Finally, evaluation must be integrated into the other aspects of the teaching-learning process.

It must be used in the motivation of the trainees; it must be used to assist in developing understanding during the training; and it must be related to employee application of the results of training.

This is distinctly the role of the supervisor.

THE BUILDING AND ITS MAKEUP

TABLE OF CONTENTS

	Page
BUILDING CONSTRUCTION	1
Introduction	1
General Construction Principles	1
Types of Building Construction	2
Building Materials and Contents	3
Building Code Requirements	7
Involvement of Ceilings	8
Building Elements	8
Interior Finish	9
MATERIALS	11
Introduction	11
Properties of Materials	11
Classes of Materials	12
UTILITY SYSTEMS	17
Introduction	17
Heating, Ventilation and Air Conditioning	18
Electrical	21

THE BUILDING AND ITS MAKEUP

BUILDING CONSTRUCTION

Introduction
In many cases the design, construction, and use of the building contributes to the initiation and severity of serious building fires. For these reasons, a knowledge of buildings, how they are constructed, and with what kinds of materials, is important to the fire investigator.

A knowledge and use of the correct terminology of building construction also is important in the writing of accurate reports, as well as in courtroom appearances. As an example, the investigator should know and be able to describe the similarities and the differences between spandrels, beams, and girders.

Sometimes in getting at the fire cause, it is necessary to "reconstruct" the arrangement and condition of the room or area of fire involvement to understand the development and spread of the fire. To do this "reconstruct", it is necessary to know what kinds of building materials and construction were likely to have been present prior to the fire damage. (Where there are similar rooms or areas available in the same or similar buildings, such as in hotels or garden apartments, a method to "reconstruct" is to examine undamaged units.)

General Construction Principles
The fire investigator should be familiar with the basic principles of building construction.

The initial concern of fire resistance provisions in building codes is that the building should not collapse as a result of a fire. Secondarily, the structure should limit the fire to an area of acceptable size.

Some elements of the system are more vulnerable to fire than others. When a fire occurs, the building is only as stable as the weakest (to fire) element.

All loads must be transmitted continuously to ground. This is accomplished by a multitude of structural components and connections in the structure. The importance of the connections varies. In some cases, the failure of a connection may have only a local effect. In other cases, the failure may be catastrophic in that a building collapse may occur.

Principal structural materials are wood, masonry (stone, brick, and concrete block), steel and reinforced concrete.

The principal elements of structures are walls, columns, and beams. Walls and columns carry the loads of the building down to the earth. Beams carry the loads generated on each floor of the building to the columns or walls.

Walls may be load-bearing, that is, carrying a load other than themselves, or be nonload-bearing, typically partitions and exterior veneer walls.

Columns carry vertical loads to the ground or foundation. Because columns take up space, suspension rods or cables in tension are sometimes used to "hang" certain loads in a building.

The system must, however, provide for the tensile load to be carried over into a column or wall and delivered to the earth in compression.

Floors and roofs are supported on beams and girders as well as on walls. A girder is a beam which supports other beams. Since beams must resist both tension (usually in the bottom of the beam) and compression forces (usually in the top), solid beams contain excess material. In many cases, the load can be carried on a lighter unit called a truss, which eliminates excess material. A trussconsists of a series of specially connected and designed load-carrying elements and open spaces, which makes it more vulnerable to fire and thus more likely to collapse than an equivalent solid beam.

Types of Building Construction

There are five basic construction types. Various building codes subdivide these types further (see table 1) The five types are:

Table 1 Types of Construction According to Model codes*

Construction Type	Basic Building Code, by Type (BOCA)	Standard Building Code, by Type (SBC)	Uniform Building Code, by type (UBC)	National Building Code, by Type (NBC)
Fire Resistive	1A	I	I	A
	1B	II	I	B
Noncombustiable Protected	2A		II (4 hr)	
	2B	IV (1 hr)	II (1 hr)	Protected Noncombustiable
None combustible Unprotected	2C	IV	II (N)	Unprotected Noncombustiable
Heavy Timber	3A	III	IV (HT)	Heavy Timber
Ordinary Protected	3B	V (1 hr)	III (1hr)	
Ordinary Unprotected	3C	V	III (N)	Ordinary
Wood Frame Protected	4A	VI (1hr)	V (1hr)	
Wood Frame Unprotected	4B	VI	V (N)	Wood Frame

* This Table indicates the type assigned by the respective codes to various construction types. It is not intended to indicate that different codes necessarily have identical requirements for any specific type.

Fire Resistive
Noncombustible
Heavy Timber
Ordinary Wood
Frame
Wood Frame

The investigator's report should use the terminology of the appropriate local code.

Note that the commonly used word "fireproof" does not appear in the list of types, though it may appear in some codes. When designers first considered fire as a problem they believed that all fire problems would be eliminated by constructing the building of noncombustible material. Such buildings were called "fireproof" and the misnomer has persisted. Early "fireproof" buildings were found deficient when put to the test of actual fires since all noncombustible materials will lose strength at sufficiently high temperatures. As technology improved, the term "fire resistive" emerged.

Fire Resistive buildings are ones in which specimens of the major structural components have been rated by standard fire endurance tests during which collapse and passage of fire, where appropriate, were resisted for prescribed periods of time. No direct relationship should be assumed between the "time" of the controlled test and an uncontrolled hostile fire. Whereas each of the elements of the building may meet fire resistance criteria, it is most unlikely that the building as a whole was ever analyzed for the total impact of a potential fire, and "the whole may be less than the sum of the parts". Fire resistance does not guarantee life safety. Fire resistance is not necessarily related to fire loss; in fact, while achieving its designed fire resistance, the structure may be damaged severely. Fire resistive assemblies are not necessarily noncombustible. Floors and walls of wood and gypsum board are assigned fire resistance ratings by UL (Underwriters Laboratories Inc.), even though the assemblies are combustible.

Depending upon how the fire resistance is achieved, different buildings of the same fire resistance rating may exhibit different characteristics in similar fires. For instance, a fire resistive floor of reinforced concrete absorbs considerable heat. A steel joist floor and ceiling assembly, of equal fire resistance, will not absorb as much heat. This can affect the propagation of a fire, as every Btu absorbed by the structure is one less available to keep the fire growing. As a second example, a rated reinforced concrete floor may act as a very effective smoke barrier. An equally rated floor and ceiling assembly with an integral air handling system could provide a path for travel of smoke and gases. This property is not considered in the test rating.

Noncombustible buildings are ones in which the walls, partitions and structural members are of noncombustible construction not qualifying as fire resistive construction.

Heavy Timber construction buildings have masonry exterior walls and heavy timber interiors. The concept is that the heavy timber is slow to ignite and burns at a slow enough rate that collapse may be delayed. The concept fails once the fire involves the building and the fire suppression forces cannot sustain an interior attack. The massive amount of timber then simply becomes a tremendous fire load.

Ordinary Construction buildings have masonry exterior walls and lightly constructed combustible interiors. The principal benefit of the masonry walls is to reduce the conflagration potential. The interior is expected to collapse in a fire and may be required by code to be so designed, the so-called fire cuts on wood joists are an example.

Wood Frame buildings are basically of wood construction. A noncombustible veneer, such as brick, does not change the nature or classification of the building.

Building Materials and Contents

Code regulations which limit the type and size of construction are predicated on the type of building, the type of occupancy anticipated, and the anticipated level of potential fire risk.

Estimates of the potential fire risk are based to a large extent on the fire load (or fuel load). For buildings of combustible construction the basic fire load is the building itself, thus such buildings are usually limited by code in area and height. In addition, for all buildings the weight of combustible contents per unit of floor area must be considered. Fire loads are usually expressed in the term pounds (of ordinary combustibles) per square foot. All weights are commonly converted to the equivalent of ordinary combustibles such as wood which has a heat value of about 8,000 Btu/lb. For instance, plastics which have a heat value of about 16,000 Btu/lb are converted at the rate of 1 lb of plastic to 2 lb ordinary combustibles.

Typical ranges of fire loads for the more common occupancy classes are shown in table 2. However, fire loads can vary considerably according to the occupancy the specific location in the building, and, other factors.

Table 2 Typical Fire Loads

Occupancy Classification	Typical Range of Fire Loads lb/sq ft
Residential	5 to 10
Educational	5 to 10
(Library)	(10 to 40)
Institutional	3 to 10
Assembly	5 to 10
Business (office)	5 to 10
(File, Storage)	(10 to 40)
Mercantile	10 to 20
Industrial	10 to 35
Storage	10 to 100
Hazardous	*

* No typical values available. Risk based on factors other than fire load

Structural fire protection requirements in building codes are based on fire resistance or fire endurance ratings expressed in hours. The ratings are basedon fire tests performed on the structural or compartmenting (separating) building components according to the NFPA 251 (ASTM E 119) standardized test procedure, The exposure is such that a temperature of 1000°F (538°C) is reached in 5 min, 1700°F (927°C) in 1 hr, 1850°F (1010°C) in 2 hrs, 2000°F (1093°C) in 4 hrs and 2300°F (1260°C) in 8 hrs. These temperatures-vs.-time points produce a curve which is referred to as the fire endurance standard time-temperature curve. The test is conducted in a special test furnace and continued until one of several criteria of failure, as appropriate, is reached: (a) structural failure (inability to sustain the applied load), (b) integrity failure (development of a crack or opening through which flames or hot gases may pass during the fire test, or a hose stream test) or, (c) insulation failure (heat transmission sufficient to raise the temperature on the unexposed surface by 250°F (139°C) average).

Although the standard fire test curve represents only one type of fire exposure, it serves as a useful means for the comparative rating of individual columns, beams, walls, partitions, and floor and ceiling assemblies. Again, it should be stressed that although the ratings are expressed in hours, the relationship between the rating hours and hours of an actual fire assault on a building may differ.

A relationship between fire load and equivalent fire endurance period was developed many years ago based on experimental burnouts of combustibles in special masonry test buildings and is shown in table 3. Table.3 indicates that the burning of a fire load of 10 lbs of ordinary combustibles per square foot (or 80,000 Btu/sq ft) is the approximate equivalent of 1 hour of the standard fire test ASTM E 119.

If these figures are used cautiously and broadly, rather than precisely, it is possible to estimate whether, in a given fire, the fire load was grossly excessive for the fire resistance of the building. Consider a building with floors rated two-hour fire-resistive. Such a building might reasonably be expected to successfully resist a fire involving a design fire load of 160,000 Btu/sq ft average. On the other hand, an investigator may estimate that in the affected area of an actual fire, the fire load was 300,000 Btu/sq ft average. It can be reasonably concluded that the fire area was overloaded from the fire endurance point of view, even though the total structural loading may have been within permissible limits.

Table 3. Fire Load versus Equivalent Fire Endurance Period in Standard Fire Test

Fire Load 1b sq ft	Equivalent Fire Endurance Period hr
5	½
7 ½	¾
10	1
15	1 ½
20	2
30	3
40	4 ½
50	6
60	7 ½

Structural members and floors are made fire resistive in a variety of ways.

Reinforced concrete has inherent fire resistance. This inherent fire resistance can be increased to the desired level by increasing the concrete cover over the "reinforcing" steel. If the depth of the concrete cover is not as specified, early failure may result.

Steel must be protected from the harmful effects of elevated temperatures (loss of strength, elongation and heat transmission). Protection can be accomplished in several ways, including encasement, sprayed fireproofing, membrane protection or by using water- filled columns. In a particular building more than one way may be used.

Encasement. Each structural steel member is encased in an insulating cover; hollow tile, poured concrete, concrete block, wire lath and plaster or gypsum board are typically used.

Sprayed "Fireproofing". In this case structural steel members are spraye or trowele with plaster containing inorganic fibers or cement. One common material formerly used, asbestos, is held responsible for health hazards due to inhalation in many buildings. In some cases this has caused its removal, sometimes without any provision for replacing the necessary fire resistance. Sprayed "fireproofing" may be poorly done and in many cases is found to have fallen off or been removed by other building trades

Membrane Protection. Large areas, such as entire floors, are protected by a membrane,"consisting typically of a wire lath and plaster ceiling or a suspended ceiling of individual panels. The problem is that, like all membranes, a single penetration may reduce the effectiveness of the entire membrane. Wire lath and plaster membranes are designed to be permanent and generally left in place but individual acoustical tile (panel) ceilings are readily removable.

The entire floor and ceiling assembly is fire rated as a unit. The presumption is that the unit is installed the same way as the unit tested. Even if this is accomplished, the ceiling tiles may be removed for many reasons. The fact that the ceiling tiles are part of the fire resistance of the building is unknown to many building owners and operators and fire inspectors. Untested penetrations as for sound system speakers are another weakness. Any tampering with the ceiling opens the entire floor area up to attack by fire. The void space between the ceiling and the floor above represents a potential for lateral fire spread between every floor of the building. There can be a substantial fire load in the void due to plastic insulation and piping, and lightweight merchandise is sometimes found stored in the void.

In one case, fire in one occupancy entered the void and extended downward to combustible shelves and contents in the next occupancy, This was detected early enough to clearly show what had happened. Had the extension not been detected, all appearances would have been of two separate fires. In fact, the fire was incendiary and successfully prosecuted. Failure to describe the development of the fire accurately might have led to a loss of the case.

Current lists of fire rated constructions and assemblies are maintained by Underwriters Laboratories -- the American Insurance Association -- and the Factory Mutual System.

Almost any structure has some degree of fire resistance, even though it is itself combustible. Table 4 is provided to enable the investigator to develop estimated fire resistance values for some common wall and floor assemblies. It consists of two parts. In the first part values are given for some common materials used as membranes (the surface finish). The second part gives values for framing members

For example, using table 4, unprotected open web steel joists are assigned a value of 7 minutes. With 1/2" gypsum wallboard properly attached and sealed, the combination could be assigned a time of 22 minutes (7 minutes for the steel joists, 15 minutes for the gypsum wallboard).

A wood stud wall with 1/2" gypsum board on both sides could be assigned a value of 50 minutes (20 minutes for the studs plus 15 minutes for each layer of the wallboard). It should be stated here again that the times referred to are estimates of how long the structure in question would continue to meet the standards of ASTM E 119 (NFPA 251) when tested in accordance with that standard. There is no necessary relationship to elapsed time in a hostile fire.

Table 4 Time Assigned to wallboard membranes

	Description of Finish	Time Assigned to Membrane in Minutes
(i)	½ in Fiberboard	5
(ii)	3/8 in Douglas Fir Plywood Phenolic bonded	5
(iii)	½ in Douglas Fir Plywood Phenolic bonded	10
(iv)	5/8 in Douglas Fir Plywood Phenolic bonded	15
(v)	3/8 in Gypsum Wallboard	10
(vi)	½ in Gypsum Wallboard	15
(vii)	5/8 in Gypsum Wallboard	30
(viii)	Double 3/8 in gypsum Wallboard	25
(ix)	½ + 3/8 in Gypsum Wallboard	35
(x)	Double ½ in Gypsum Wallboard	50(1)
(xi)	3/16 in Asb. Cem. + in Gypsum Wallboard	40(2)
(xii)	3/16 in asb. Cem. + ½ in Gypsum Wallboard	50(2)
(xiii)	Composit 1/8 in Asb. Cem. 7/16 in Fibreboard	20

1) No. 16 s.w.g. 1 in sq wire mesh must be fastened between the two sheets of wallboard.
2) Values shown apply to walls only.

Time Assigned for Contribution of Wood or Light Steel Frame

Description of Frame	Time Assigned to from in Minutes
i. Wood Stud walls	20
ii. Steel Stud Wall	10
iii. Wood Joist Floors and Roofs	10
iv. Open Web Steel Joist Floors and roofs	10(07)

Building Code Requirements

In many cases a building is not required by code to be fire resistive but the designer chooses to use components which resemble rated fire resistive units (or which may in fact be rated). For instance, structures recently observed in the Washington, DC area are rated as Type 3C (unprotected ordinary) under the BOCA (Building Officials and Code Administrator's International, Inc.) Basic Building Code. The floors are of bar joist construction with concrete topping on corrugated metal. The suspended ceilings need only meet Fire Hazard (flame spread) requirements. When the job is finished its appearance will be similar to a rated floor and ceiling assembly and protected with the same surface finish. Wood joists would have been acceptable under the code and the floor as installed may not be as resistive to collapse as a wood joisted floor.

In a fire investigation it may be necessary to determine whether or not a fire-resistive structure or structural element reacted to the fire in a manner consistent with its rating. This can be extraordinarily difficult. Assuming that the building was required to meet fire resistance standards, there can be several reasons for determination of the reason for failure to perform adequately. Information developed may be of use in prosecution, civil actions, code changes or fire suppression planning.

Did the building meet code requirements? This requires a thorough knowledge of code requirements at the time the building was built and access to original drawings, change orders and officially authorized variances.

Possibly, in fact, the building met modern code requirements but when given the ultimate test, the fire, the code requirements were proven inadequate. Such information, properly developed and carefully documented, is vital to translating costly experience into recommended code revisions.

Valuable information also can be developed to aid fire suppression forces in preplanning and combating future fires in the same or similar buildings. For example, the investigation may develop information that the sealant of the floor slab to the panel exterior walls was made of foamed plastic which lacks "dimensional stability" (that is, it melts). If this was permitted in one building, it may exist in other buildings built about the same time.

Involvement of Ceilings

Fires generally burn upward. Thus, the ceilings and upper parts of walls are generally exposed to higher temperatures than the lower parts of walls and floors. Fire exposed ceilings can fail early in fires, sometimes considerably earlier than a fire test rating would indicate. The fact that a particular ceiling fell may be an important element in an investigation. It cannot be assumed that the ceiling stayed in place for as long as one might conclude from its quoted fire rating.

Recently there have been a number of cases of fires burning downward (10). Many plastics when ignited form a pool of fire on the floor. The plastic may be from building contents or it may have been installed as part of the wall or ceiling.

Material falling from the ceiling may extend the fire beyond the area of origin. Consider a noncombustible building with steel bar joists with combustible tile ceiling mounted on the bottom side of the joists. There is a gap atop the masonry partition wall equal to the height of the top chord of the joist. Heated gases passing through this gap into the adjacent space may ignite the combustible tiles on their upper side. They may fall, extending the fire beyond the masonry wall.

Building Elements

Historically the chief consideration in building fire problems has been given to the Structural Elements of the building, but in building fires three elements can be identified:

- Structural Elements
- Nonstructural Elements
- Contents

The structural elements are those which are necessary to the stability of the building. The nonstructural elements may be more important in the development and extension of a fire than the structural elements. Nonstructural elements which contribute to the fire are independent of the type of construction and may be found in any of the five structural types discussed. For instance, a high flame spread interior finish of plywood and fiber tile may be found in any type building. The life hazard due to rapid flame spread over the surface will be the same. In the case of a combustible building the interior finish may be the kindling which ignites the structure. In the case of a noncombustible or fire-resistive structure, the structure will not be ignited, but substantial damage may be done to structural elements.

Nonstructural elements can include the electrical system, interior finish on ceilings, walls, and floors, air handling systems, openings from floor to floor such as shafts, stairways, interior courts, and combustible exterior surfaces and insulation.

In the majority of fires the initial fuel is the contents. Only rarely is the building directly ignited.

Interior Finish

Up to World War II there was only one significant interior finish, plaster installed over either wood lath or metal lath. It is noncombustible and, when properly installed, provides a degree of fire resistance for combustible structural elements. If the plaster is penetrated and if wood lath is present, the wood lath may provide substantial fuel.

The interior finish of the building may be the most important single element in the development and spread of a fire. In a number of cases interior finish has been a major factor in the rapid spread of fire and resultant loss of life.

Interior finish may be applied to the ceiling, walls or floors. Building codes have applied specific limitations on the flame spread classification of wall and ceiling materials. Floor coverings are less likely to be regulated but flame spread over carpeting, for example, has been an important factor in a number of serious fires. Standards and techniques for measuring carpeting flame spread have been developed recently and these regulations have begun to appear in the codes.

There are a number of ways in which the restriction of high flame spread interior finishes can be circumvented which do not appear in the code regulations. Materials which would not be permitted by the code if attached to the building may appear in significant amounts as furniture, in exhibits, as free standing office dividers, and in merchandise displays.

Alterations are sometimes accomplished without a building permit and buildings properly built have been altered with the use of high flame spread ceiling or wall materials.

Even the building permit does not guarantee safety. Consider a building with a combustible acoustical tile ceiling. It is planned to "modernize" the room by installing a ceiling grid with tiles and light fixtures mounted below the existing ceiling. A local code may require the new tiles to meet flame spread requirements but there is no requirement to remove the old combustible ceiling hidden in the void. Such a hidden ceiling can generate heat and gases which can move upward through available openings.

The investigator must try to get an accurate description of the wall and ceiling surfaces before the fire. Often only very slight clues are available, for example, nails holding scraps of furring strip to joists may indicate that there was a combustible acoustical ceiling. Adhesive beading on a wall may indicate where paneling had been secured with adhesive. Small pieces may be found behind unburned baseboard.

Table 5 contains a listing of selected materials commonly used for interior finish in buildings and a rough classification according to flame spread rating by ASTM E 84. This tabulation is intended only as a general guide and the reader should not assume that all material of the same

10

Table 5 Approximate Spread Raing (E-84 Tunnel Test)

Ceilings

Gypsum Plaster	0
Sprayed Mineral-base plaster	0-20
Enameled metal	0-20
Mineral fiber tile	10-25
Glass or mineral fiber bord or title, coated	10-40
Wood-base acousical tile (flame proofed)	20-75
Wood-base acoustical tile (untreated)	75-300

Walls

Brick, concrete, asbestos-cement board, ceremic tile, gypsum plaster	0
Enameled st eel, aluminum	0-20
Gypsum board, various facings	10-50
Wood, fiberboard (flame-retardant treated)	20-75
Plastic Paneling (flame-retardant-treated)	20-75
Wood, at least 0.5 in thick, various species	70-200
Plywood paneling	70-300
Hardoard	100-250
Cork	200-500
Cloth, paper, wood veneer, fiberboard (untreated)	200-500
Shellac finish on wood	500+

Floors*

Concrete, terrazzo	0
Vinyl Asbestos Tile	10-50
Red oak	100
Linoleum	100-300
Carpeting**	50-600

* Use of E 84 Tunnel Test on Floor Covering Materials is no longer recommended. See other Methods, for example, NFPA 253 and ASTM E648
** Depends on type of face fiber, uunderlayment, method of attachment if glued down, loose, etc.

all materials of the same generic type will perform in a similar manner. Furthermore, although a flame spread classification rating or label denotes that a test has been performed on a sample of the material, there is no assurance that the material will not contribute in a major way to the spread of a fire in an actual building situation. A fire investigator should not hesitate to request that tests be performed on samples of unburned material removed from the building where the finish material appears to have contributed significantly to the fire.

In removing materials for testing the investigator should understand how the test is done so that proper samples will be obtained. If it is possible that criminal proceedings will develop, the samples must be treated as any other criminal evidence.

ASTM E 84, the Steiner Tunnel Test, is the usual basis for legal regulation of flame spread. The sample required is about 22 in width and 24 ft (565 mm x 7.32 m) in length. It may not be easy to get a sample of this size, but it may be necessary.

The fact that the method of attachment is important to the actual flame spread of combustible tiles was discovered when a full size sample of tiles glued to gypsum board showed a much greater flame spread than the same tiles, removed from the board for shipment

ASTM E 162 requires a sample only 6 x 18 in (15 x 46 cm). Samples this size is easier to get. For some materials, results from this test can be correlated in a general way with ASTM E 84 but no direct relationship should be assumed. The information developed can be useful in developing better code requirements. If the question of discrepancy in the installed material is going to be criminally significant, the prosecutor should be made aware of the difference in these tests because it might be critical to the case that the test be performed under the same conditions as the code requires, which would almost invariably be ASTME 84.

Carpeting should first be tested to the requirements of FF 1-70 (11), al so known as the "pill test". The "pill test" only measures the ignitability of the carpet from small flame sources, such as a dropped, burning match. If the carpet passed the "pill test", and it was thought to have contributed significantly to the fire, it may be useful to test the flame spread properties of the carpet, properties which are not involved in the "pill test". One flame spread test procedure is that given in NFPA 253, Standard Method of Test for Critical Radiant Flux of Floor Covering Systems Using a Radiant Heat Energy Source. For this test, samples 10 x 42 in (25 x 107 cm) are required. If a pad was used with the carpet, this pad should be included with the carpet in the test.

Nearly all carpets will spread fire if the exposure is sufficiently intense. However, some carpets spread fire under less heat exposure than others. If a pad is used under a carpet, the pad generally will cause an increase in the carpet's flame spread characteristics. The purpose of conducting the NFPA 253 test is to determine whether the carpet spreads fire easily or is more resistant to this spread than other carpets. The results of NFPA 253 will be a number called the critical radiant flux (CRF). To compare this number against other carpets, one should then refer to reference which lists the CRF's for many different types of carpets, with and without padding.

MATERIALS

Introduction

Knowledge of the effect of fire and high temperature on all types of materials -- construction, interior finish, furnishings and contents is essential to the job of the fire investigator. In searching through a burned building, the investigator should make note of the materials which were relatively unaffected as well as those which burned, charred and melted. The historical patterns of fires in buildings should be recognized and comparative differences or similarities noted.

Properties of Materials

There are many properties of materials which determine their response to fire and high temperature, as well as the contribution they may make to the growth of a fire. The principal fire properties of organic materials are heat of combustion and ignition temperature. Other thermal and mechanical properties include heat conductivity: ·specific heat (heat absorption capacity), melting and softening points, coefficient of expansion (elongation due to heating), shrinkage, cracking, etc. Some typical thermal properties are listed in table 6.

The high thermal conductivity of metals can be a means of spreading fire, for example, through sheets, ducts, joints, connectors and fasteners. Specific heat (or more accurately volumetric heat capacity) is a measure of the capacity to absorb and store heat. A material with a high heat capacity will heat up slower and may keep the maximum air temperatures lower but it will also retain the heat longer. Where high temperatures exists, thermal radiation is important and shiny surfaces (aluminum, steel, mirrors) may reflect the heat to other surfaces. While reflective surfaces would be expected to remain cooler, in most cases smoke deposition, oxidation and other changes often occur on shiny surfaces so that they eventually absorb as well as most other materials. Melting and softening points are obvious indicators of fire scene temperatures, provided allowance is made for fallen ceilings (which may protect materials at floor level), heat sinks (metals, for example, or water) and exposure to heat prior to the fire.

Classes of Materials

Masonry. In common usage, this term includes precast or cast-in-place concrete, concrete and cinder block, brick, stone, cement and clay tiles (terra cotta). Under fire exposure, many masonry walls will remain intact. However, due to thermal expansion caused by severe heating of the exposed surface (usually the interior surface), ordinary brick, block and stone walls may sometimes lean out at the top and collapse. The integrity of masonry walls depends to a large extent on the quality of the mortar bond at the joints. Collapse also may occur for other reasons, including failure of a non-masonry supporting element, thermal expansion of floors, beams or trusses, or impact loading due to collapse of a floor, a roof, another building, or an explosion. A brick veneer wall depends for its integrity on the wooden structural wall to which it is fastened. If the wooden wall is damaged, the brick wall may collapse.

Table 6 Typical Thermal Properties of Selected Materials

Materials	Density Lbs/Cu Ft	Thermal[1] Conductivity Btu-in Hr ft2 °F	Spefic[2] Heat Btu/lb °F	Percent Increase in Length for each 100° Temp Rise	Melting Point °F
Air	0.06	0.2	0.24		
Water	62	5	1.0	0.01	32
Aluminum	165	1400	0.22	0.14	1220
Brass	530	720	0.09	0.11	1650
Copper	560	2600	0.09	0.09	1980
Cast iron	440	320	0.13	0.06	2466-2550
Steel	490	310	0.12	0.06-0.15[3]	2370-2550
Glass	160	6	0.20	0.04-0.06	2600
Brick	120	5	0.22	0.05	--
Concrete, normal Weight	140	9-12	0.16-0.25	0.06-0.08	--
	120	4	0.2		
Asbestos-cement board	45	1.1	0.30-0.55	0.03-0.05	--
	32	0.8	0.33-0.45	0.02-0.03	--
Wood (oak, maple)	65	1.0	0.33	--	--
Wood (fir, pine)	35	0.8	0.29	--	--
Hardboard	15	0.35	0.30	--	--
Plywood	70	3-6	0.23	--	--
Fiberboard (wood or cane)	50-60	1.5	0.26	--	--
	0.6	0.5	0.2	--	--
Plaster	3	0.3	0.2	--	--
Gypsum Board	3	0.3	0.25	--	--
Glass fiber batt	-	1-2	0.2-0.3	0.3-1.0	--
Mineral wool	-	0.7-1.0	0.32-0.35	0.3-0.4	--
Plastics, rigid Vinyls	2	0.26	0.32	0.3-04	--
Styrene Polystyrene foam Polyurethand foam	2	0.18	0.38	0.4	--

Note: Values listed are estimated values at ordinary temperatures, or over typical temperature ranges in fires, if available.
   Actual values vary considerably with temperature, particularly where moisture is involved.
[1] The number of Btu transmitted in one hour, through one square foot, one inch thick, for each degree of temperature difference.
[2] Specific Heat is the number of Btu required to increase the temperature of one pound of the material one degree F.
[3] Steel elongation increases at higher temperatures.

Concrete. Concrete is typically composed of portland cement, sand and coarse aggregate, for example, gravel, stone, cinders, slag, shale, vermiculite. The proportions may vary, for example, from 1:1:3 for columns to 1:3:6 for foundations. Concrete has high compressive strength but low tensile or shear strength. When exposed to elevated temperature under load, the compressive strength decreases and is one-half of its normal value at a temperature of about 1100°F (593°C). When exposed to rapidly rising temperatures, concrete is susceptible to spalling which is the (sometimes violent) loss of surface material. Spalling is attributed to the rapid generation of steam and depends upon moisture content (generally above 5%) in the concrete, type of aggregate and compressive load. Spalling is more likely in concrete which has not had sufficient time to lose its initial water of hydration, a process which continues for years in heavy concrete sections.

Ordinary concrete contains no steel reinforcement (or only light reinforcement). Concrete blocks may be made from cement sand and gravel, or from cement and sand alone, or from cement, sand and cinders.

Reinforced concrete is a composite mixture in which steel rods or bars are used to provide tensile and flexural strength. Fire may cause the concrete to spall away from the reinforcing steel. The strength of the concrete structural element depends upon the close bond between the steel and the concrete. Damaged concrete may be structurally unsafe. The tendons used in prestressed concrete totally lose their prestress at 800°F (427°C).

Steel. Steel has high tensile and compressive strength and is used in buildings in many sizes, shapes and products. Steel loses strength at elevated temperatures. When used as a structural member its yield, tensile and compressive strengths decrease to one-half of its normal value at a temperature of about 1000 to 1100°F (538° to 593°C). The color of heated iron and steel is sometimes used as a measure of temperature (see table 7). Steel is used in rolled or built-up members, in bar and thin sheet "C" joists, as channels, tees and angles, and as a variety of connectors such as nails, screws, bolts, hangars, and gusset plates. The fire characteristics of the steel, including high heat conductivity, substantial thermal expansion and decrease in yield strength at high temperatures, may be critical factors in a fire. For instance, a 20 ft steel member will elongate almost 2 in when heated to 1000°F (538°C). If restrained, it will buckle to accommodate the expansion. The buckling may cause structural collapse and may be well removed from the point of origin of the fire.

Gypsum. Gypsum is used both for plaster and for manufactured wall boards. Gypsum is one of the few materials which absorb heat from a fire, rather than contributing to the fire. It performs well in fires. It is widely used in fire-resistive assemblies. If the question of fire resistance is an issue, careful examination of the rear of several full sections should be made to determine if the board has a label or marking indicating it was listed by UL (Underwriters Laboratories Inc.) or FM (Factory Mutual Research Corp.). If the board is listed, then the installation should be compared with the code requirements, particularly in type and spacing of nails, cement cover over the nails, taping of all joints and firestopping of the structure.

Wood. Lumber is sawn wood used for construction purposes, although the word timber is often applied to large cross sectional pieces of lumber. Under fire exposure, wood undergoes dehydration, followed normally by a burning and/or charring process. Charred wood has readily defined layers or zones. The charring rate is roughly 0.025 or 1/40 in/min, but varies significantly with species, density and moisture content. The relatively thin wood members of frame construction may lose structural strength rapidly on fire exposure. Thick structural members may retain their strength for long periods but the structure itself may fail because of failure of the connections.

Table 7 Approximate color of Glowing Hot, Solid Objects

Appearance	Temperature	
	°F	°C
No emission detectable	Less than 885	Less than 475
Dark red	885-1200	475-650
Dark red to cherry red	1200-1380	650-750
Cherry red to bright cherry red	1380-1500	750-815
Bright cherry red to orange	1500-1650	815-900
Orange to yellow	1650-200	900-1090
Yellow to light yellow	2000-2400	1090-1315
Light yellow to white	2400-2800	1315-1540
Brighter white	higher than 2800	Higher than 1540

Wood cannot be "fire proofed" or made "noncombustible". However, it can be treated to reduce its rate of burning by a variety of surface treatments and impregnations with mineral salts. Pressure impregnation is one of the most effective methods of reducing surface flame spread, rate of heat release and smoke generation. If there is an apparent poor performance of impregnated or surface-treated wood, samples should be removed and tested for adequacy of the treatment.

Plastics. This term refers to a group of organic substances (resins) of high molecular weight which can be shaped or molded into finished solid products. Cellulosic plastics, which include cellulose acetate, ethyl cellulose, methyl cellulose and cellulose nitrate, are produced by chemical modification of cellulose. Some plastic products are blends, combinations or composites with unique properties; some can be compounded to be thermoplastic or thermosetting. Thermosetting plastics are those which undergo chemical reaction and cure during molding and do not melt. Some thermoplastics melt at temperatures only slightly above 212°F (100°C) and may form liquid pools and burn intensely in a manner similar to flammable liquids. Examples of the two types of plastics and quoted values of service temperatures and ignition temperatures are given in table 8. These temperatures may not relate directly to actual performance of products in fires, since the test methods do not take into account specimen size, heat transfer properties, aging, etc.

The fire performance of plastics depends upon type, use and level of exposure. Some plastics form a char structure which may inhibit further burning, but most plastics will burn rapidly and generate heat, smoke and potentially toxic gases at fire temperatures. The plastics may be almost completely consumed, and the investigator should investigate for the presence of plastics in fires which reached high intensity early.

Table 8 Pastics

Typical Uses	Continuous Service Temp [1] °F	Ignition Temp [2] Flash °F	Self °F	Decomposition Temp Range °F
Thermoplastics				
ABS — Piping, refrigerators, telephones	175-212	--	--	--
Acrylic/Methyl Methacrylate — Glazing, light diffusers, furnishing	170-23	540-570	830-860	340-570
Cellulose Nitrate — Throwaway test tubes	120-160	285	285	--
Polyamide (Nylon) — Carpeting, clothing, appliances	180-250	790	795	590-715
Polycarbonate — Glazing, appliances, light diffusers	250	--	930	--
Polyethylene — Containers, vapor barriers	160-230	645	660	635-840
Polypropylene — Wire insulation, appliances, piping	190-280	650	730	625-770
Polystyrene — Appliances, furnishings, thermal insulation (foam)	140-175	650-680	910-925	570-750
Polytetrafluorethylene (Teflon) — Cooking utensils, wire insulation	500	--	985	950-1000
Polyurethane — Furniture cushioning, coating, thermal Insulation (foam)	250-300	590	780	--
Polyvinyl chloride — Floor and wall covering, wire insulation, piping, Upholstery, clothing, coating	150-175	735	850	390-570
Thermosetting				
Alkyd — Paints, lacquers	350			
Epoxy — Protective coating, reinforced plastics	210	--	--	
Melamine — Tableware, laminates	280	885-930	1150-1190	
Phenolic — Laminates, appliances	250-350		900	
Polyster — Partitions (Glass-reinforced), boats	350-525	635-750	810-910	
Silicone — Electrical Insulation, coatings, grease	120	--	--	
Urea Formaldehyde — Thermal insulation		--	--	

Flame retardants added in manufacture may be used to reduce the ease of ignition and flammability of some plastics.

Insulation. The principal types of thermal insulation used in buildings are (1) mineral wool batts, blankets and fibrous loose fill, (2) foamed plastics, (3) inorganic (vermiculite, perlite) loose fill, (4) organic (wood or cane fiber) boards and (e) organic (macerated paper) loose fill.

Batts and blankets may be supplied with an integral vapor barrier (asphalt-treated or aluminum-foil-faced Kraft paper) which is intended for application to the warm-in-winter surface of the wall or ceiling interior finish board. The paper facing"is flammable and should never be left exposed. The batts are held together with a combustible binder. Plastic foam, which is combustible, should never be left exposed and most building codes require that a layer of 1/2 in (1.3 cm) gypsum board or equivalent barrier protection be provided.

Loose fill cellulosic insulation is commonly made of ground-up paper with chemicals added to reduce flammability. The more common chemicals used are boric acid, borax, and various sulfates and phosphates and these are added in amounts ranging generally from 15 to 30% by weight. If the chemicals are not added properly, they may segregate and leave portions of untreated paper. Loose fill insulation may be poured or blown into attics or blown into walls. Unless care is taken to maintain clearances around light and heat fixtures, and around flues and other heated surfaces and heat-producing appliances, smoldering of the cellulosic insulation may occur.

UTILITY SYSTEMS

Introduction

Brief descriptions of the types of utility systems found in buildings are provided. Those features and materials of the various systems which have resulted in fires and fire spread are discussed. The principal utility systems are:

1. Plumbing systems;
2. heating, ventilation, and air conditioning systems;
3. electrical systems.

Plumbing Systems

Plumbing systems include water supply and waste removal (sewage). Water supply systems, as the wording indicates, supply water to the building's fixtures and equipment. Sewage systems remove the waste products, usually accompanied by water for ease in movement, from the building.

Piping for both water supply and waste removal systems may be either metallic (copper, steel, or cast iron) or nonmetallic (plastics such as chlorinated polyvinyl chloride, polyvinyl chloride and acrylonitrile-butadiene-styrene, or CPVC, PVC, and ABS, respectively).

In some code jurisdictions, gas piping is included under the local plumbing code provisions and, as such, is a plumbing system. Piping for gas supply systems includes wrought iron (black pipe) and zinc-coated pipe (galvanized).

The major concerns with plumbing systems from a fire standpoint are with:

1. Piping, if metallic, providing an accidental ground for stray electrical currents;
2. piping, if nonmetallic, providing a fuel for nearby fires with the resultant spread of the fire;
3. penetration of fire-resistive walls and floors without proper protection (firestopping) leading to the spread of the fire;
4. leaks or ruptures in fuel gas piping and the possibility of ignition of the leaking gas.

Gas leaks have contributed too many accidental fires. The leak does not have to be within the building to pose a fire problem. Gas from leaks in the underground piping outside of a building has been known to follow the piping through the wall of the building and contact an ignition source within the structure. Also, gas leaking outside of the building has been known to have entered the sewage system and flowed back into the building through untrapped floor drains, reach an ignition source within the building and explode. Natural gas and liquefied petroleum gas have no natural odor. They are odorized artificially. The odorant may be removed as gas leaks through the earth or it may be absorbed in the scale in the inside of the pipeline. As a consequence, the absence of any reported gas odor does not necessarily mean that gas was not present. Gas leaks in the underground gas utility systems which result in accidents should be reported to the National Transportation Safety Board. While the Board must investigate any accident in which a fatality occurs, the Board also will assist in the investigation of any serious gas utility accident.

The major concerns from fire in plumbing systems are with:
(1) leakage from joints, especially in gas piping or sewer systems, where sewer wastes may produce methane; and (2) improperly constructed penetrations of fire-rated assemblies by the piping or appurtenances. Under fire exposure certain installations of plastic piping, either water or waste, may contribute to spread of fire or emit toxic gases.

Heating, Ventilation and Air Conditioning

Heating. The basic types of heating systems are hot water, steam, hot air and electricity. Hot water and steam systems utilize water usually heated by coal, gas, or oil-fired boilers. The hot water or steam is conveyed to radiators and/or convectors by piping. In hot-air systems, the air is heated by coal, oil, or gas-fired burners, or electric-resistance heaters, and conveyed throughout the building through ducts. Electrical heating systems generally utilize either radiant panels (resistance heating cables) built into the floor or ceiling or baseboard heating coils (convective panels) with electrical service supplied directly to the heating units.

Ventilation. Mechanical ventilation is provided either in conjunction with the air conditioning systems, or is in the form of ventilating fans installed in exterior walls or roofs and exhausting directly to the outdoors or into exhaust shafts which lead to the outdoors. Supply or makeup air is usually obtained through grills in doors or exterior walls, or by air leakage through openings.

Air Conditioning. There are two primary types of air conditioning: (1) central systems with distribution ducts or piping, utilizing compression or absorption-type refrigeration equipment or (2) packaged room or zonal air conditioners with free air discharge.

Central air conditioning systems utilize electricity, natural gas, or fuel oil to operate the compressors and a refrigerant as coolant in the coils and condensers. Either cooled air is circulated through ducts or chilled water is circulated through piping to individual room or zone convectors.

Individual packaged room or zonal units are generally electrically operated with closed refrigerant circuits self-contained within the units and may, depending on the conditions of usage, take fresh air from the outside or recirculate the inside air.

Heating, ventilation and air conditioning systems may be the cause of the original fire or the systems may contribute to the growth and spread of the fire. Fire initiation may include:

1. Explosive ignition due to the accumulation of gas or oil vapors within the equipment from failure of equipment controls;
2. ignition of fuel gases or oils from leaks in the piping or in the equipment;
3. ignition of combustibles near flue pipes, combustion chambers, and radiant heating units.

In air duct systems, most codes require fire dampers at points where ducts pierce fire-resistive walls and floors (where not in a shaft). In fire investigations, it is sometimes important to determine whether these dampers operated properly. As noted below, air conditioning and ventilation systems are sometimes designed to perform specific functions, such as smoke removal from the area of the fire. It is sometimes necessary for the fire investigator to determine whether such a system was installed and whether the system operated as intended.

Smoke Movement

The explanation of heated smoke and gases rising and mushrooming under the roof, if not vented, is adequate for simple structures. In tall buildings a number of factors may cause the movement of smoke to locations far beyond the area of origin, without necessarily affecting the areas in between.

Smoke movement may be caused by:
1. Thermal energy of the fire;
2. wind;
3. stack effect;
4. air handling system;
5. special built in smoke removal equipment;
6. openings in the building;
7. atmospheric conditions.

Wind. The wind exerts a pressure on one side and suction on the opposite side of the building. It may be powerful enough to overcome any of the other forces discussed here. It may change direction a number of times during the fire. It may blow in different directions at different levels of a high-rise building, particularly in congested areas where "canyon effects" may occur. The effect of the wind is increased when openings occur in the building. It is important to note that the wind at the fire may not have conformed to the information recorded at the nearest official weather station.

Stack Effect. This is due to differences between the inside and outside temperatures. The greater the difference, the greater the stack effect. Under cold weather conditions, normal air flow in the lower part of the building is from floors into shafts. The flow will decrease on successively higher floors until there is a "neutral zone", one or more floors where the flow is minimal. In the absence of wind, this generally will be from 1/3 to 1/2 the height of the building. Above the neutral zone the flow reverses, from the shafts onto the floors, with the pressure (and thus the flow) increasing with height. The greatest flow therefore is from the lowest floors into the shafts and out from the shafts onto the highest floors. Thus top floor occupants sometimes may be the first to report a lower floor fire. In air conditioned buildings on a hot summer day, the flow may be reversed, that is downward. It should be kept in mind that the stack effect exists due to temperature difference and height. The fire does not cause it, the fire gases simply are transported by it. As an example of stack effect on fire gases, a rubbish fire on the ninth floor of a high-rise building under construction ignited PVC (polyvinyl chloride) air conditioning connectors. The fumes greatly distressed workmen on the 35th floor. They started to walk down the stairs but the stairwell was so full of noxious fumes that they got out at the 25th floor. They smashed the glass windows to get relief. This movement of gases from a lower to an upper floor was due to stack effect.

Air Conditioning. The investigator should determine the effect of the system on the fire. If the system was supposed to react to the fire in some way, the suggestions in the next paragraph are pertinent.

Special Smoke Removal Equipment In some buildings special equipment is provied to vent the fire area. It may be triggered automatically or manually. In other buildings the air conditioning system may have been designed to assist in controlling the spread of smoke.

There are two questions the investigator can ask:

"Did the special smoke removal equipment operate as designed? If it did operate as designed, were the results adequate?"

Openings in the building. Openings in the building, particularly large ones, can disrupt stack effect, multiply the wind effect, and disrupt the operation of mechanical equipment. When and why openings occurred might be important information as the fire investigation develops.

Atmospheric Conditions. When the temperature of the atmosphere is constantly decreasing as height increases, the condition is called "lapse". Under "lapse" conditions smoke will move up and away from the fire. If there is a layer of air warmer than the air below, this layer is called the "inversion layer". It acts as a roof to rising smoke. A high rise building may penetrate an inversion layer. This causes substantial differences in the smoke situation above and below the layer.

Wood-Burning Stoves and Furnaces

In recent years, there has been a growth in the use of wood-burning stoves and furnaces to provide either primary or supplemental heating. Such equipment, if not installed with adequate clearances to nearby combustible materials is potential sources of accidental fires. The burning of wood leads to the production of creosote which tends to deposit in the flue pipes and chimneys. This is particularly true of the newer so-called air-tight stoves. Operation of these stoves at low-firing rates enhances the production of creosote. The buildup of creosote in the flue pipes and chimneys can lead to a severe fire in the flue and chimney as the creosote is combustible. Flues and chimneys, be they masonry or the newer all-fuel triple-wall metal variety, should be able to withstand a total burnout. However, they may not due to deficiencies which may have been built in or have occurred with the passage of time.

ELECTRICAL

Electrical service consists of the following:

1. Service drop wires, either overhead or underground (from the public utilities' lines to the building);

2. service-entrance wires (from outside of building to equipment on the inside);

3. meter;

4. service entrance switch (to disconnect entire installation from public utilities' lines);

5. panel boards providing fuse or circuit breaker protection as well as disconnect means for each of the individual branch circuits;

6. grounding system;

7. distribution system - individual circuits, for lighting, appliance, and equipment operation.

There are six different types of wiring systems in common use. They are: (1) rigid conduit; (2) thin wall conduit; (3) flexible conduit; (4) nonmetallic-sheathed cable; (5) armored cable; and (6) knob-and-tube (which is seldom used today). Electrical codes are very specific with regard to where each of these systems may be used.

Junction boxes and outlet boxes are required at every location where wiring is spliced or insulation is removed, and at fixture locations.

In older buildings, electrical installations may have been made without outlet boxes at all splices and where insulation had been removed. In these locations, and where the wiring has been run in joist or stud spaces, dust, cobwebs and other easily ignitable materials may be present. If the splices and joints have not been properly made, there is a possibility of either short circuits or overheating of wire junctions thus leading to fire.

Another common cause of electrical fires, particularly in single-family dwellings, is the replacement of fuses of one rating with those of higher rating, that is, replacement of 15 ampere fuses with 20 or 30 ampere fuses. This practice may result in the overloading of the electrical wiring causing overheating and breakdown of insulation, and, if in close proximity to combustibles, eventually to smoldering and possible flaming ignition.

THE SCIENCE OF FIRE

Chemistry and Physics of Fire

CONTENTS

	Page
FRIENDLY AND UNFRIENDLY FIRES	1
FUEL, OXYGEN, IGNITION SOURCE	1
CHEMISTRY OF FIRE	1
Introduction	1
Gaseous Fuels	2
Liquid Fuels	2
Solid Fuels	4
Oxygen Requirements for Combustion	5
Heats of Combustion and Maximum Flame Temperatures	6
Products of Combustion	7
Reference	8
HEAT TRANSFER IN FIRES	8
Introduction	8
Convective Heat Transfer	8
Conductive Heat Transfer	8
Radiant Heat Transfer	9
Other Methods of Fire Extension	10
FIRE DEVELOPMENT	10
Introduction	10
Ignition	10
Flame Sptread	12
Effect of Enclosure	13
Flashover	14

THE SCIENCE OF FIRE
Chemistry and Physics of Fire

FRIENDLY AND UNFRIENDLY FIRES

Combustion may be defined as a chemical and physical reaction between a fuel and oxygen from the air which generates heat. Combustion usually produces light, smoke, and combustion gases as well. Controlled combustion, or friendly fires, has been of enormous benefit to mankind but when uncontrolled can be a terribly destructive force. Many destructive, or unfriendly fires, grow out of controlled, useful combustion.

FUEL, OXYGEN, IGNITION SOURCE

Three conditions are necessary to have a fire: a fuel must be present; it must be in contact with oxygen (usually from the air), and there must be a source of energy to raise the temperature of the fuel and oxygen to a point where they react rapidly (ignite). Fuels and oxygen coexist safely everywhere in nature. As an example, gasoline, which forms a highly flammable mixture in air, is handled safely in enormous quantities every day in the United States. Only when an ignition source, such as a spark, heat or flame, is present can a fire result.

CHEMISTRY OF FIRE

Introduction

Fuels may be classified as gases, liquids, or solids. Each behaves differently in fires. Most fuels are organic in nature; that is, they are made up of carbon and hydrogen. They may be natural products such as coal, oil, or plant materials. Or, they may be products derived from these sources, such as coke, gasoline, lumber, paper, or the wide range of chemicals and plastics produced by industry.

When organic fuels burn with an abundant supply of air the principal products are carbon dioxide and water vapor.

Nitrogen-containing plastics, such as nylon, produce nitrogen gas among the products of combustion in addition to carbon dioxide and water vapor. Similarly, plastics containing chlorine, such as polyvinyl chloride, produce hydrogen chloride, an acid gas, when they burn along with the carbon dioxide and water.

When combustion takes place in a limited air supply, as is the case . in building fires, combustion will be incomplete. Incomplete combustion produces toxic gases such as carbon monoxide and hydrogen cyanide (from nitrogen-containing materials), along with other irritating and toxic gases and smoke particles.

In burning buildings incomplete combustion is the rule, with a large variety and quantity of toxic, flammable, even explosive, gases being generated. Overall, then, there is no "perfect combustion" in a building fire.

Gaseous Fuels

Fuel gases, such as natural gas, since they mix readily with air, present a very serious fire hazard. They are readily ignited by a very small ignition source, such as a spark. As they flow freely, they can reach remote ignition sources. Once ignited, the flame spreads rapidly through the fuel/air mixture, generating high temperatures, igniting other combustibles, and creating a destructive pressure wave (explosion).

Fuel gas/air mixtures will burn only if their composition lies within certain limits. If the fuel concentration is too low (below the lower or lean limit, and often called the lower explosive limit, L.E.L.) insufficient fuel is present to sustain the flame. If the fuel concentration is too great (the upper or rich limit and often called the upper explosive limit, U.E.L.) not enough oxygen is present in the mixture for combustion. The region between the upper and lower limits is called the flammable range. From a fire safety standpoint, generally it is only the lower limit that is of practical interest since a mixture above the upper limit will always have to pass through the flammable range to bring the mixture to within safe limits.

Liquid Fuels

When the surface of a combustible or flammable liquid is exposed to the air, some of it converts to a vapor and mixes with the air. In a closed container the concentration of vapor in the air reaches an equilibrium value (the saturated vapor pressure), which depends on the composition of the liquid and the temperature. The vapor pressure of a liquid increases with increases in temperature until, at the boiling point of the liquid, the vapor pressure is just equal to-atmospheric pressure and rapid vaporization (boiling) occurs.

The combustion of a liquid actually takes place in this fuel/air mixture above the liquid surface rather than at the surface of the liquid. In this respect, it resembles the combustion of a gaseous fuel. For ignition to take place, the concentration of fuel vapor in air must exceed the lower flammability limit; that is, the temperature of the liquid must be high enough for the equilibrium vapor concentration to be within the flammable range.

The minimum temperature at which vaporization is sufficient to produce a flammable liquid fuel/air mixture is called the flash point of the liquid. It is measured by gradually heating a sample of the liquid in contact with the air and periodically bringing a small ignition flame near the surface . The minimum temperature at which a flash of flame spreads over the surface is recorded as the flash point. It is one of the most important properties in determining the fire hazard of a liquid.

The initial flash seen when the ignition source is brought near to the liquid surface may consume the fuel in the fuel/air mixture and the flash will die out. At a slightly higher temperature, vaporization of the liquid is sufficient to sustain the flame. This temperature at which the sustained flame is observed is called the fire point. The flash point is more widely used than the fire point to characterize the flammability properties of a liquid.

A liquid fuel is not readily ignited by a small ignition source if the liquid's temperatures is below its flash point, but it can be ignited by a larger ignition source which is capable of heating the surface of the liquid to the flash point. Once ignited, radiation from the fire will increase the temperature of the liquid, increasing the rate of vaporization and the intensity of the fire.

Liquid sprays and mists (for example, from a leak under pressure) are more easily ignited and burn more vigorously than the bulk liquid because of the larger surface area per unit volume in contact with air. An example of this is the pressurized oil burner of an oil-fired heating plant.

Another measured property of liquid fuels is ignition temperature, also referred to as autoignition temperature. The ignition temperature of a liquid fuel is that temperature to which the fuel, in air, must be heated to ignite spontaneously. The ignition temperature of a specific substance can vary widely depending upon many conditions. The following information is quoted from reference (2):

"Ignition temperatures observed under one set of conditions may be changed substantially by a change of conditions. For this reason, ignition temperatures should be looked upon only as approximations. Some of the variables known to affect ignition temperatures of flammable liquids and gases are percentage composition of the vapor or gas-air mixture, shape and size of the space where the ignition occurs, rate and duration of heating, kind and temperature of the ignition source, catalytic or other effect of materials that may be present, and oxygen concentration. As there are many differences in ignition temperature test methods, such as in size and shape of containers, method of heating and ignition source, it is not surprising that different ignition temperatures are reported for the same substance by different laboratories.

As illustration of the effects of test methods, the ignition temperatures of hexane determined by three different methods were $437°$ F, $637°$ F, and $950°$ F, respectively. The effect of percentage composition is shown by the following ignition temperatures for pentane: $1,018.4°$ F for 1.5 per cent pentane in air, $935.6°$ F for 3.75 per cent pentane, and 888.8F for 7.65 per cent pentane. The following ignition temperatures for carbon disulfide demonstrate the effect of size of space containing the ignitible mixture: in a 200 ml (milliliter) flask the ignition temperature was $248°$ F; in a 1,000 ml flask $230°$ F; and in a 10,000 ml flask $205°$ F. That materials of the container walls in which the flammable mixture is in contact may affect the ignition temperature is illustrated by ignition temperature determinations for benzene conducted in various containers: $1,060°$ F in a quartz container, $1,252°$ F in iron, and $1,330°$ F in zinc."

These variations in ignition temperatures for a given liquid fuel should be kept in mind by the investigator should he encounter a fire where ignition of a liquid fuel by an external heat source is thought to be involved.

Flash points are used to provide for legal regulation of liquid fuels. Liquids with flash points below 100F ($38°$ C) are classified as "flammable" under most codes, while those with flash points above $100°F$ ($38°$ C) are classified as "combustible". Regulations for the handling and storage of "combustible" liquids, for instance, are more lenient than for "flammable" liquids. There is much misunderstanding of these terms. People accustomed to obtaining information from handbooks and tables, often take the published figures as physical constants, which they are not. They are merely observed phenomena and are truly valid only for the sample tested in the apparatus in which tested.

Floor wax, nominally "combustible", ignited from the spark of a floor resulting in a large fire. Tests of a similar material gave an actual flash point of 74° F (23° C). A flammable liquid mixture, such as alcohol and water, may or may not ignite under ordinary temperatures depending upon the percentage (or proof) of alcohol. Whiskey will ignite; wine will not. However, if the wine is heated, it will ignite. The relationship between the fire point and proof of various alcoholic beverages is shown in table 1.

Table 1 Fire Points for Various Alcoholic Beverages

Beverage	Fire Point °F	°C
Whiskey		
80 proof[2]	100	38
100 proof	95	35
Gins		
80 proof	100	38
95 proof	98	37
Rums		
80 proof	100	38
140 proof	80	27
Brandies		
80 proof	100	38
140 proof	80	27
Wines		
20 proof (10%)	above 180	83
40 proof (20%)	135	57

[1]Fire points typically are only a few degrees higher than flashpoint.
[2]For alcohol percentage, divide proof by two.

Published characteristics of flammable liquids must be used with caution in attempting to determine what part a particular flammable liquid played in the development of a fire.

Solid Fuels

The combustion of solid fuels is more complex than the combustion of a liquid or gas. For example, as wood is heated certain gases are given off. The wood is decomposing even though flaming has not yet developed. The reaction moves from the surface into the wood. Gas continues to evolve. The wood is still absorbing heat (endothermic reaction). When enough gas is emitted (temperatures of about 600° to 900° F or 316° to 482° C are required), the gas ignites. The wood is now burning and contributing heat to the fire (exothermic reaction).

Surface area is important in the burning of solids. Materials with large surface-to-volume ratios, such as paper or wood shavings, are readily ignited by a match while a solid block of wood may be difficult to ignite. As plywood and plywood paneling burn, the plywood layers separate increasing the surface area. The total amount of fuel is not increased, but increasing the surface area increases the rate of burning.

For a long time it was thought that the damage to structural elements would be equal in fires where the total amount of heat generated was equal. More recent work indicates that short, hot fires may be more destructive to some materials than long, cooler fires, even though the total amount of heat given off is the same.

Many solid fuels, particularly plastics, will volatilize and burn almost completely when subjected to high temperatures. Other materials, particularly those made from wood, may be only partially volatilized and leave behind a carbon-rich char. The carbon is non-volatile but it will react with oxygen which diffuses to the solid surface, giving off a large amount of heat and causing the solid surface to glow brightly (glowing combustion). The glowing combustion of charcoal is an example. This is a relatively slow process and may continue for a long time after the more volatile flame-producing gases are used up.

Because of the low volatility of most solid fuels, flame spread over surfaces in the downward direction is relatively slow. Flame spread in the upward direction, where the fuel is heated by the rising flaming gases, is much more rapid. Flame spread in the horizontal direction falls between these two extremes. The flame spread, however, may be influenced by a variety of other factors, for example, reradiation from nearby surfaces or air flows.

Oxygen Requirements for Combustion

Since oxygen combines with fuel in the combustion process, the size of a fire may be limited by either the amount of fuel available or by the amount of oxygen which can reach the fire.

Oxygen will usually be supplied to the fire from the surrounding air. Air normally contains 20.9 percent of oxygen by volume or 23.2 percent by weight. The remainder (79.1%) consists of nitrogen and traces of other gases. Nitrogen is not consumed in the combustion process. One cubic foot of air contains 0.0175 lbs of oxygen (0.28 kg/m^3). The amount of oxygen required to burn a fuel will depend on the nature of the fuel. Hydrocarbons, such as gasoline, have the highest oxygen requirement, needing approximately 3.5 lbs of oxygen per pound of fuel or 200 cubic feet of air per pound of fuel. Paper has a much lower oxygen requirement, needing approximately 1.2 lbs of oxygen per pound of fuel or 69 cubic feet of air per pound of fuel. Most other common fuels will have oxygen requirements between these limits.

As an example of what this means, consider a fire started in a pile of paper in a closed room 10 by 10 by 8 ft (3.2 x 3.2 x 2.5 m). The 800 cubic-foot-room will initially contain about 14 lb (30.8 kg) of oxygen, sufficient to burn less than 12 lb (26.4 kg) of paper. The actual amount of fuel consumed, however, would be less since the fire will go out when the oxygen concentration drops to around 8 or 10 percent. The rest of the oxygen would remain unconsumed.

Thus, a fire in a tightly-closed compartment will go out due to lack of sufficient oxygen and will not grow to a dangerous size. Most fires, however, will have access to an unlimited air supply through open doors, windows and other openings. In such circumstances the fire will continue to burn until all of the fuel is consumed, unless the fire is extinguished.

Heats of Combustion and Maximum Flame Temperatures

The complete combustion of a pound (or gram) of a specific fuel yields a fixed quantity of heat. This quantity is known as the heat of combustion and will differ for different fuels. Among the common fuels, hydrocarbons (such as gasoline) have the higher heats of combustion while oxygen-containing fuels such as paper (cellulose) have lower values. Heats of combustion for typical fuels are listed in table 2.

The heat given off in a fire goes first to heat the gases coming off and then the nitrogen and any excess oxygen in the air. When the supply of oxygen is exactly sufficient to consume the fuel present, the flame temperature will be at a maximum. Maximum flame temperatures for typical fuels are listed in table 3. If the air supply is insufficient to burn the fuel completely, not all of the heat available will be released and the flame temperature will be reduced. If an excess of air is present, part of the heat will go to heat this excess air and again the flame temperature will be reduced.

The maximum flame temperature is probably never reached in a fire. Usually, the temperature will be much less due to mixing of the cooler surrounding air with the flame gases, incomplete combustion, and the loss of heat through windows and doors as well as to walls, ceilings, floors and room contents.

Table 2   Approximate heats of combustion of typical fuels

Fuel.	Heat of Combustion	
	kcal/g	Btu/lb
Methyl Alcohol	5.3	9,600
Ethyl Alcohol	7.1	12,800
Isopropyl Alcohol	7.9	14,200
Ethylene Glycol	4.5	8,100
Octane	11.4	20,500
Benzene	10.0	18,000
Gasoline	11.5	20,700
Kerosine	11.0	19,800
Fuel Oil	10.5	18,900
Crude Oil	10.8	19,500
Rubber	10.8	19,500
Wood	4.2 - 5.0	7,600 - 9,000
Paper	4.5	8,100
Polyethylene	11.1	20,000
Polystyrene	9.9	17,800
Polyurethane	6.2	11,200
Polyvinyl Chloride	4.0	7,200

Table 3   Maximum flame temperatures of typical gaseous fuels in air

Fuel	Flame Temperature	
	°F	°C
Methane (natural gas)	3400	1871
Propane (LPG)	3500	1927
Octane (gasoline)	4050	2232
Acetylene	4350	2399
Hydrogen	3700	2038
Benzene	4150	2288

Products of Combustion.

The products of combustion from a hostile fire are as great a threat to humans as is direct exposure to the fire. The combustion products from all fires are toxic; the level of toxicity will depend on the concentration, the type of fuel, and the specific conditions of the fire. In a hot fire with a good air supply, the principal products will be carbon dioxide and water vapor. Carbon dioxide is mildly toxic while water vapor is not. The low oxygen content of the fire gases, due to the consumption of the oxygen in the fire, may make them dangerous, even in the absence of significant quantities of toxic gases. Around a free-burning fire, however, material being heated is generating quantities of toxic and combustible gases. Carbon dioxide in fires is always accompanied by some carbon monoxide. The ratio of carbon monoxide to carbon dioxide increases as the oxygen supply is decreased. Carbon monoxide is highly toxic and is the direct cause of a majority of fire deaths. A concentration of 3,000 ppm (parts per million) can cause death in half an hour while higher concentrations will cause correspondingly more rapid death.

When the supply of air to a fire is limited, combustion will be incomplete and, in addition to carbon monoxide, large quantities of other combustion products, including hydrocarbons and soot particles, will be produced. This mixture of products will contain insufficient oxygen for further combustion but can accumulate in a building. When additional oxygen (air) is introduced (if the window breaks or the door opens), rapid combustion can occur. A sudden and dangerous pressure rise, called the back-draft, is created. The back-draft resulting from the rapid combustion may be reported as an explosion by witnesses to the fire. (However, the investigator should be aware that there are other sources of explosions in fires, such,,as aerosol cans, which may mislead witnesses.)

Incomplete combustion also produces a variety of toxic and irritating gases, in addition to carbon monoxide. Nitrogen-containing materials such as wool, nylon and polyurethane, can produce highly toxic hydrogen cyanide and nitrogen oxides. Sulfur-containing materials, such as wool and rubber, produce sulfur dioxide. Chlorine-containing materials, such as polyvinyl chloride, produce hydrogen chloride, a choking, irritating gas. When dissolved in water, hydrogen chloride forms hydrochloric acid, a corrosive liquid which attacks metal surfaces. All fuels can produce aldehydes such as formaldehyde and acrolein. These are strong irritants which attack the lungs and may produce delayed respiratory complications. Toxic gases may remain at the scene of a fire after the fire has been extinguished. For this reason, breathing apparatus should be used in examining the site until it has been thoroughly ventilated. Ventilation may not, however, thoroughly clear cellars, basements and other low points. (The investigator should keep this in mind.) Fire gases may cause incapacitation of the victim before death occurs. In such cases escape is prevented and death may follow due to continued toxic gas exposure or burns from contact with the fire.

Smoke is the visible product of a fire. It consists of soot particles, partially burned fuel fragments and liquid droplets. The visible smoke serves as a warning of the presence of toxic gases, and the smoke particles themselves may contain toxic and irritating substances.

Reference

Methods for measuring the flash points of various liquids can be found in the most recent edition of the following ASTM standards:
D 56   Flash Point by TAG Closed Tester
D 92   Flash and Fire Points by Cleveland Open Cup
D 93   Flash Point by Pensky-Martens Closed Tester
D 1310   Flash Point by TAG Open-Cup Apparatus

HEAT TRANSFER IN FIRES

Introduction

Heat energy generated by a fire first heats the fire gases (flames) to a high temperature. It must then be transferred to other materials to spread the fire. This energy transfer can take place through convection, conduction and radiation, either singly or in combination.

Convective Heat Transfer

Convective heat transfer is the movement of the hot fire gases upwards and away from the fire source. Heat flows from regions of high temperature to regions of lower temperature. The rate of flow is proportional to the temperature difference between the two regions. As these gases come in contact with solid surfaces, such as walls, ceilings and building contents, heat energy is transferred to these surfaces and the gases are cooled in turn. Since the hot gases tend to rise, the ceiling and upper walls of a room will be heated first and most strongly. The flow of convective energy will follow the flow of fire gases, the temperature decreasing with distance from the fire source.

Conductive Heat Transfer

When a solid surface is heated by contact with hot gases, heat is carried from the surface into the interior of the solid by conduction. The conductivities of materials vary widely. Metals have high thermal conductivities (conduct heat readily), followed by other dense materials such as masonry. Porous and lightweight materials, such as wood and particle board, have still lower thermal conductivities while insulating materials, such as mineral wool or foam plastic, have very low thermal conductivities. The amount of heat absorbed by a wall, and thus the amount of cooling of the fire gases, will be greater for materials with high thermal conductivity. On the other hand, the surface temperatures of materials with low thermal conductivity or materials backed by insulation, such as a carpet with a pad, will rise more rapidly since the heat cannot be conducted rapidly from the surface to the interior. This may result in more rapid fire spread over the surface of these materials, providing they are combustible.

The rate of heat transfer to an object immersed in a flame will decrease as the temperature of the object increases until, as its temperature approaches that of the flame, the rate decreases to zero. Thus the temperature of any object in the fire can never exceed that of the flame heat source.

Radiant Heat Transfer.

Radiant heat transfer takes place without direct contact between the heat source and the receiving surface. The transfer takes place by electromagnetic radiation or waves. Radiant heat transfer follows line-of-sight and does not turn corners. The warming of the earth's surface by the rays of the sun is one example of radiant heat transfer.

The quantity of heat transferred per unit of time by convection and conduction is approximately proportional to the difference in temperature between the heat source and the receiving surface. As a consequence, small changes in the temperature differential produce small changes in the rate of heat transferred. However, in radiant heat transfer, small changes in the temperature differential between the heat source and the receiving surface can produce large effects due to the nature of the laws of electromagnetic radiation which govern radiant heat transfer. This explains the danger from overheated stoves and heaters, particularly the black-colored, radiant-style, wood stoves currently in vogue. Clearances from combustibles that were more than adequate when fuel is burned at a low rate, rapidly become inadequate when fuel is burned at a high rate.

As in convective and conductive heat transfer, objects cannot be heated in a fire by radiation to a temperature higher than that of the flame source.

The amount of heat radiated also is a function of the area of the radiating surface. A small fire will have a relatively small radiant output. But as the fire grows, the radiation will increase. In addition, the upper part of the room will fill with a layer of hot, radiating smoke and gas, and the walls and ceiling surfaces will become heated and contribute further to the radiant energy falling on the floor and other objects in the room. Temperatures of easily-ignited materials (such as paper or fabrics) may reach the point where they burst into flame without direct contact with the fire due to this radiant heat transfer. Thus, radiation can play a very important role in the spread of a fire. Figure 5.4.4-1 depicts the effect of radiation from the hot gas layer at the ceiling on the floor and other objects in the room.

Radiation also heats the burning fuel surface, increasing the rate of burning and the intensity of the fire. Radiation from the ceiling, ahead of the fire, is important in the spread of fire along carpeting in corridors. Differences in ceiling height, however, may cause significant differences in the flame spread on identical carpets, with the radiation from lower ceilings being more pronounced than that from higher ceilings. Similarly, it is thought that one of the causes for rapid flame spread in mobile homes is the relatively short distances between vertical surfaces, which promotes high levels of radiation and reradiation.

Other Methods of Fire Extension

Radiation, conduction, and convection are the classic methods of heat transfer and have long been cited as the methods of fire extension. This overlooks another important method of fire extension "Moving Flaming or Heated Material".

Burning shingles, when carried by the up-draft of the fire, have long been recognized as a potential method of fire extension What is not often recognized is that the same phenomenon can occur inside of a building. Take, as an example, an office where papers are scattered around on the tops of desks, file cabinets and tables. In the event of a fire in this room, burning papers are likely to be lifted by the hot plume of the fire and deposited in different locations around the room. If the fire department arrives at this point, they may conclude that there were several different fires instead of just one and suspect that the fires were incendiary. It is appropriate, therefore, for the investigator to consider what types of materials were involved in the fire and their likely behavior under fire conditions in the process of determining the fire cause and origin.

Heat transfer also can result in secondary fires, fires away from the original point of origin. This can mislead if the investigator is not aware of this phenomenon. For example, consider a chair burning in a living room. As the chair burns, the room begins to fill with hot gases from the ceiling down. There are cloth draperies on windows and these draperies extend up close to the ceiling, into the hot gas layer. Before the room flashes over, the top of the draperies ignite, burn free of the drapery rods, and fall in a burning pile onto a sofa. Assume a few minutes later, the fire department arrives and extinguishes the fire. In a casual examination of the room, the investigator might conclude that there were two fires, independent of each other, and suspect a malicious intent when such was not the case.

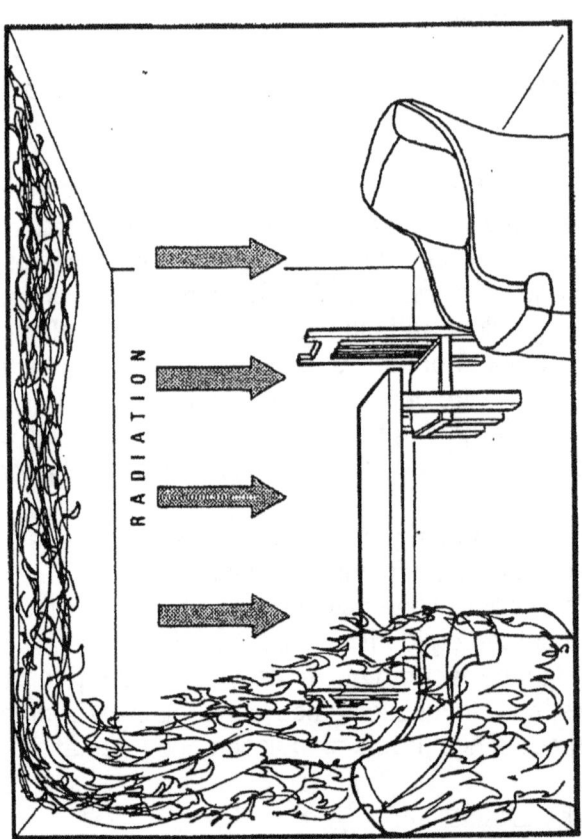

Figure 4

While fire usually moves upward, fire can fall down through hollow walls and cause confusion as to the point of origin. Many fires have been started by heated metal falling from cutting torches, falling, in some cases, several stories.

FIRE DEVELOPMENT

Introduction

The severity and duration of a fire, as well as the hazard involved and the extent of damage, will depend on many elements. The nature of the ignition source, the proximity, type, and amount of fuel present (whether there is sufficient air available to sustain the burning), are just a few of the elements determining the behavior of the fire. In spite of the seemingly endless number of variations of elements which will affect the outcome of the fire, there exist several general characteristics common to most fires, a knowledge of which will aid the fire investigator in understanding fire development.

Ignition

The nature of the ignition source, combined with the first fuel item involved, will determine the initial fire development. For example, one extreme might be an explosion and the resulting fire from operating an electrical switch in a room filled with a natural gas/air mixture caused by a leaking gas main. At the other extreme might be a piece of combustible material located close to a furnace or stove flue. Upon being heated over weeks, months or years, the material could begin to smolder and finally burst into flame.* The ignition source for most fires would generally fall between these extremes. A cigarette dropped into the folds of an upholstered chair or bedding could cause the chair or bedding to smolder for several hours before one might observe a flame. A pan of cooking oil being heated and left unattended on a kitchen stove could ignite in a matter of minutes.

The intensity or strength of the ignition source in reference to fuel is important. A light switch is generally not thought of as an ignition source nor would a cigarette placed on a plank of ordinary lumber be considered dangerous. Yet by switching to a gas, liquid, dust or easily ignitable plastic, ignition can and does take place from quite weak ignition sources. For example, flaming ignition (the direct contact of a flame with the material or fuel), is potentially dangerous for any fuel. The temperature of an open flame, be it a match, candle, torch, fireplace, furnace, or kitchen stove, is generally higher than other sources. Obviously the larger the flame the more the heat transfer and the greater the risk of ignition.

Simple theories of ignition require only that the material reach a certain critical temperature for ignition to take place. The item can be heated indirectly (for example, with a heater) until it reaches a high enough temperature and bursts into flame (autoignition). Or, the item can be heated directly with an open flame (piloted ignition). The material is raised to the required temperature and ignited by the flame. (Autoignition generally requires higher temperatures than piloted ignition.) The two processes, indirect or direct heating, are identical. The presence of the flame simply is faster in initiating the chemical chain reactions in the combustible gases (flaming) given off by the material at these high temperatures.

In reality, ignition is a more complex process than that described above. However, the concept of raising the temperature to high enough values is an easy one to understand and provides a simple means of ranking ignition sources as to their strength. An electric spark will produce extremely high temperatures but generally only for a very short time and only in a small volume. If there is a flammable mixture surrounding the spark, then there will be an explosion. At the other extreme is heating due to spontaneous ignition, mild frictional heating, and other lower temperature heat sources.

Flame Spread

Whatever was ignited, the next phase of the fire involves flame spread. The growth of the fire will involve both flame spread along the ignited or initial item, as well as from one item to the next. In the beginning stages of flame spread, the fire usually will be small and growing. The important elements again will be the material properties as well as the item's location. Generally, sufficient air is available in the initial stages of flame spread.

Heat transfer from the flame will raise the temperature of the unburned fuel adjacent to it causing the area of involvement to increase. As the area increases, the flames will become larger, resulting in larger heat transfer rates and larger areas of involvement. If conditions are favorable, a self-sustaining chain reaction occurs. How rapidly this takes place will change from material to material. A flame will spread across the surface of gasoline in seconds. On the other hand, a flame will not spread across an oak floor and the chain reaction will stop, unless heat is supplied from some other nearby fuel. Carpeting may react like the oak floor, like gasoline, or somewhere in between, depending on the carpet material, the presence of padding, if any, the radiation from the ceiling, and the energy of the ignition source.

Heat loss from the material is also important in flame spread. If underlayment (pad) is placed under the carpet, increasing the thermal insulation between the carpet and the floor, the flame spread rate will increase since less energy would be lost from the burning area. This is the reason it is much easier to keep two or more logs alight in a fireplace since the radiant energy given off by the logs will be "captured" by the others and not lost to the surroundings as in the case of a single log.

Location is extremely important. The results of a small waste basket fire, located at the base of a combustible wall or at the edge of a bed or sofa, will be vastly different than the same waste basket fire placed in the center of the room. In general, upward flame spread rates will be significantly higher than horizontal or downward flame spread rates due to the heating by the hot combustion products flowing upward over the unburned fuel. The more closely spaced the items or fuel elements are in a given region, the higher the potential for fire spread from one item to the next. The further a nonburning item is from a burning one, the larger the flame must be before the nonburning item will ignite.

Flame spread tests are available to rank materials as to their potential hazard, that is, how easily flame will propagate along a given sample of the item when one end is lighted. They are described in reference

Effect of Enclosure

After the fire is started, the fire development will be determined by the room or building or, simply, the enclosure. Up until this point nothing has been said about where the fire is taking place, only that there was sufficient air available. From this point onward, fire development will be dominated by the effects of the room, building, or the enclosure.

Consider a lighted candle safely placed on a table in a room. The candle will burn continuously until it runs out of wax. It will not change conditions in the room and it will not be changed by the room. The amount of oxygen used up in the room will be made up by normal air infiltration and similarly, the combustion products will leave the room through leaks. Any heating effects in nearby items will be small.

For a larger fire, however, the effect of the enclosure will begin to be felt. There are two primary effects that will now determine the course of the fire; one is ventilation, the other is called reradiation. The fire, beyond the size of a candle, will be consuming oxygen at a much greater rate, such that normal leaks will not be sufficient. For a completely sealed room the fire will go out due to a lack of oxygen.

Doors are not always closed or even present in open-plan homes or offices. Hence, a ready supply of air is generally available to a fire and the fire will grow. Fresh air will be drawn in through the lower part of the door opening at the same time hot gases from the fire will be collecting at the ceiling, filling the upper portion of the room and spilling out under the top of the door frame. (In older buildings, transoms were often installed over doorways for ventilation and light. This permitted the room fire to spread quickly to the corridor. After several hotel fires in which transoms were a factor in fire spread many codes were changed to require the permanent closure of the transoms, and they are not installed in modern buildings.)

The second effect of the enclosure will begin to be realized. The trapped hot gases in the upper portion of the room will heat the ceiling and walls. These surfaces, together with the gases themselves, will radiate down onto the unburned fuel in the room raising the fuel to the required temperature necessary for burning. An additional acceleration process (reradiation) now will be operating making the fire spread and grow further (see figure 4).

The larger fire will draw more and more air through the doorway. If the opening is large enough relative to the potential fuel supply, the controlling mechanism for further development is the amount of fuel present, the so-called fuel-controlled or fuel-limited fire. The fire will continue to grow until all of the fuel elements are burning inside the enclosure as long as there is more than an adequate supply of air coming through the door. This fire will continue in a more or less steady manner until the fuel is consumed.

Flashover

Consider the same sized opening, with considerably more fuel than in the previous case. The fire would continue to get larger, drawing more and more air, burning more and more vigorously. Temperatures and corresponding radiation feedback would rise until rather dramatically a phenomenon known as "flashover" occurs. Items in the room not in direct contact with the original flames suddenly burst into flame due to the high radiation levels. The rate of burning for all items in the room becomes so high that the amount of air coming through the door is inadequate. Flame lengths become longer and reach out through the door in search of more air to burn the additional combustibles and the "inferno" inside becomes controlled by the amount of air entering. This is called a ventilation-controlled fire. The fire cannot get any larger in the room because all the air entering is being utilized. The fire will continue in this fashion until all the fuel is burned up.

Flashover can be abrupt, unpredictable and highly dangerous. Firefighters are warned about entering rooms or buildings not knowing the state of things. For a growing or fuel-controlled fire one might be able to crawl into the room for rescue purposes. If the room has "flashed over," the flames coming out the door will prevent entry. It is likely that the fire will extend to the corridor and adjacent parts of the building are now in grave danger. Inspection of the enclosure after a fire often will reveal the telltale signs of flashover—every combustible in the room will exhibit some degree of fire damage, if not totally destroyed, even to charring of the paint and paper on gypsum walls.

www.ingramcontent.com/pod-product-compliance
Lightning Source LLC
Chambersburg PA
CBHW081809300426
44116CB00014B/2289